NEILL! NEILL! ORANGE PEEL!
A Personal View of Ninety Years

A.S. NEILL

QUARTET BOOKS   LONDON, MELBOURNE, NEW YORK

Published by Quartet Books Limited 1977
A member of the Namara Group
27 Goodge Street, London W1P 1FD

First published in Great Britain by
Weidenfeld and Nicolson, London, 1973

Copyright © 1972 by Hart Publishing Company Inc.

ISBN 0 7043 3112 8

Printed in Great Britain by litho at The Anchor Press Ltd
and bound by Wm Brendon & Son Ltd
both of Tiptree, Essex

A.S. Neill, who died in 1975, is world famous as the founder of Summerhill School. His anti-authoritarian approach to education and belief in self-government and freedom for children have had a profound and far-reaching effect on both orthodox and experimental teaching methods. His book *Summerhill* has been translated into fifteen languages and sold more than a million copies in the English language.

The *Guardian* called *Neill! Neill! Orange Peel!* 'an autobiographical memoir shelved some years ago, and now joined with a series of shrewd and gentle essays.'

ALSO BY A.S. NEILL

A Dominie's Log
A Dominie Dismissed
The Booming of Bunkie (fiction)
A Dominie in Doubt
Carroty Broon (fiction)
A Dominie Abroad
A Dominie's Five, or Free School
The Problem Child
The Problem Parent
Is Scotland Educated?
That Dreadful School
The Last Man Alive (fiction)
The Problem Teacher
Hearts not Heads in the School
The Problem Family
The Free Child
Summerhill
Talking of Summerhill

Contents

A NOTE ABOUT
THE TITLE

Years ago, Hetney, a little boy at Summerhill, went round muttering to himself: 'Neill! Neill! Orange Peel!' The phrase caught on and has lived for more than twenty-five years. To this day, small children follow me around chanting the words, and my usual reaction is: 'Wrong again. Not orange peel – banana peel.'

I have selected this rhyme as the title of my book, because it sums up my life with children; indeed, it might be the motto for Summerhill, if we believed in mottoes. These words tell the whole story of my school and my life. They show how the gulf between generations can be bridged – or rather abolished – for they do not connote *cheek* or *hate*: they mean love; they mean equality. If every kid in the world could call his teacher Orange Peel, or an equivalent, my mail would not be filled with letters beginning: 'I hate my school; can I come to Summerhill?'

The little boy's chant shows that there is no necessity for a gulf separating pupils from teachers, a gulf made by adults, not children. Teachers want to be little gods protected by dignity. They fear that if they act human, their authority will vanish and their classrooms will become bedlams. They fear to abolish fear. Innumerable children are afraid of their teachers. It is discipline that creates the fear. Ask any soldier if he fears his sergeant major; I never met one who didn't.

The Summerhill rhyme tells the world that a school can abolish fear of teachers and, deeper down, fear of life. And it is not only

Neill that the kids treat with equality and fun and love; the whole staff are treated as pals and playmates. They do not stand on their dignity, nor do they expect any deference because they are adults. Socially, the only privilege the teachers have is their freedom from bedtime laws. Their food is that of the school community. They are addressed by their first names and seldom are given nicknames; and if they are, these are tokens of friendliness and equality. For thirty years, George Corkhill, our science master, was George or Corks or Corkie. Every pupil loved him.

Years ago, in one of my books, I wrote that when interviewing a prospective teacher, my test was: 'What would you do if a child called you a bloody fool?' It is my test today, except that *bloody* – never a real swearword outside British realms – has been changed to a more popular expletive.

More and more, I have come to believe that the greatest reform required in our schools is the abolition of that chasm between young and old which perpetuates paternalism. Such dictatorial authority gives a child an inferiority that persists throughout life; as an adult, he merely exchanges the authority of the teacher for that of the boss.

An army may be a necessity, but no one, barring a dull conservative, would argue that military life is a model for living. Yet our schools are army regiments or worse. Soldiers at least move around a lot, but a child sits on his bottom most of the time at an age when the whole human instinct is to move.

In this book, I explain why the powers that be try to devitalise children as they do, but the mass of teachers do not understand what lies behind their discipline and 'character moulding', and most do not want to know. The disciplinary way is the easy one. ATTENTION! STAND AT EASE! These are the orders of the barrack square and the classroom.

Obey! Obey! they say, but people do not *obey* equals; they obey superiors. Obedience implies fear, and that should be the last emotion encouraged in a school.

In the USA, it is the student's fear of bad grades – idiotic grades that mean nothing of importance – or fear of not passing exams; in some countries – Britain among them, I hate to admit – it is still fear of the cane or the belt, or the fear of being scorned or mocked by stupid teachers.

The tragedy is that fear also exists on the teacher's side – fear of being thought human, fear of being found out by the uncanny intuition of children. I *know* this. Ten years of teaching in state schools left me with no illusions about teachers. In my time, I,

2

too, was dignified, aloof, and a disciplinarian. I taught in a system that depended on the *tawse*, as we called the belt in Scotland. My father used it and I followed suit, without ever thinking about the rights and wrongs of it – until the day when I myself, as a head-master, belted a boy for insolence. A new, sudden thought came to me. What am I doing? This boy is small, and I am big. Why am I hitting someone not my own size? I put my tawse in the fire and never hit a child again.

The boy's insolence had brought me down to his level; it offended my dignity, my status as the ultimate authority. He had addressed me as if I were his equal, an unpardonable affront. But today, sixty years later, thousands of teachers are still where I was then. That sounds arrogant, but it is simply the raw truth that teachers largely refuse to be people of flesh and blood.

Only yesterday, a young teacher told me that his headmaster had threatened him with dismissal because a boy had addressed him as Bob. 'What will happen to discipline if you allow such familiarity?' he asked. 'What would happen to a private who addressed his colonel as Jim?'

I believe that in the Russian Army after the Revolution there were no barriers between officers and men. They were all pals. But the system failed, I am told, and the army returned to its old ways of class division and stern discipline.

'*Neill! Neill! Orange Peel!*' is a title that may shock the 'dead' teachers. But it will be understood by students in all lands – barring those in Iron Curtain countries who are never allowed to hear of Summerhill.

Why do I get hundreds of letters from children? Not because of my beautiful eyes – nay, but because the idea of Summerhill touches their depths, their longing for freedom, their hatred of authority in home and school, their wish to be in contact with their elders. Summerhill has no generation gap. If it had, half of my proposals in our general meetings would not be outvoted. If it had, a girl of twelve could not tell a teacher that his lessons are dull. I hasten to add that a teacher can tell a kid that he is being a damned nuisance. Freedom must look both ways.

I do not want to be remembered as a great educator, for I am not. If I am to be remembered at all, I hope it will be because I tried to break down the gulf between young and old, tried to abolish fear in schools, tried to persuade teachers to be honest with themselves and drop the protective armour they have worn for generations as a separation from their pupils. I want to be re-membered as an ordinary guy who believed that hate never cured

3

anything, that being on the side of the child – Homer Lane's phrase – is the only way to produce happy schooling and a happy life later on. As I am 'Neill! Neill! Orange Peel!' to my little pupils, so I would like to be to all the children in the world – one who trusts children, who believes in original goodness and warmth, who sees in authority only power and, too often, hate.

Soon I must shuffle off this mortal coil, but I hope that coming generations will look back at the education of our time and marvel at its barbarity, its destruction of human potentialities, its insane concern about formal learning. I hope against everything that makes me pessimistic: the wars, the religious suppression, the crimes. Cannot those who yell for the hanging of criminals see that they are treating a ruptured appendix with aspirin? Will not society recognise that it is our repressive system, plus the poverty of our mean streets, plus our soulless, acquisitive society, that is making criminals and neurotics?

I confess to dithering. One day, when I think of the challenge of the young, I am optimistic; next day, when I scan the newspapers and read of rape and murder and wars and racialism, I become engulfed by pessimism. But I guess that ambivalence is common to us all.

Alexander Sutherland 'Orange Peel' Neill

Summerhill
1972

Part One

THE MacNEILL CLAN

I was born on the 17th of October, 1883, in Forfar, Scotland. Forfar, which today is the Angus County seat, is not far from Dundee and the Firth of Tay. The MacNeill clan originally came from the island of Barra and later joined Bonnie Prince Charlie. Those said to have deserted him before or after the battle of Prestonpans – before, I should guess – settled down in and around the village of Tranent near Edinburgh.

The MacNeills became coal miners, and my grandfather William MacNeill, worked in the pits for many years. But as I first remember him, he had already left the pits and set up a fish shop in Edinburgh. He came to visit us sometimes, a tall, distinguished-looking man with a fine profile and long-fingered, sensitive hands. His hobby was fiddle-making. As a boy, I was afraid of him, for he had a sarcastic tongue and I still recall one occasion when I fell under its lash after trying to sharpen a pencil with his new hollow-ground razor. I think my father was afraid of him, too, for he was always a little strained when the old man came to stay with us.

Though all my uncles had gone to work in the pits, my father was of less tough clay and, having a flair for learning, was sent to be a student-teacher. I never knew why he dropped the Mac from his name. Indeed, I never knew much about my father's early life, for he was not a communicative man. But I recollect his being very angry when his sister Maggie told us about his boyhood days.

My mother was Mary Sutherland. Her mother had been a Sinclair, and her maternal grandmother a Gunn. Granny Clunes Sinclair was one of a family of about twenty sons and daughters, born to a farmer with a small holding in Caithness. They all died of tuberculosis except herself. My Granny went to Leith (now part of Edinburgh) as a servant girl, married Neil Sutherland who had something to do with the docks, and began to rear a family on fourteen shillings a week. Then one night my grandfather was found drowned, and Granny had to take in washing to support the family.

How it came about that my mother – her only daughter – became a teacher, I do not know. It must have meant tremendous self-sacrifice on the part of Granny. My father and mother taught in the same school in Leith, and so their courtship began.

I have one or two of my father's love letters, beautifully written in copperplate. They are not real love letters and resemble the letters I used to write home: 'Today it was raining . . . Jim Brown sprained his ankle last week.' My mother had kept them all tied up in pink ribbons, but she had taken care to burn all her letters to him. Only as a postscript did my father usually send his love, yet I have a hazy memory of once uncovering something more. This happened at the age of twelve when I was prowling about the lumber room and found a box of Father's letters. I recall being a little shocked at one of them. He had just been reading *Venus and Adonis*, and his letter showed the eroticism aroused by this poem. Reading it then, I was sure my mother must have been morally outraged; now I am not so sure.

Granny Sinclair lived with us until her death when I was fourteen. As her favourite grandchild, I think I must have loved her as much as a boy can love an old woman. She used to suck peppermints, and her way of showing her love was to kiss me while shoving a peppermint from her mouth into mine. She was very religious, read much in the family Bible, and liked to tell us that as a girl she had walked nine miles to church every Sunday and nine miles back. Her faith was a simple one of sheep and goats, with no doubts, no scepticism whatsoever. I remember discovering the word 'bugger' when I was about seven, and Granny making me kneel down beside her to ask God for forgiveness. My early fear of hell must have come from her.

She made us read aloud to her from various books of sermons, including Boston's *Fourfold State*. Boston, apparently, had no doubts either. For me, the most terrifying passage of that book was one in which the Man of God, as Granny called him, gave a minute description of the pains of hell. It began in this fashion: 'If you want to know what the torments of hell are like, just light a candle and hold your finger in the flame.' And because Granny and Boston had no doubts about what was going to happen to sinners, I also had no doubts, but knew, as if by instinct, that hell was my destination. Yet there was no hate in Granny. She was a very human, loving old woman, and one of her joys was to listen to the often obscene gossip of the woman from the cottage over the road.

My sister Clunes (named after Granny) had less timidity and faith than I had. She wouldn't have hell at any price; and when she took the next step and wouldn't have God and his heaven, I actually feared that she might be struck down dead on the spot. My fright was caused by a grim story in Granny's annotated *Shorter Catechism* about a servant girl accused of stealing a silver spoon. 'May God strike me down dead if I stole the spoon!' she cried; and, of course, she fell down dead there and then, the silver spoon tinkling on the floor. I reminded the atheistic Clunie of this tale more than once, but she laughed me to scorn, and threatened to commit the unforgivable sin – blasphemy against the Holy Ghost. She never did, but when my oldest brother Willie, at the age of thirteen, stood out in a thunderstorm and invited the Almighty to strike *him* down dead for asking God to perform an unnatural act on the Holy Ghost, I was terrorstruck. As the thunder crashed, I shut my eyes tight, opening them to whatever degree of scepticism I was capable of having in those days, for Granny's silver-spoon story had lost some of its glory. It is of interest to note here that Willie became a minister.

When the psychologists say that our early experiences rule our lives, one is apt to question. But I have had no doubts about this since 1918, when my dearly beloved sister Clunie died of pneumonia at the age of thirty-four. In all her years, she had never compromised her atheism. To her the Christian religion was both superstition and a cruel humbug. Yet on her deathbed she kept muttering the prayers she had learned as a baby, imploring God to save her soul. In the weakness of dying, she returned to emotions that had slumbered for thirty years. To me, that was convincing proof that the feelings of early childhood live on for a lifetime.

My Granny was psychic. She had none of that second sight so often mentioned in Scottish tales I heard all my youth – tales like the one about Old Tamson touching Mrs Broon on the shoulder in the kirk, and whispering: 'Better go home for your laddie has

7

just broken his neck'; after which Mrs Broon drives the seven miles home to discover that exact calamity. Many such stories were told in my boyhood, but it was always a case of 'I know a man who heard about it from the beadle'. No, Granny contented herself with more simple phenomena: her special department was knocks. 'I'm no' long for this life,' she would say, coming down from her room of a morning, very very depressed. 'I heard three warning knocks, loud and clear. My Maker has called me.' And she would go upstairs again to get her death linen in order. Naturally, we grew accustomed to her premonitions, but suffered some remorse in the end when she died after hearing her knocks.

It is difficult to look back and come to any conclusion about the overall influence the old woman had on me. She used to say to my mother: 'Allie will be the best of the family to you in your old age'. And it is true that I never neglected my parents in their old age, although other members of the family may have given them more practical help than I did. I do think that what older folks say to a child may have a great effect on later behaviour and thought. One of our neighbours once looked sadly at me when I was about ten. 'Eh, Mrs Neill,' she said, 'that laddie has death written in his face. He winna live lang.' That remark haunted my life for years.

Death was no stranger to me. I had been at the burial of little members of the family more than once, and knew the trappings of death and the tears – yes, and the airy relief after the body was left in the grave. I must have attended three funerals before I was ten. Counting a still-born infant, my mother had thirteen children in all. Years later, when we used to criticise her for having so many, she indignantly told us that it was God's will, and she got furious with Clunie for saying: 'That's all very well, but you had no right to have me eleven months after Allie; and if you call that God's will, He is to blame for my poor health.'

Father walked back and forth to his school at Kingsmuir, two miles out. Later, when I was about eight, we moved there after a new schoolhouse had been built. My earlier memories of Forfar are vague and hazy. We lived in a third- or fourth-storey flat, and one of my pleasant recollections is playing trains in the long hall. Saturday morning was market time for the farmers' wives who brought in their butter and eggs; a hopeful time for a small boy who might get tuppence for holding a horse, though my fear of horses then makes me wonder how I had the pluck to go near one. To this day I pass a horse's heels uneasily. Sometimes on those Saturdays, we did manage to pick up a penny or two, largesse

8

from kindly farmwives whose bairns were at Kingsmuir School. This had to be accepted surreptitiously, for one of my mother's stern rules forbade us to accept money or food from other people under any circumstances. For her, to have the children accept little presents from others would have been classing her family with the lowest orders. But we children found it hard to give a reasonable excuse for refusing Mrs Findlay's offer of a delicious piece of bread with thick fresh butter and damson plum jam.

One day when I proudly told Mother that I had refused such a tempting dainty, she smiled and told me I was a good boy.

'Of course you said you weren't hungry, didn't you?'

'No,' I said with confidence, 'just "Thank you, but my ma says I mustn't take it." ' And she slapped me hard.

She was a proud wee woman, my mother. To us her rule seemed cruel: naturally, we did not understand the fear of patronage that lay behind it, a fear that came from her lowly upbringing in a humble Leith home. Mother had high ambitions for herself and her family. She was a snob, and she made us snobs.

The brothers and sisters of both my parents were poor folk of the working class, speaking in dialects you could cut with a knife. Gradually, we came to believe that they were beneath us, and we acquired the well-known 'poor-relation' complex. My mother dexterously managed to keep her own relatives from visiting us – they were a hundred miles away – with one exception.

Eccentric Uncle Neil was a barber in Brechin – a most unsuccessful one. He would suddenly lock up his shop and go for a long walk. Legend said that on one occasion he went off for a stroll in the midst of shaving a customer, leaving the man with one cheek unshaved. He talked to himself a lot, which may explain his lack of success: a barber who talks to himself while handling a razor will not build up a large business. But he was a harmless man, and we were all very fond of him. When his business failed shortly after Granny's death – she had been helping him with her saved-up coins – he came to live with us. After a while, Mother began to suggest it was time he did something for a living. One morning he got annoyed with her, bundled up his few belongings, and left. We never saw nor heard of him again. The children missed him, for he was always generous with sweets. I often wondered what happened to him.

Father's people, apparently, were less immune to hints and sometimes would come to stay with us. Old William MacNeill, my grandfather, was a man of strong convictions. He had all the dourness of the Scot, and any subtle suggestion made him stiffen.

My mother could not forgive him his neckwear; he refused to wear a collar but wore a black handkerchief instead. As I have said earlier, he was a distinguished-looking man; in my mother's eyes, however, a man whose neckwear betrayed his low-class origin. He could make a fine fiddle with a penknife; he could make wonderful furniture with hidden dovetails; he could tackle any mechanical job with skill and some art, but he would not wear a collar. Worse yet, he always had a hechle in his throat and would spit anywhere. Even as a child, I felt a tense atmosphere between my mother and him. He had definite ideas about women: they were something lower than men in the scale of humanity; they had to be kept in their place. Possibly Mother could have forgiven him his neckwear and his spitting if only he had given her the right to be at least as important as he was.

There also was some confused story of my father's family having spoiled Mother's wedding in some way: something about the MacNeills keeping Father to themselves when he ought to have started on his honeymoon. To her, the old man remained a bossy old interferer.

Saturday mornings stand out as happy times. I can still smell the fresh, unsalted butter in the market, still see the farmers' gigs with their smart ponies. By midday, the ponies had all taken their masters home – literally – for in those days many of them got so drunk that the pony had to find its own way without guidance. When motors came in and an agent tried to sell Farmer Mosside one, Mossy looked at him beerily. 'Here', he said, 'if you can sell me a car that'll bloody well take me home when I'm fu', I'll buy it.'

Glory departed with the gigs; Saturday afternoon was dreary and dull. We wandered around the grey streets, often searching the gutter for treasure. Sammie Clark averred he had once found a penny, but search as we might, we never found money. The richest treasure I recollect was a cap gun with a broken trigger. Sometimes the town band would play, and we would march along the street to the music. Clunie and I followed the band one day to the Market Muir, a long way from home for toddlers' feet. I had a sanitary accident; and when I got home, my irate mother marched me down to the outside washing house, took off the offending pants, and sent me running home with a hearty slap on the bum. I must have been about six, yet I still can recall my fear that someone would meet me in that pantless sprint. Mother seemed to get some amusement out of the incident, for years later she referred to my speed that day as a criterion for swiftness.

Sundays always seemed a depressing time, when we were

rigged up in Sabbath clothes with starched collars and cuffs. We were accustomed to the collars, because Mother prided herself on the fact that her boys wore genuine stiff collars even on weekdays. She spoke bitterly of the lazy limmers who dressed their sons in ordinary waterproof ones.

Getting ready for the kirk was hateful to us. We struggled with clumsy cufflinks: we resentfully stood to have olive oil rubbed into our hair. We were all dressed up with nowhere to go – nowhere, at any rate, that we wanted to go. We knew there lay before us an hour and a half of extreme boredom, of sitting on a hard pew with upright back – only the rich had cushions – of listening to dull psalms and hymns and a seemingly interminable sermon by Dr Caie. The one bright spot in the sombre picture was the tight-laced woman who had the pew in front of ours. Her waspish waist had been gained at the expense of internal gurgles, and we beguiled the time during the sermon by counting the intervals between gurgles. As the sermon dragged on, we found that we had enough to do just keeping our sense of gravity. Occasionally, I imagine, the sounds from the wasp-waisted one were drowned by our own unsuppressed splutters of merriment. I don't think the lady was conscious of our ribald attentions, for she often turned around and gave us peppermints.

I was just getting on to Sunday School age when, luckily, the schoolhouse (our new home) was finished, and we moved to Kingsmuir. Evidently my parents did not think it necessary to send us to a Sunday School two miles away. Moving to the country stands out as a happy milestone in my life. At five, I had gone to school from Forfar, daily toddling the long two miles while holding my father's hand. He was always a fast walker – even at seventy-five he could outpace me – and my childish steps must have irritated him.

My father did not care for me when I was a boy. Often he was cruel to me, and I acquired a definite fear of him, a fear that I never quite overcame in manhood. I see now that Father did not like *any* children; he had no contact with them. He did not know how to play, and he never understood the child's mind. The boy he admired was the boy who could beat the others in lessons; and since I never had any interest in lessons and could not learn, I had no hope of gaining Father's interest or affection. But in the time I am writing of – the time I attended school as a toddler – the lesson element had not yet appeared on the horizon. To him, I was merely a drag who made him late for school. He had a lady assistant at that time, a long-legged girl who kept up with him

11

athletically, and I still see myself falling behind and whimpering in dread of being left.

I also remember another fear of those days: cattle. The Forfar cattle market was held on Mondays, and the roads were full of cattle droves. I soon found that the droves frightened Father, who sometimes even jumped a dyke with me when we met what looked like a dangerous beast. In the manner of all boys, I believed that my father could fight a score of lions, and to see him scuttle ignominiously over a wall to escape a herd of bulls must have pricked the bubble of my faith. Like his father before him, he was a timid man.

Old William MacNeill was so afraid of the dark that when he was courting my grandmother, she had to come from her village to meet him in his. My father always feared the dark, and in later years when he returned from Edinburgh by the midnight mail, my brothers and I had to meet him at the station about two in the morning.

My mother was fearless, partly because she had less imagination than Father. I recall the day she set off to town, presumably to shop. She returned, having had all her top teeth extracted. Local anaesthetics were then unknown, and only the rich could afford gas.

We certainly were not rich. My father's salary was never more than £130 a year, and how they brought up eight children, sending three of us to the university, is a mystery. Only great self-sacrifice could explain it. My mother augmented our meagre income by dyeing and curling feathers, and my father spent nothing on himself. He neither smoked nor drank. Other teachers could have their golf and their bowls; he had no games and no hobbies. Once he tried to join in a village game of quoits, but my mother put her foot down: 'George Neill, think of your position! You can't lower yourself to play games with ploughmen and railwaymen.'

I fear that Mother's emphasis on social position cramped our style. In summer, when the whole school went barefoot, we children alone had to wear hot stockings and boots – also those stiff starched collars.

Mother had a mania for laundry, and she washed well and ironed perfectly. If her family did not become ladies and gentlemen, it would not be her fault. We had to speak English in the house, but of course we spoke broad Forfarshire outside. How we managed to change slickly from one to the other is astounding: we never seemed to make a mistake. The inside *boots* automatically became *bates* when we talked to Jock Broon.

12

One of our grievances was not being allowed to work as the common children did. In the potato-harvest holidays, they all went gathering on the farms. In the berry season, they all went picking strawberries. The 'aristocratic' Neills could not be allowed to behave as menials. But a day came when economic circumstances overruled snobbery. Then thirteen, I was sent to the strawberries and potatoes, and hated the toil. Snobbery gave way because my oldest brother Willie was acting the spendthrift at St Andrew's University.

Moving to the new schoolhouse in Kingsmuir broadened our view of life. In Forfar, our horizon had been the churchyard; here it extended farther. The smell of new wood always takes me back to that house; to us it was heaven, and for many years, the centre of my world. Later, Clunie died in the wee bedroom where I had slept for years – Clunie, the playmate I loved so much; for my two elder brothers left me out of things and I was forced to make her my chum. The strange thing is that I can look at that schoolhouse now without any emotion. I cannot sentimentalise what has gone, and perhaps that is a good thing, for hankering after the past often denotes a disappointing present. If we go backward to find our emotions, something is far wrong; equally wrong is the forward look, toward bliss in the next world.

Father's school was on one side of the road; our dwelling, the schoolhouse, on the opposite side. The house had a parlour, dining-room, kitchen, and five bedrooms. Our loo was an earth closet far up the garden. I cannot remember if we appreciated the fact that instead of a two-mile uphill walk to school each morning, we simply had to cross the road. I may have, but my brothers soon had to go to Forfar Academy and walk two miles again, morning and evening.

The penny-farthing bicycle was then in use, though we never knew it by that name and simply called it a 'high' bicycle. The 'safety', growing in popularity, had solid rubber tyres, rather like those of a baby carriage, and was displaced by the 'cushion', a bicycle with thicker solid tyres. I cannot remember when the 'pneumatic' came in, but have a vague recollection of seeing the great racer Killacky riding a cycle with inflated tyres about as big as the modern low-pressure automobile tyre. But bicycles were unknown to the poor in those days, and my brothers had to walk.

Forfar Academy was the stepping-stone to a university education. To my father, advancement in life meant advancement in learning. We were to be scholars, and Willie led the way. In the Academy, he topped his class in most subjects, and won the gold medal – or, rather, tied for it with a boy called Craik, son of an important jute manufacturer in town. My mother strongly believed that Craik was in the tie only because of his bigwig father, a natural opinion for her to have. But Willie was the hope of the house. His brilliance as a scholar seemed remarkable. Without visibly doing any work, he managed to go to university at sixteen and win further medals there. His method was to sit up for three nights before the exam with a wet towel around his head, and his memory was prodigious.

Willie's brilliance had unhappy effects on all the members of the family. Neil, who became between Willie and me, also went to the Acadamy. He was no great scholar and he did not worry much when the teachers made nasty comparisons between his work and Willie's.

When it came my turn to go to the Academy, I was not sent. I was the only one of the family who never went to the Academy. The sad truth is that it would have been useless and hopeless to send me there, for I could not learn. My father still did not care much for me and little wonder: I was obviously the inferior article, the misfit in a tradition of academic success, and automatically I accepted an inferior status. If there was a particularly hard and unappetising heel to a loaf, my father would cut it off with a flourish; with another flourish, he would toss it over the table in my direction, saying: 'It'll do for Allie'.

Clunie used to wax indignant at the way I was treated, but she never had the courage to attack my father on the subject. I recall her vigorous protest against my having to wear Willie's cast-off clothes; but adoring Willie so much at that time, I may have given her a clump on the ear for interfering. In all fairness, I still do not know why all the others were sent to the Academy. Clunie was clever but no prizewinner, and the other sisters did nothing important academically.

I was the only one who began and completed his schooling in the village. This was unfortunate, for it kept me tied to the old folks too long and prevented my measuring myself against the more sophisticated boys in the town. Not that Forfar Academy would have helped me at all educationally; there I surely would have been near the bottom of every class.

EARLY SCHOOLDAYS

Kingsmuir School was a two-roomed building divided into the 'big' and 'little' rooms. In the big room, my father had Standards IV to ex-VI, ex-VI being composed of the few boys who remained in school after age fourteen. The 'Missy' kept the younger children in the little room.

If Father was to give Class V a lesson in geography, he told a boy to hang the map on the blackboard. While this was being done, test cards in arithmetic were given out to Standard III. Standard IV might be ordered to learn its spelling, while Standard VI read. Heaven only knows what the ex-VIs were doing. My father would stand at the map, and I can still hear the geography class shouting in unison: 'Leeds, Bradford, Halifax, Wakefield'. After a few minutes, he would leave this class to its own devices and take the reading of the VIs. Naturally, it was a noisy room. We spent much of our time talking, also drawing on our dirty slates, which we cleaned by spitting on them and then rubbing them with the palm of the hand. We never seemed to tire of tilting our slates so that the spittle would make slimy designs.

It was in the main a happy school. Sometimes my father used the strap a lot, especially when exasperated by the dunces, for his salary depended on the number of Standard V students he passed. For some obscure reason, Standard V came to be the parking place of dunces; as Inspection Day approached, and my father got more and more irritable, the blows of the strap grew many and hard. Lest he be accused of favouritism, he punished his family

15

as severely as the others, and I came in for more than my fair share when the strappings were given for noise or mischief: as a Neill, I ought to have kept away from the bad boys.

I feared my father much at that time. He had a nasty habit of taking me by the cheek and pinching me hard between thumb and forefinger. Often he pinched my arm painfully. There must have been something very unlikable about me then, for the other members of the family received fairer treatment. I was clumsy, preoccupied with scraps of iron in my pockets, and my unprepossessing appearance did not help. My stuck-out ears earned me the nickname Saucers, and my feet grew suddenly to the size they are now. I was much ashamed of the enormous boots I wore. Because my toes turned in, I clattered along the road with those great boots hitting each other, sometimes tripping me up. I was certainly not the kind of son desired by a father who sought high academic distinction for his family. This aim was apparent in our evening homework. The rural scholars, destined to be hewers of wood and drawers of water, had none. But we were different. Every night at a certain hour, our games with the village lads were sadly and roughly interrupted by a dog whistle my father blew at the back door.

'Time for the dogs to ging hame,' cried our chums, and the dogs went home with their tails between their legs – Neilie and Clunie and me. Willie, a law unto himself, required neither driving nor coaching. The rest of us trooped into the nursery and attempted to turn our thoughts from 'smuggle the gig' to Allen's *Latin Grammar*.

How I hated that book! Tags from it still linger in my memory: *A dative put with show and give, tell, envy, spare, permit, believe: to these add succour, pardon, please*. Neilie and Clunie had no great difficulty in learning such things, but I never could; and often I had to sit poring over the stuff when they had been allowed to go back to the village lads and their play.

On Sundays my mother took command, and we had to stay in until we had learned set verses of a psalm or paraphrase. Again I was left behind, tearfully muttering to myself the meaningless lines. Sometimes dear old Granny Sinclair would surreptitiously slip me one of her peppermints to show that she was on my side.

I know that my ability as a teacher came from watching my father's methods. In those far-off days the village dominie was the oracle, for, apart from the minister, he was the only educated man in the village. Since Kingsmuir was too small to have a kirk my father was the adviser, materially and spiritually. Like the school-

16

master in Goldsmith's 'The Deserted Village', he had a fund of information.

> 'And still they gazed, and still the wonder grew
> That one small head could carry all he knew.'

And although so far as his own family was concerned, he was not a man of good judgement, with the villagers he seemed to give the best advice. True the matters he was asked to solve were minor ones but not to the askers. 'Should I send Wullie tae the Academy or let him work as a loon on the farm?' Sometimes old pupils, now at a higher school, brought him most intricate sums to solve, the kind where a man rows up a river at three miles an hour against a current flowing at one mile an hour; he stops for lunch for half an hour and meanwhile the current has changed . . . awful sums that I could never solve, but my father never failed once. My father certainly had the knack of drawing out his pupils. Long before modern methods in teaching geography, he kept telling them to ask why . . . why is Glasgow where it is? Why London? Why is there more rain on the west coast of Scotland than on the east? In geography he had no way of knowing how foreign names were pronounced. For him, the capital of Iceland was *Reeky-a-veek*, Bucarest was *Boo-carest*, Arkansas was pronounced with the final 's'. He had his own pronunciation; pencil was *pincil*, a lantern was a *lantren*, a physician was a *physeecian*. Yet he always knew the meanings of even the most uncommon words. If crosswords had existed in his day he would have been adept at them.

He used to have a class which he called Intelligence. We formed a half-circle and if the boy or girl at the top did not know the answer the one who did went up top. On one occasion I reached the top. The word was 'evident', and I said 'easily seen', but I had a very bad conscience later, for I had just learned the word from a saying of my brother Willie:

'That's quite evident, as the monkey said when he shat on the table cloth'.

I had a vague, frightening idea that the word was associated with shit and that my father knew it.

His method certainly gave us a vocabulary. And my father gave us a sound training in grammar, so that, even today, I have a mild shock when someone says: 'He spoke to Jim and I' or 'These sort of things are useless'. In teaching us Latin he showed us how it helped spelling; we knew that committee had two 'm's' because it came from con (with) and mitto (I send). That was all I ever got

17

from Latin. I had just got to an appreciation of the lines of Virgil when I passed an examination and never opened a Latin book again.

That is the absurd feature about learning the Classics. One spends dreary years over the grammar and unless one takes Classics at the university the whole subject disappears from memory.

My father's teaching of geography consisted mainly of lists of names. I knew all the rivers of Britain, the cotton, the pottery, the iron towns. Snippets remain . . . Hexham famous for hats and gloves, Redditch for needles, Axminster for carpets. Yet, as I say, he asked us to ask why. To this day I feel that if I motor to Scotland I am going uphill; it was uphill on the hanging map.

I cannot recall having drawing classes in Kingsmuir. We had few books to write in; we had slates with wooden frames that did not last long. I can still hear the clatter of them on the floor, when we piled them to see who got the answer to a sum first. Later they were condemned as being unhygienic because we licked them clean, but I cannot recall that any of us caught germs from them.

My father had little humour but some imagination. He made history live for us. His selection of poetry, however, may have had some bearing on my later inability to appreciate poetry. Sentimental ballads . . . 'Little Jim', 'Lucy Gray', 'Mary, go and call the cattle home . . .', they all seemed to deal with early death and family grief. But he did give us 'The Deserted Village' and no doubt we identified him with the schoolmaster in it; 'He was a man stern to view'.

I have sometimes wondered why he did not give us the lovely Border Ballads. Much later when head of a Gretna Green school I used the Ballads a lot; especially liked by the pupils was 'Helen of Kirkconnel', 'I wish I were where Helen lies . . .' Kirkconnel Lea was a few miles from my school and I took the children to see Helen's grave. When a rival shot to kill her lover, Helen threw herself in front of him and died.

'I lighted doon my sword to draw,
I hackit him in pieces sma.'

Tut, tut, I was as bad as my good father in selecting poems about death. To counter it I gave them 'Young Lochinvar' and his merry abduction of the bride-to-be. His Esk River was also near the school.

My failure to learn Latin angered my father, but my inability to learn even two lines of a psalm gave my mother more sorrow than anger. What did anger her was my forgetting 'messages' when sent to town. As the only child who didn't go to the Academy, my job of a morning was to walk to Forfar with the Academy lot and fetch household supplies.

'Now are you sure you can remember the list?' my mother would ask. 'Pound of flank and a marrow bone, two pounds of sugar, mustard, bottle of vinegar, and' – here my mother whispered – 'a bottle of aqua.' In those days, aqua – our word for whisky – was 2/10d. a bottle, Melvin's best; but when Grandfather was coming, or when Donald Macintosh, the School Board Clerk, was expected, we had to have it in the house. It was always a luxury.

So off I'd trudge to town in my big boots. When I got to the East Port, however, I had completely forgotten the items. Sometimes I made wild guesses, but the result of bringing home sugar when I had been told to get salt was too painful, and I took to telling feeble lies about Lindsay and Low being out of sugar at the moment. Then I was given a written list, though sometimes I lost even that.

Coming back from town with my awkward parcels was an unpleasant experience. No one ever thought of inventing a rucksack, and although I could have taken a basket, it seemed an effeminate thing to do. So I trudged up the braes with my heavy parcels, pausing every few steps to see if Will Clunie's milkcart was coming, for Will was always kind to the children and never passed without giving me a lift.

Often empty gigs would pass, but my plea for a hitch: 'Hi, mannie, see a lift fae ye,' was met by indifference. They were a dour, unfriendly crowd, the Angus farmers. Most of them wouldn't allow even a 'hing ahent', when you gripped the backboard and ran behind.

Those farmers, most of them long since dead, affect me to this day. When motoring, I seldom pass a child or an old person on the road without offering a lift. On long journeys, like going to Scotland, I often give lifts to tramps, partly for company but mainly because I suffered so much as a child from selfish drivers.

I got into the way of lingering on the road until Will Clunie came along to pick me up. He left town rather late, however, and Father got exasperated because I was too long in bringing him his *Scotsman*. Then I was forbidden to wait for milkcart lifts.

This 'going messages' to Forfar was not only tiring but alarming. Every boy who did not live in one's own village was regarded as an enemy; and if a Letham boy walked through Kingsmuir, we did our duty; that is, we chased him with stones.

19

In Forfar, of course, we Kingsmuir 'skites' were the strangers, and therefore regarded as enemies.

The way into town was through a street called the Ha'en, a queer name in an inland town. The Ha'en had its squad – gang, nowadays – and every morning there were dangers to face. I cannot recall being severely beaten up, possibly because I ran like hell when I saw them. But there are also vague memories of sometimes being friendly with the Ha'en squad, and I can only guess that immunity was won by flattery and humility.

This hatred of strangers was very strong when I was a boy. A few sons of well-to-do farmers had ponies on which they rode to the Academy. We continually attacked them with sticks and stones. I don't know why, for they were harmless fellows who gave no offence.

Kingsmuir and Lunanhead were both called Landward schools, the only two in the Forfar area. They had a common school board, and this board stupidly arranged a joint picnic for the two schools during the celebration of the Queen's Jubilee in 1897. Students of each school marched to the picnic grounds, and there we stood staring sullenly at each other. The Lunanhead lads were bigger and beefier than ours, so when one of them, seeing me, asked what I was laughing at and did I want 'my face ca'd up amongst my hair', I looked away hurriedly. Unfortunately, our bruiser Jake Hanton had left school a few weeks before. When competitions began, and the rival schools began to express their enmity by charging and kicking, we looked at Lunanhead's shock brigade as we whispered to each other: 'Oh, if only Jake Hanton was here!'

Suddenly, a small boy came running to us, and told us that not only had Jake Hanton come down after his day's work but also that Dave Wyllie, another pugilist, was with him. Then, I fear, we smaller, weaker ones behaved in a lowdown fashion. We began to make insulting remarks to the Lunanhead louts; whereupon they took off their coats, turned up their sleeves, and told us they would 'knock us into jelly'. We smiled and signalled to our champions. The Lunanhead lads lost the battle, and as they sidled away, pretended not to hear Jake's sporting offer to 'fecht any five o' them with one hand'.

Jake Hanton was a dunce, with one talent – fighting, and he fought like a bulldog. His name alone could quell any boy in the neighbourhood. He liked me and became my protector, and for some months my life was made soft and easy by the magic phrase: 'If you touch me, I'll tell Jake Hanton.'

20

We seem to have fought a tremendous lot, though seldom in anger. For example: I would have a quarrel with Jock Broon about anything at all, maybe a marble or a piece of skiley – a slate pencil. I'd threaten to sock him in the nose; and Jock, who of course was younger than I, would reply: 'Ye wudna say that to Dave Wyllie.'

Now Wyllie was a hefty lad, a good fighter who could beat me to a standstill in a few seconds; but when Jock insinuated the truth, that I was afraid of Wyllie, honour compelled me to say that I had no fear of Wyllie. So Jock would tell Wyllie, who would look over the schoolroom at me, put his fist to his nose, and say: 'Wait till fower o'clock'. And so at four o'clock I would be facing the champion Wyllie up the Back Dykes, scared stiff and hopeless, beaten before the fight began. The shattering effect of that 'wait till fower o'clock' is with me still.

Like my father and grandfather, I was a coward, but a coward with a difference. Like my father, I feared the dark, but unlike him, I did not avoid the dark. A dread of the dark haunted me in those early days, especially when I had to walk home from Forfar after dusk, a distance of two long miles with only one house. This house was kept by two old women, but to me it seemed a sort of halfway sanctuary from the dangers of the road. I never doubted that the two old women could protect me when 'the man wearing the cheesecutter bonnet' came after me with a knife. He had sprung out on Jeem Craik, a grown man. He had held up ploughmen with the demand: 'Your money or your life!' His favourite spot was the stile at the bottom of Welton Brae. Needless to say I never saw him, for he existed only in the imagination of Eck Smith.

My fear was proportionate to the lateness of the hour. Winter nights seemed safe until six o'clock, for the factory girls were on the road then. Seven wasn't so bad because one of the girls might have stayed behind to do some shopping, and sometimes lovers wandered slowly along the Kingsmuir Road. One night a couple, annoyed because I walked close behind them, accused me of trying to listen to their conversation. I hadn't the courage to tell them the truth, that I was afraid to be alone.

Leaving the town was the worst of it. I trailed slowly up Easter Bank Brae, fearful to leave the light of the gas lamps. At the last lamp I would stop and stare into the black night ahead of me, glancing back in the hope that a gig would be coming along behind. There was small hope of getting a lift, but if I hurried into the dark road, I'd get as far as the High Dykes before the gig

21

passed me. Then, when the pony had to walk up Welton Brae, I could overtake the gig by running. Once up the brae, I was within sight of the first twinkling lamps of Kingsmuir. In any event, the man with the cheesecutter bonnet had not been known to operate above the brae.

Although the major terror was the road from Forfar, there were minor fears attached to shorter journeys. I had to go to Granny Hutchison's every night for the milk. Her place was just round the corner, and I never had any fear going there; but when I turned to come back, it seemed that all the murderers in the world were after me. I had a similar emotion about going to the water closet, or rather the *closet*, for it was a dry one at the top of the garden. Going up there in the dark made me uneasy, for who knew who might be sitting on the seat? But coming back was something like the speed of the wind. Taking a lantern was doubtful help. It certainly gave a kind of protective companionship; on the other hand, it told the man with the cheesecutter bonnet where you were.

Somewhere back in this period, I discovered that on a lonely dark road it was advantageous to stop and urinate; for I had only to begin when someone's footsteps would be heard. Of course, I had to move on hastily. Nevertheless, it seemed an infallible way to attract company.

I must have relied mainly on my legs to escape the terror, but I can recall arming myself. Willie brought home a real skullcracker that could slip easily into an overcoat pocket. I also had a Gamages water pistol filled with cayenne-peppered water, and must have been somewhat disappointed that I never got the opportunity to test its efficiency on some bad man's eyes. Later, our Skye terrier completed my armament, although he was a poor bodyguard. Boulot kept at my heels all the way to town, when I didn't need him, but went off on his own when we entered the town, and straggled home hours later, wet, bedraggled, and very, very guilty.

Still, Boulot gave me ideas. When passing the worst danger – the stile at the foot of Welton Brae – I kept whistling for an imaginary dog, calling 'Wolf' or some such name that would let the man with the cheesecutter bonnet know that my dog was a huge man-eater. Another technique was to shout back to an imaginary companion: 'Come on, Jock', when I thought that that danger was near.

I never knew if the other children had similar fears. We did not mention such things, because we knew that to be a coward was the greatest of all social sins. Like the sin against the Holy Ghost, it was unforgivable. I do not know how we acquired this standard. It may have had something to do with our literature, which was of the penny-dreadful variety. (We called the booklets *penny horribles*, or *bloods*.)

Our school readers always contained a few stories of heroes, inclined to moral courage. One was the tale of a British officer in a far-out Empire post, sick with fever, speared in the leg by the natives – gangrene had set in – and facing a tribal uprising with no other weapon than his belief in God and Queen Victoria. I cannot recall how he triumphed, but he did; and with his dying breath he thanked God that he had done his duty. I'm afraid we preferred the godless heroism of the penny horribles.

It cannot be easy for younger generations to imagine village life at the end of the last century. Every village boy of today is within reach of a cinema; he has, or he can hear, a radio; he watches television, and he sees the world go by in automobiles, trucks, and buses.

In my childhood, life went by slowly, in gigs and on bicycles. The only entertainment was a very occasional concert in the schoolroom, or a visit from an itinerant juggler. There was, other times, old Professor Thomson, unwashed and smelling of drink. He usually arrived in the morning. My father told us to bring our price of admission (a ha'penny) in the afternoon. We were thrilled, of course, to see the professor draw ribbons from his mouth by the yard, and find eggs in Jock Broon's pocket. When the magician breathed forth fire after swallowing balls of coloured paper, I was at once excited and alarmed. To this day, I have the same attitude toward conjuring: I simply stare like a rustic, vainly wondering how it is all done.

Once a year, we had a school picnic. That was a swell affair. We went in farmers' carts, and the ploughmen spent nights polishing their harnesses and grooming their horses. Of all the days in the year, that one was nearest heaven; the day following was the deepest hell. On the day after the school picnic, I invariably plumbed the depths of bitter despair, weeping in sheer misery. The glory had departed and would never come again. I tried to perpetuate the emotion of the picnic by attaching some of it to the people who had been there. Because a man called Jake Kenny had driven the cart I rode in, Jake became my hero for weeks. I had a vague feeling that Jake and I were bound together for eternity as two souls having shared a great spiritual experience.

On the other 364 days of the year nothing happened in Kingsmuir. This monotony of life was broken only by an occasional

23

wedding or funeral. We welcomed both but preferred marriages. They were often forced ceremonies, the couple having 'cut the wedding cake before the marriage', as the saying went. Sometimes a boy was present at his parents' wedding. Kingsmuir had no false modesty about such marriages.

The part of the ceremony that interested us was the departure of the bridal pair. Not that we had any special interest in them, but their departure was the proper time for the best man to 'scatter'. He had a bag of sweets, and sometimes he included a few coppers. Thees he scattered on the road as the carriage drove away, and we all scrambled for the goodies in the mud or dust. We had no fine feelings about eating the sweets: any of us would lift one from a pile of horse dung and shove it into his mouth. I compromised by spitting out the first suck, but one lad considered it a sentimental waste to spit out anything.

It was the chance of picking up coppers that drew us to the marriages. Money was almost unknown to us, for we had no pocket-money as most children do nowadays. The possession of a ha'penny marked a red-letter day. Then we went to Nanzy Tam's wee shop window and glued our little noses to the panes. The window was not a good window as shop windows go: all it contained was a row of sweetie bottles, a few laces or sticks of sugarella and jaw-sticker, and one or two lucky bags. These last were my favourite purchase. I never got anything lucky in them, but never lost hope of finding a new golden ha'penny wrapped up in tissue paper. Later, lucky something-or-others appeared with red bits of toffee in thin paper. They had ha'pennies inside. I once got a lucky one – and then lost the golden ha'penny.

Games had their special periods: marbles when the March dust was blowing, tops later in the spring. We all had marbles and tops, and iron hoops which we called girds, but I never knew how we got them. Marbles in the shops were expensive – ten a penny at one time – yet when the season began, poor ragged boys would appear suddenly with their 'pooches full of bools'. Some at least were stolen from Nanzy Tam's shoppie, and more than once I helped raid the coal-shed where she kept empty lemonade bottles. We took the bottles to a dark corner and broke their necks to get out any glass marbles inside. We made poor catapults from the rubber rings. It never occurred to us that poor Nanzy would have to pay for the empties. Possibly the marbles originated from small sons of the more well-to-do farmers.

I cannot recall many other attempts on our part to steal from shops. We'd ask Nanzy for something we knew she kept in the kitchen, and while she was away we'd pinch chewing gum or chocolate, but that was petty crime. A milk-delivery boy, who freely supplied me with penny horribles and *Chips* and *Comic Cuts*, had some elaborate system of robbing a newsagent's shop. Exactly how he managed this I was not curious enough to inquire, no doubt because knowledge would have made me a guilty accomplice. We were an honest crowd, mainly because there wasn't anything to steal. We did the usual raiding of orchards; our moral standard made stealing money a heinous offence, whereas orchards were pure sport.

Money was a very necessary adult concern on two Saturdays of the year – the May and November 'Terms'. Those were the days on which the ploughmen were engaged or fee'd. (I was brought up among words or phrases that no Englishman or American ever knows: *fee, public roup, ashet, ground to feu, avizandum,* for example.) Twice a year, on Market Day, masters and men met in town to bargain. Ploughmen were engaged from term to term, but why they changed masters so often I cannot understand, for the wages were standard (very low) and the perquisites of meal and milk seem to have obtained on all farms. For us children, *any* Market Day meant entertainment. Each Friday we peeped excitedly at booths and tents going up in the High Street – at hobby-horses and swing boats. The anticipation made us sleep badly every Friday night.

The sons of the farmers had a lot of money to spend at the Market, the Adams family as much as half-a-crown each. We poor Neills never had more than sixpence apiece; it was all our parents could afford. Sometimes I augmented mine by looking soulfully up into Mrs Adams' eyes and asking if her rheumatism were better. She was always kind to us bairns. On Market Day, I displayed quite a lot of anxiety about the health of farmers and their wives, and could turn my sixpence into eightpence, or sometimes even ninepence. The spending was a ticklish business. Hobby-horses cost a penny, so did the swinging boats. The boxing saloon, from the front of which Jimmy Lavin bellowed an offer of five pounds to any man who would knock out his boxer, was too dear; and I had to take the easier road of sneaking under the tent canvas when Jimmy Lavin was concentrating his attention on the boxing. No one ever won the five pounds. The ploughmen went in with their arms swinging like flails, and the scientific boxer knocked them down easily with straight lefts.

I was conservative in my spending on Market Days. My procedure was always the same: I went straight to Laing's shop and bought a tuppeny pencil with blue lead at one end and red at the other, then a penny ice-cream; and walked up the street to the hobby-horses. I trembled as I mounted the steps, and when the horses started and the organ blared, I felt that the end had come. The sickly smell of hot oil did not tend to make me happier. I had a terrible phobia that the machinery would break down and the horses carry me round for ever and ever. My terror and delight were so great that I sat on and had another pennyworth – a pennyworth I could ill afford. I never had the nerve to try the swing boats, but got some vicarious thrills out of watching drunken ploughmen try to swing themselves over the top. I always turned away disappointed in the end, as I did after every thunderstorm, because no one was killed.

What a great day! Even after all one's money vanished, Market Day was still exciting. I soon got a sharp nose for potential trouble, and when a fight started, with bloody noses and black eyes, I often managed to squirm into the front rank of lookers-on.

At the Cross, a public square, there were always one or two cheapjacks selling eighteen-carat gold watches for 'any price you like, gentlemen'. Their technique was always the same: 'I didn't come here to make money. I came here to do you a favour. Will any gentleman give me a penny for this half-crown?' Now the half crown was always genuine, yet these slow-wits stood and gazed at him with open mouths. In the end, he practically had to force someone to buy the coin for a penny. The next stage of building confidence was to sell a set of genuine gold studs for two shillings – 'But don't go away, sir: each and every man will have his reward' – and sure enough, the buyer got his studs and his money back. I spent a long time each Market Day studying the technique. The difficulty was to know the exact point at which the real business of fleecing the yokels began. The first few got their money back; the next lot got the gold watch, plus a beautiful set of gold dress studs; and for the rest of the day, the buyers merely got dud watches in exchange for their pound notes.

One Market Day, I had half-a-crown saved up. Brushing aside the temptation to invest in my usual red-and-blue pencil, I went straight to the Cross. This time the man was selling purses, not watches, and held one up when I approached. 'Half-a-crown for this beautiful purse. No offers? Good, then watch me make it more valuable.' And he proceeded to drop shillings into the purse. 'Still half-a-crown', he cried; 'Who will have it?' I went nearly mad with excitement and had my half-crown in a very sweaty hand, but my pluck failed me; I simply couldn't risk it. A ploughman bought the purse while I watched with mad chagrin as he counted out the coins in it. There were about ten shillings in all. But already the cheapjack was dropping coins into another purse, and I pushed forward and held out my sticky half-crown. He gave me the purse but admonished me not to look at it until he told me to. Gripping the bulging purse tightly, I made for the outskirts of the crowd, where I finally opened it. There were three pence in coppers. Only then did I absorb that the man was not ever trying to be kind to the people of Forfar. Presently Clunie found me in tears and gave me half of the money she had left, while unkindly reminding me of her warning about these men the night before. Though I swore Clunie to secrecy, she gave me away, and I had to undergo a second humiliation, the mocking laughter of my brothers.

About the age of thirteen, I decided that my genius lay in invention. By this time, I had a secondhand cycle with cushion tyres, which I spent much time taking to pieces, carefully putting the balls in a saucer that my dog Boulot always managed to upset. At one period, I was riding with only four balls in the front axle. My dismantling mania had a grim purpose; I was studying the cycle to see how it could be improved. For many years, I believed that I had invented the rim brake, but I think now that that was sheer fantasy. What I did create was a rim brake with caliper action. When I described it to a patent agent, he wrote back that it was a fine invention, and if I would forward him my cheque for fourteen pounds . . . I had to consider other ways and means.

My brother Willie, just returned from summer teaching in a prep school at Bexleyheath, happened to mention one of the boys called Bowden. I pricked up my ears. 'The Bowden Brake man?' I asked.

Yes, Willie was sure that the boy's father was the Bowden Brake man. I said nothing but sat down and wrote to Mr Bowden of Bexleyheath, enclosing a sketch of my invention. After a week, a reply came. I could scarcely open the envelope for the trembling of my hands. It was a nice letter – so nice, I failed to grasp at first that it was not the kind of letter I had hoped for. He had only replied because he was curious to know how I had got his address. Moreover, he was not the 'Bowden Brake' Bowden at all, but a distant relative, and knew nothing about mechanics. About a year later, I found a caliper brake in a cycle catalogue.

Cast down I was, but not beaten. I next turned my inventive skills toward power as applied to cycles. I had read about levers and concluded that if the pedal cranks were about three feet long,

27

the power of driving would be enormous. The difficulty of getting two long cranks to revolve without touching the ground would be overcome by a mechanism that made them fold up telescopically as they reached the bottom of their strokes. After an engineer had laughed heartily at this idea and had explained its impossibility, I gave it up.

But power still held my imagination. When a semi-relative, versed in mechanics, hinted that the cycle of the future would be driven by compressed air, the idea set me going. I saw the whole thing in a flash. I would invent a cycle whose tubes formed an air chamber. On the back wheel would be an air pump, and when going down hill, this pump would fill the air chamber. Then, as the cycle climbed the next hill, a lever would open the air port, and the compressed air would work a small motor to drive the machine bravely up the brae. But again a tiresome and interfering practical engineer blew my invention sky-high by demonstrating that you can't get more out of a machine than you put in; as for pumping air into a cylinder going down hill, the pumping would bring the damn machine to a standstill. I think that was the last invention I attempted.

What I was going to miss in giving up invention were the bulky catalogues that came by post, especially a thumping one like Gamages'. I began to read advertisements, favouring those with coupons for free samples. I wrote to all sorts of firms for prospectuses, especially those that offered to train you by correspondence for thousand-pound-a-year jobs. There was nothing of the plodder about me; my motto was simple: GET RICH QUICK.

About this time, Neilie had a spell of body-building. Every morning he did strenuous exercises with Sandow's dumbbells and developer, and his muscles grew big and strong. I wrote a friendly letter to Sandow saying that I could not afford to take his advertised course at six guineas, but if he would let me have the course for nothing, I should be eternally grateful. The body-builder did not reply – much to my surprise, for in spite of swindling cheapjacks, I still retained my belief that men were good, loving, and always willing to help the poor and deserving.

I still have fleeting fantasies that a millionaire will step in and build me a new school after I have written him a nice, friendly letter. The fact that I don't write the letter, and never will write it, only proves the sad truth that age robs one of anticipations. Think of the interest with which I should look for the post if I were expecting a reply from a millionaire!

The letter to Sandow made me uneasy, however, after a boy

28

told me how Sandow, when attacked by two toughs in America, had thrown them over a wall and broken their backs. I wondered dimly if there was any probability of his coming five hundred miles north to chuck me over a wall for my impertinence.

About this time, I also had considerable anxiety over a firm who offered to teach you How to Write Advertisements. I had sent for its prospectus, only to learn the usual grim fact that the fee was about as much as two months of my father's salary. The firm kept sending me stiff letters, demanding to know why I was not replying. I saw myself in a lawcourt being mulcted for untold damages. When I told Willie, he took the matter in hand and wrote them a snorting letter. That was the end of my attempts to get rich quick.

Looking back on the boy that I was, I can fully appreciate my father's irritation. What could Latin verbs matter to a boy whose name was going to be known the world over as the inventor of a new cycle or a new trouser-button? 'Mary', Father said again and again, 'the boy will come to nothing', and my mother seemed to agree. Yet on one occasion I became a scholar. Kingsmuir school had a special annual prize for arithmetic – the Angus Club – which I made up my mind to win, although my chum, Frank Craik, was better at sums than I. It was a long, grim fight, but in the end I won. I still have the prize, a gilt-edged volume entitled *Ferdinand and Isabella*, but have never succeeded in getting past the first chapter.

When a boy, I seldom read a book. I can't remember Neilie reading much then either. Any book I did read was one recommended by Willie or Clunie. Willie read everything he could find, and at an early age had a fine taste in books. Clunie also was an omnivorous reader, and although a year younger than I, read Dickens and Thackeray and *Jane Eyre* when my level was the penny horrible. It was through them that I discovered H. G. Wells, W. W. Jacobs, Anthony Hope – *The Prisoner of Zenda* delighted me – and Rider Haggard. After reading *She*, I knew that my future lay in Central Africa. I also read Marie Corelli. Clunie and I agreed that she was the greatest writer who ever lived; and together, we wrote her a letter to this effect. If she would only send us her signature, we should cherish it until death. She never replied, and soon we grew critical of her work.

Today, when I get letters telling me that I am easily the greatest man alive, I always answer them, hypocritically disclaiming the compliment but wishing the senders all luck in their own futures. Marie Corelli lost two earnest admirers by not answering them; I have so few that I dare not lose any. If any youth thinks that I am greater than Shakespeare and Shaw rolled into one, it would be brutally unkind for me to contradict him. The heroes of my youth often let me down, but perhaps my tactics were all wrong. Had I written: 'Dear Miss Corelli, you can't write for nuts, and your characters are dead sticks, and your philosophy is tripe', I am sure I should have had an answer.

I indulged much in hero-worship as a boy. Willie was my demigod for many years, and my identification with him had much to do with the line my life took. At school I always had a protective hero – usually a stupid lad. I helped him with his sums, and he repaid me by beating up any boy who attacked me. All the best fighters seemed to be dunces. They hadn't the brains to argue, and the easiest reply for them was 'a scone on the lug'– what we'd call today a cuff on the ear.

My heroes were the waggish ploughmen who used to congregate in the evenings at the bridge. Indeed, I used to imitate their typical rolling walk; and, to me, it was always a matter of infinite regret that when my mother made my breeches, she would never sew on the front pockets all the ploughmen had. To my mother, such pockets were 'common' and slightly vulgar. I remember her once saying that she considered the flies on male trousers indecent, and that her father had always worn trousers whose flies were hidden by a flap. We called flies *spavers*.

At that time, Killacky was a national wonder, winning most of the prizes in cycle racing; and when a rider passed the bridge, these local wits would shout after him: 'Go on, Killac,' or 'Yer wheel's gaein' roond!' I never seemed to tire of the latter remark, nor its companion to a pedestrian: 'Hi, loon, ye've missed a step!' But it was an ordeal for me to pass the bridge when the ploughmen sat on the dyke. Perhaps I dreaded a witty line about my enormous feet or my hen toes.

I was feeble at games and, at football, always had the dishonour of being the last chosen when sides were tossed for. Yet I cannot recall ever making an athlete my hero. It must have been about the age of fourteen that I began to seek importance as a wag, and I have a faint recollection of making my schoolmates laugh easily. Their standard was not high; in geography, the River Po – *po* was toilet slang to us – kept them sniggling guiltily for the whole lesson.

Like most children, we did not appear to be conscious of the changing seasons. My haziest memories are of the winters, when there seemed more snow than now, and we made slides on the roads, skating clumsily as frogs. Sometimes when the frost was good, we tried to skate on a local pond, but never efficiently. Our skates were partly to blame, being so blunted by cart tracks that they would not grip the ice. We hated the old men and women who put salt on our slides overnight.

To us – first of all – spring meant dust, blowing with the March winds, and then the joy of bird-nesting. We all had egg collections, but harried every nest we came across, no matter how many specimens we already possessed. This search for nests was exciting, because it led us into forbidden areas where gamekeepers were savage and terrifying in voice. I still can feel the agony – as I prepared to climb a tree – of hearing a voice cry: 'What the hell are you doing there?' We had all heard tales of gamekeepers beating boys up, but these tales must have been legends, for these men never touched us. As a timid lad, I often had to stand guard for the others; that was far worse than actually taking part in a raid.

In late summer, we also came up against the gamekeepers when we went gathering raspberries. Here we were slightly fortified by the knowledge that we were poaching with parental approval. It was an economic necessity for my mother to make as many pots of raspberry jam as possible, and there were berries in the woods for the taking. The local squires did not prohibit the gathering of berries out of arrogance; their defence was that pickers disturbed the pheasants and partridges.

These raspberry expeditions were pleasant. To hold the fruit, we took milk flagons and baskets lined with cabbage leaves. I never ate the berries, and used to despise Eck Fraser for nibbling at his on the way home. Often when he had an almost empty flagon to show his indignant mother, he told her that the gamekeeper had emptied it out.

My mother slaved during the berry season. The jam pot was seldom off the fire, and we loved the delicious smell of the skimmings. She was really a wonderful housekeeper; how she managed to make just the right amount of jam to supply us for the whole year makes me marvel, even now. She was proud of all her jam-making, especially that she was the only woman in the village who could get her strawberry jam firm. Equally satisfying to her was her washing and ironing. She slaved at the washtub and ironing board, using a charcoal iron, and I fear her criterion of whiteness in linen has made me consider most steam laundries inferior ever since.

During the years when I was a boy, she suffered extreme pain –

31

often agony – from gallstones, but she never made her illness an excuse for shirking her housework. I think her proudest moments were on Sunday mornings when she stood at the garden gate and watched us troop off to the kirk: my father in his chimney hat and starched shirt; the boys in their well-brushed clothes and stiff collars, with their snow-white hankies showing from their pockets; the girls with their well-ironed dresses. She had become stout, and seldom made the long walk to town herself, only on special occasions like the Sacrament Days.

BOYHOOD

Not long after we had moved out to Kingsmuir, the Auld Kirk was completely renovated. An old Forfarian had presented a marvellous four-manual organ, and the whole interior of the kirk had been changed. With a pew in the front seat of the gallery, going to church seemed more pleasant for us children than it had been in the days of the woman with the internal gurgles. Ours was easily the best vantage point in the kirk, and it was fun to look down and watch folks during the sermon; how they nodded, or couldn't find the place when the reading was from Amos or Daniel, or dropped their pennies for the collection. On Sacrament Day, we watched eagerly to see if anyone would drop the communion chalice and we knew who took just a sip or who emptied nearly half the cup. The loud blare of the organ fascinated us. I got into the way of sitting until the final voluntary was ended in the empty church, and whatever musical taste I have dates from that time. The organist became my Sunday hero; my ambition was to sing in the choir.

I shall have much to say about religion in my youth, but somehow it is not connected with going to the kirk. That was a social function, associated with showing off clothes and making contact with people. The sermons meant nothing to me: Dr Caie read all his prayers, but without much conviction. To me, his prayers were words, stereotyped phrases about the pitcher broken at the fountain, or the silver cord being unloosed. Looking back, I wonder if anyone felt any religious emotion in that kirk. In my teens, it certainly became a place of worship, for the girl in the front seat of the opposite gallery was my goddess – cold, lovely, unattainable. My chief impressions of the kirk were sex and death. My most outstanding colour memories are the pretty faces and hats of the girls in the choir, and the black weeds of bereaved families when they were 'kirkit' after funerals. The whole family sat in a black row, the widow wearing a heavy veil.

Our chief desire was to see how they reacted when the minister made his remarks at the end of his sermon: 'I cannot conclude today without alluding to the tragic loss we have sustained through the death of one of our best-known townsmen. John Brown was . . .' With emotions that had no connection with grief, we children watched the hankies coming out. The younger members of the bereaved family generally seemed to enjoy the publicity, but to the elders it must have been painful. After church, the family wended their way to the cemetery. Some families never seemed to get out of mourning blacks, especially those like the Craiks, who had all their uncles and cousins living – or, it seemed, dying – in the town.

Sundays were rather dull, for we were not allowed to play games, and the only permissible recreation was a staid walk in kirk clothes and tight boots that blistered my toes. But, negatively, Sunday was desirable for its respite from Allen's *Latin Grammar*. We enjoyed another respite on Wednesday nights, when my father, an elder of the kirk, had to attend a meeting. He usually assigned us some pages of Allen or Caesar to do, but no sooner had he gone down the road a hundred yards than we were out with the boys. My mother often threatened to report us, yet she never did. I cannot remember what my father said or did when he found that we hadn't prepared our homework. Clunie stood up to him, at this period, and my second sister, May, positively bossed him. We believed that she was his favourite because she was named after his mother. May knew what she wanted and usually got it. Mother, who constantly was having trouble with her – 'the strong-willed hussy' – tried to 'break her will' when she was quite small. I cannot exactly recollect how, but I have a faint memory of May sitting very red and defiant in the parlour, while my irate mother yelled: 'You *will* do it!' and May screaming back: 'I tell you I won't'. And she didn't.

Willie and May prospered, simply because they went their own ways, whereas we timid ones, fearful of discipline, did what we were told. I was obedience personified, although in the long run, my passive obedience backfired. Obedience made me stare at

34

Allen's *Grammar*, but something inside me negatived my passive response by refusing to allow me to learn anything.

I am trying consciously to be objective about my parents, trying to look back at them without sentimentality. As a boy I loved my mother deeply – loved her too much – but at that age I could not love my father. He was too stern, too far away from me. As a model for us children, he used to hold up a frail little chap with glasses, who never played a game in his life but was an earnest student, actually weeping if he weren't at the top of the class. We hated that lad; he became a railway porter.

Many years later, I came to love the old man. His ambitions for us had long since gone, and he accepted us as we were. But in the times of which I speak, he held himself aloof from us boys and would never talk about his childhood. It was only before his death at the age of eighty-four (a fortnight from eighty-five) that he told me of his first great tragedy, his mother's death of cholera when he was a boy. 'I grat (wept) for weeks,' he said, as the tears came to his eyes and my own.

I do not know why he was so strained and unhappy when we were young. True enough, he was trying to do all he could for his family with very inadequate means. I am convinced, however, that economic circumstances never go deep enough to affect individuals fundamentally. I am sure, for instance, that no man ever killed himself because of loss of fortune, the reason given so often in the newspapers. For many, money comes too late in life to have any deep significance. My father's youngest brother, who never had a bean, was always cheerful. Father's pessimism must have sprung from an abnormal fear of life, and a sense of its disappointment. But how his fear arose cannot be known. Certainly his ambitions for us must have been a transfer of his own.

He was the soul of honesty, and I do not think he could tell a lie easily. Absolutely conscientious in his work, he must have felt keenly that he did not get his due recompense. His salary depended on inspection reports, and Her Majesty's Inspector at that time was a sour, unfriendly man who begrudged my father any praise for his work. This man would give glowing reports of the neighbouring school of Inverarity – a school in which my father had his first appointment as assistant – but Elder of Inverarity was no better a teacher than Father.

Inspection Day was an agony for my father. I see him yet, his white strained face looking out of the window to watch the HMI and his assistant come down from the station in the morning. Father's obvious fear infected us, and we also trembled before the mighty authorities. The inspector was a bad examiner, who attempted to find out what we did not know, rather than draw out from us what we did know. He kept writing notes in a pocket diary, and all of us, including my father, believed them to be notes of damnation.

Afterward, the stern inspector softened a little when he came over for lunch at the schoolhouse. Mother was a good cook, and on Inspection Day she always gave the guest his favourite pudding. We children were never at table. To this day I cannot meet an HMI easily, although I realise that the modern ones are different from the old, and much less powerful.

Inspectors had special arithmetical test cards on pink cardboard, and the only piece of dishonesty I can ever remember in my father occurred when test cards were once purloined from Dominie Deas's inspection the week before ours. Father worked out the tests on our blackboard, but dishonesty had its own reward, for the inspector brought a new edition when he came to us. I conjecture that he missed a few cards when he left the Dominie's school and was taking no risks.

Later on, Hunter Craig came on the scene as a new assistant inspector. He had been an elementary-school teacher himself, and not, like the usual senior inspector, an Oxford graduate who had never taught in his life. Craig was a genial fellow who inspired neither fear nor respect. You could argue with him as an equal, and we all liked him.

I never knew how much my father suffered from his school-board governors. They were mostly farmers, and I recall the chairman coming to sign the register and writing at the bottom 'Number presant, 98'. An odd custom called 'The Examination' always followed the HMI inspection. This was the last day before summer holidays, when prizes were given out. The farmers' wives brought bunches of flowers, and school-board members sat in state behind the book-laden table. My father saw to it that every child got a prize. He used to scratch his head when he came to Jake Hanton, and finally would give him a small book with the inscription: 'John Hanton, for Reading'.

The board chairman began in a businesslike fashion, 'James Young, First Prize for geography – that's fine, Jeemy, I'm glad to see you stick to your learning.' But after a few books had been given out, the chairman gave up trying to make helpful comments, and simply called out the winner's name when handing out the prize. Examination Day was one of the brightest of the year to us. It meant the prelude to weeks of freedom when we could catch minnows all day long in the Back Ditch, or go farther afield to the Vinney where we tried to 'guddle', to catch trout with our hands – but never got any. We never attempted to use a line and hook, no doubt because they were too expensive.

Many years later when cycling Vinney way as a student, I looked over the bridge and saw my youngest brother Percy with rod and line. I asked him how long he had been standing there. 'Two hours,' he said, 'and not even a nibble.'

'I'll show you how to fish', I said, with all the superiority of an elder brother, while casting the line. A trout jumped at it, and I whisked it out.

'That's how to catch fish', I said, and left him. It was the only fish I ever caught in my life, but to his dying day I am sure Percy considered me an expert angler.

We were continually catching minnows with the kitchen drainer. We shoved them into jam-jars, and by the time we got home most of them were dead. We knew that the fun was in the catching, so I don't know why we didn't throw them back in the water. To see a large stickleback or red gabbie struggle in the drainer would still give me a thrill, only nowadays I'd throw it back.

In our summer excursions, we always took the shortest way. When crossing fields, we fearfully watched the cattle to see if there was a bull among them. None of us had any illusions about bulls; we knew them as dangerous brutes, not to be trusted even when quiet. Farm dogs, too, gave dangerous spice to our adventures, and we grew accustomed to the friendly farmer's wife who stood at her garden gate and cried: 'He winna touch you!' when an evil collie was showing us all his teeth. I learned early in life that a dog never forgets. When Fraser's collie was a puppy, I hit it playfully with a halfbrick. The collie never forgot, and years later I could not go up to Fraser's door.

When we first moved to Kingsmuir we had a Newfoundland bitch called Myrtle; that is, my father bought her as a Newfoundland, only to find she was a mongrel. When she was on heat, we had great sport collecting piles of stones and gleefully pelting the suitors who came from neighbouring farms – some as far as two miles. We threw lots of stones as boys, but I cannot recollect our ever hitting anything.

We must have displayed more than a little cruelty, yet we never went so far as one or two pathological specimens, who cut off the heads of young birds and blew up toads by sticking straws up their anus. Nor did we ever kick hedgehogs to death as other boys

37

did. Our limit was chasing Bell Eggie's cat with the Skye terrier Boulot. We also followed the cattle drovers' custom of hitting stots (castrated bulls) with sticks. Cattle had a poor time then: at the Forfar mart, the drovers used to twist their tails cruelly, a practice later stopped by law.

We were very unconscious of the reasons for things. Though we saw cattle around us all the time, we never connected them with moneymaking. They were good for rounding up with a collie dog; a stick sounded lustily against their dung-caked haunches. To us, in fact, they seemed like toys, playthings. Pigs were different. We all knew that Martha Ramsay kept a pig for the bacon and hams, and we were there at first frost when the animal was led out to its death.

The tub of boiling water steamed in the morning frost. The ladder to which the carcass would be strung was against the wall. Ay, and Georgie Marshall stood there with the knife in his hand. Then the screeching began when many hands dragged the beast from its sty. If it was a large pig, some time and energy were needed to get the animal tumbled on its back, ready for the knife at its throat. The holders sprang away at the first spurt of blood, and the brute struggled to its feet, taking a few grunting steps. After the gore rushed out in a strong stream, the pig collapsed and all was over, so far as we were concerned. Seeing Marshall rip open the carcass was a secondary excitement. We must have been a morbid lot.

Seeing a hen's neck wrung was almost a daily occurrence. When I was about fourteen, my mother asked me to kill a hen. I had just seen experts kill thousands after the Forfar Christmas sale, and it all seemed too easy. They simply took the fowl by the head, gave it a slight twist, and threw the fluttering thing down. But when I caught the hen, took it by the head, and gave a slight twist – at least so intended – the body went flying over the cabbage patch. I stared at a bloody head left in my hand, and suddenly felt rather sick.

Most country people can kill an animal without any feeling; I never acquired the indifference necessary to do the thing well and cleanly. When Boulot was old and half blind, my mother asked me to kill him with chloroform. I got a bottle from the chemist's, put the dog in an old trunk, and shoved a soaked hankie beside it. I heard the poor brute struggle against the fumes, and in my excitement upset the bottle on the floor. I knew that I could not kill the dog by chloroform. Luckily there had been enough on the hankie to send him to sleep, so I held his head in a pail of water till the bubbles stopped gurgling up. It was a ghastly experience. I buried him 'darkly at dead of night' with the wind and rain driving down, and finally crept into the house, feeling more like a murderer than I have ever felt in my life. It was the utter helplessness of animals about to be killed that shattered me.

Recently, I had to kill a kitten because it was obviously in great pain with some internal inflammation. I used the gas oven as the only painless method I had within reach, but although I knew that death was necessary and a kindness, I had that uncanny sense of guilt that comes from knowing that you have complete power over something weaker than yourself.

We really do attribute humanity to our own animals. They seem different from ordinary beasts, because they have our personalities. When my sister Hilda's pet lamb grew up and had to go away with a flock to the slaughterhouse, I felt – as the whole family did – that it would feel the knife much more than the other sheep. This I truly believed, even though I hated the spoiled brute. Of all animals, a pet lamb seems most objectionable. Within its native stupidity is a queer, demanding sort of arrogance beyond description. Big animals should never be made pets. I have known pet horses; they are always self-willed and unreliable. Pet bulls can be highly dangerous when they grow up. I have never seen a pet pig so don't know what its evil characteristics are.

We had the usual pets as boys, generally rabbits. Like all children, we fed them for a few days and then neglected them. That was to be expected, for a rabbit is the dullest of all pets. Only their sex life really interested us. Now and again we had guinea-pigs, and later, homing pigeons. Neilie specialised in 'homers', and he and I got much joy from flying them. We learned, however, that their homing instinct is exaggerated. A homer has to be trained, and the usual method is to send it in one direction by rail, beginning with a near station and gradually increasing the distances. One can easily train a homer to fly from Carlisle to Land's End, but the chances are that if you send the bird north instead of south, it will not be able to find its way back to Carlisle from Edinburgh. Perhaps sight helps them more than instinct – a guess only, for I am no authority.

Dove-keeping afforded some excitement in raiding other dovecotes. Occasionally, in the wall-dovecote of Findlay the joiner, we would see among all the mongrels a lovely dove with a ring on its leg. Then we would go to Findlay, tell him that one of our 'doos' had got in among his, and could we catch it? Because he had no interest in doves and no idea of the number he kept, he would give us permission. Later, at dead of night, we would climb up and steal the bird. It was usually a stray, lost in a race, and therefore worthless, but to us it was a thoroughbred. Would a mongrel have a silver ring on its leg? So we'd carry the dove home triumphantly; but the first time we let it out, back to Findlay's dovecote it would fly. Findlay must have got rather tired of our nightly retrievings.

Some of the happiest days of our childhood were spent at the seaside. We were taken by train to Arbroath and then on to Easthaven. We never knew where Easthaven was when we were young; to us it was heaven, to be accepted without thought of criticism. We had rooms in the row of fishermen's cottages, very cheap and very primitive with their old boxed-in beds. To this day I always visit 'The Ha'en' when I go north. It is a small bay, and in those days there were many fishing boats on the sand.

This was an ideal spot for children, one of those beaches where low tide shows long stretches of rock pools, whelks and shells, and farther out, lobsters in holes. We bathed – my mother with us in a long gown. She loved the water but never learned to swim. Because her own father had been drowned accidentally, she kept warning us not to go out too far, and in this way gave us a complex about water. None of us learned to swim till much later in life; and although I can swim, I never have that feeling of confidence that the good swimmer has. My fears were attached to my mother. I used to stand on the beach, a miserable little lad of seven or eight, and scream: 'Come back, Ma, you'll be drowned!' My father never bathed; he disliked the water and seldom even waded. Willie also disliked bathing, but the rest of us enjoyed it.

Easthaven must have been dull for Father. His one recreation was searching for agate-type pebbles as the tide went out, and many a beauty he found. Later on, after the rock-pool stage, I also took to pebble-finding, and went a step farther than Father in grinding and polishing the best ones.

Clunie and I had ambitions. Our first hope was to find a human body in the pools, preferably one that had been long enough in the sea to be half eaten away by sharks. We were indeed a morbid couple. The body did not materialise, and we fell back on a second-best wish: to find a treasure trove washed ashore from some noble galleon. We selected our exact burial spot in the sand where we were to keep our booty a secret from the others until we could dispose of it with great profit. Our imaginations did not go to the length of spending the money.

Searching for buried treasure played a big part in my young life.

I remember reading a story in *Chatterbox* about a boy hero who happened to find a secret panel in a room. With his sister, he went down a flight of stairs to find skeletons and treasure in plenty. Clunie and I were not fools enough to imagine there could be any secret passages in our newly-built schoolhouse, though we knew of old castles not far away and one day we might . . . But we were never quite sure what we would do or find. The changing sea at Easthaven was never final; tomorrow a high tide might wash in the treasure or, better still, the drowned corpse. We tried to get the fishermen to tell us thrilling tales of wrecks and sharks, but they were a dull crowd and had no adventures to relate. One old man told us a few tall tales about wrecks and pirates, and then we learned that he had never been to sea in his life.

Time did not exist in Easthaven. There, a week or fortnight was a million years. Time hardly existed anywhere when we were young, and a year seemed a long, long time because we lived every moment of it. Our life was drawn in blacks and whites; there were no greys. We were either up or down, joying or sorrowing.

My mother's constant illness gave me many black days. I was much attached to her, and when she was ill I could not play. Her bilious attacks were generally heralded by severe vomiting. Her face turned a jaundiced yellow, and pain showed in her weary eyes. Only when she got very bad did we call in the doctor. To poor people, this was the last resort, and my mother nursed us all through the usual epidemics without having the doctor to see us. This time, however, it was often my sad task to go to Forfar for Dr Wedderburn, a stately old man who drove out with a groom in his spanking gig. He had ushered us all into the world, and apparently at each birth told my mother that her baby was the finest he had ever seen. Mother adored him.

My fear was that my mother would die. Her dreadful stories about stepmothers made me believe a stepmother was a fiend incarnate. Which of the most hateful women in the village, I wondered, would my father marry if he became a widower? It never struck me that he might choose one of the nice ones; and if he did, I knew that even the best of women leather their stepsons. So when I sat by Mother's bed and held her clammy hand, wetting it with my tears, I was vaguely aware that my grief was not wholly disinterested. I kept torturing the poor sufferer with my despairing cry: 'Will you die, Ma?'

Sometimes I dried my eyes and stared into the thought of death. One day I said to her: 'Won't it be awful for Pa and you when you are both in heaven and we are all in hell?'

41

'No', she said simply, 'for God will change our hearts so that we won't care.'

This answer disturbed me greatly, but it did not alter in any way my firm conviction that we children were booked for hell with a single ticket. I never had any doubt about the destination of my parents, although I had grave doubts about the salvation of other adults. When Jake Wilson died, Clunie and I discussed his chances in hushed whispers. Said Clunie: 'I'm sure he's gone to heaven, 'cause he always went to the Sacrament and sometimes to the kirk services.'

'But Clunie', I cried, 'he swore!'

She considered this for a bit. 'Yes, I know he swore, but he didn't mean it.'

That comforted me; I was sure that Jake had gone to heaven.

But then Clunie frightened me again by bringing forth her accustomed argument that there wasn't a heaven anyway, and maybe no God. I always edged away from her in horror when she began to utter such blasphemies.

The Scots religion of my boyhood was a modified Calvinism. I cannot remember ever being taught that the doctrine of pre-destination separated us forever as sheep and goats, without our having any say in the matter at all. No, we had free will. We could choose heaven or hell, but might reach heaven only after praying to God or Jesus and getting sanction. The road to hell was easy enough. You had only to be a sinner to go there.

I got my emotional religion from the home, not from the kirk. Dr Caie did not preach heaven and hell. True, he read the lessons, and in the kirk I heard about the place where the worm dieth not and the fire is not quenched, but old Caie never drew any moral from that. His Christianity was basically a department of social status. Caie was a gentleman who looked it, and his religion was gentlemanly: conventional, skimming the surface, avoiding the grim realities of sin and damnation.

It was Granny, I think now, who kept my parents up to the mark in religion. To her, everything was so simple. Since God's word was inspired – true from first to last – you had only to 'believe' and you were safe for heaven. My mother and father stuck to this religion until mellowed by age. Then they lapsed for many years, finding their salvation at last in spiritualism.

We were not specifically taught religion; it was in the air, an atmosphere of negation of life. My father said grace before each meal, but only when my mother was there. It was she who paused

42

after she had served us all with soup. 'Now, George', she would say, and he would thank the Lord for His mercies. I can still hear her voice change when she said: 'Now, George'. It makes me think of the BBC announcer who, after cheerfully telling us about floods in China, suddenly hushes his voice to report: 'It is with great regret that we announce the death of . . .'

On Sunday nights, just before bedtime, we had family worship. We all sat around on chairs while my father read a chapter from Scripture. Then, after singing a psalm or a paraphrase, we went down on our knees as he thanked God for sparing and taking care of us, asking Him to bless us in all our doings. It was always difficult to restrain our laughter then. Neilie would pinch me, or I would pinch Clunie, and we rammed our mouths hard against the seats to keep from spluttering aloud.

Sunday was a holy day; only necessary work could be done. Our reading was censored, and we had to read our penny bloods within the protective pages of a 'good' book. Granny, with her sharp nose for deception, sometimes caught us. All games were taboo; our walks were not much joy. Village boys played football with tin cans on the road, but even these heathens did not play an organised game with a real ball.

Without being told, we knew precisely the milestones on the broad road 'that leadeth to destruction'. They were sex, stealing, lying, swearing, and profaning God's day. (The last named included nearly everything that was enjoyable.) I cannot remember that such virtues as obedience and respect were milestones on the other way – the straight and narrow path that 'leadeth unto life'. At any rate, disobedience did not come into our line of vision; we were too well trained to attempt it.

When I was thirteen, two itinerant preachers came to Kingsmuir, pilgrims from the Faith Mission. They were breezy, handslapping optimists, always bright and merry. Indeed, you almost forgot that these were *saved* men until they interjected a 'save the Lord' into their ordinary conversation. The pilgrims became unpaying lodgers in our home, and we must have resented their presence, for when Boulot took a chunk out of the leg of the more cheerful one, we were decidedly pleased.

The whole family trooped to their meetings in the school. The Mission's gospel was simplicity itself: we were born in sin and doomed to eternal torment. *But* – there was a way to escape it – the only way. All we had to do was stand up in the meeting and say fervently: 'Lord, I believe', and we would be washed automatically in the blood of the lamb. My father stood up, then my mother, and the pilgrims praised the Lord. Clunie was also saved, but I couldn't bring myself to stand up, though I tried hard. Lying in bed after the meeting, I would say over and over again with fearsome passion: 'Oh Lord, help me to believe'.

Someone had told me that the human heart was like a fiddle with millions of strings, many as thin as a spider's web, and if one string were to break, death would be instantaneous. When I felt I could not believe, I suddenly thought of this, and terror seized me in its icy grip: I may die before morning, before I can stand up and give my testimony that I am saved. Yet even in subsequent meetings, I could never do so. Clunie very soon lapsed from salvation and was highly sarcastic about the whole affair. She and I tittered when village reprobates stood up and told how they had been washed in the blood. Within a week of the pilgrims' departure, the whole village had reverted to its sinful ways, and old Dave went on singing his drunken way home every Saturday night.

But Father was a changed man. He bought up all the old books of sermons he could find in the penny trays at the secondhand bookshops, and announced that he would carry on the salvation meetings at the school every Sunday. We had to attend, but we realised that he had not the fire and the quick repartee of the original pilgrims. He did not give up his eldership of the old kirk, although he shook his head sadly over the deadness of what passed for religion there. This phase lasted perhaps a year, then the meetings stopped, and apparently my father was no longer saved. His father's death may have had something to do with it.

Old William MacNeill was no religious man – I knew that because he once had honed his razor on a Sunday – and when he died, I was a little perturbed about his future. I timidly mentioned this to my father as we walked to evening service.

'Will Grandpa go to heaven?' I asked. 'He was a good man but he wasn't saved, was he?'

'Maybe—' answered my father in an embarrassed sort of way, 'maybe there are lots of things we don't know. Your grandfather was an upright, sober man, a man who never spoke an ill word against anyone.' It was clear to me then that he had begun to doubt the efficacy of being saved.

Death cast a dark shadow over our lives. In a small village of many funerals, each was an event, a form of grim entertainment. The plumed hearse, with carriages behind it, drew up before the bereaved home. The minister read a short, tear-compelling service in the parlour while the coffin was being carried out to the hearse. In small cottages, a window had to be taken out, for it was impossible to get a coffin through the door. The women of the family did not go to the burial, but stood at the gate wiping their eyes until the last carriage had disappeared over Bunker Brae. Every blind in the village was drawn, and women stood at their doors and sighed, saying, 'Ay, but he was a guid body'. They said that even when the most hated person in the village was buried.

The first funeral I recall attending was that of my younger brother George. His illness had been diagnosed as water on the brain. I cannot recollect having any special emotion about George, but wept in sympathy with others I saw weeping at his funeral. When the first spadeful of earth sounded hollowly on the little coffin, I shuddered. Granny Sinclair's burial at Rosebank Cemetery in Leith was a more pleasant affair, for it meant a trip by train to Edinburgh. My Uncle Neil, her griefstricken youngest son, was a teetotaller, so could not join the subsequent pub crawl, in which some of the mourners got exceeding merry. Although allowed only lemonade as a boy, I became infected with their gaiety. As mentioned earlier, a relieved feeling resembling pleasure always came over me after family funerals. It began as we left the graveyard, and was intensified when I returned to the room where the coffin had stood on two dining chairs.

Death, to us, was more than the ugliness of the grave. It meant the great judgement, a kind of grand 'school inspection' which I, for one, expected to fail, for my copybook was all blots. Knowing that I would roast in the burning fire for eternity, I tried to figure how long eternity might be. It was appalling to think that I would go on burning for millions of years.

In my early teens, I began to have a phobia about disease. I pored over medical books and, like Jerome K. Jerome, the playwright and humourist, had every disease in the books. A pimple on my face spelled smallpox. A student we knew had just died of inflammation of the bowels – appendicitis, it must have been, but that disease was not known then. At once, I felt a pain in my belly, and was certain that God would deal me a similar death.

Feverishly seeking some of Granny's religious books for salvation, I had the dire misfortune to come across the story of a bad man who suffered paroxysms on his deathbed.

'It will soon be over', he said, groaning.

'Nay', said the stern minister who stood at his deathbed, 'the agony is just beginning.'

I have often wondered why each of us was affected in a different

45

way by the unholy beast we knew as religion. It did not seem to have any effect on Willie. He entered the church later, not because he was ever religious – but because it offered a job. He had no fears of death and hell that I ever saw. My next brother, Neilie, seemed also to escape religion's dire influence, and Clunie, as already mentioned, was frankly sceptical. I alone appeared to have taken as my burden the sins of the whole family.

Mingled with my fear of death was a strange, contradictory element of taking risks. We boys had competitions to see who could run over the Black Box, a viaduct spanning the deep ravine of the railway. A fall would have meant death or serious injury: yet, with the others, I went over again and again, running or attempting to run on the edge of a two-inch plank. We took risks on the railway itself, bragging about how long we could stay on the ties when the train was approaching. We put pins on the tracks and barely sprang to safety. We climbed trees without any fear, but fear became associated with trees when Eck Hutcheon broke his neck raiding Findlay's gean (wild cherry) tree. Frank Craik and I debated solemnly about Eck's destination; Frank thought he had gone to heaven because he was a nice loon, but I was not so sure. A fearful thunderstorm came on as his funeral procession went down the road, and Frank told me I had been right after all, for the thunderstorm was clear proof that God was sending Eck to the burning fire.

Thunderstorms terrified me as a boy. Granny told me very early in my youth that thunder was God's voice in wrath, and knowing well that it was me he was angry with, I fled from thunderstorms like a frightened rabbit. My parents must have been afraid also, for during a storm there was always a hushed atmosphere in the house and my father had a violent headache. I was always scared, yet disappointed after the storm that no one had been killed. Clunie shared this morbid desire with me, and we sometimes made a list of the people we'd like to be struck down by lightning.

Old Nanzy Tam, the sweetshop wifie, told us she had once seen a baby killed by lightning that had come down the chimney. 'It was like wadding (cotton wool), soft like butter: ye could put yer finger on its belly and it went in just like that', and she demonstrated on a cushion. We liked that story, and wondered how far we could press our finger into the belly of the fattest woman in the village if she were killed by a flash. We feared death but we jested at it.

One of my worries was the danger of sudden death, the most

frightful of all, because there would be no time to repent. Consumption seemed an ideal death, with months to repent in, but poor Eck Hutcheon had had to go to his Maker without one second to cry: 'Oh, God, forgive me my sins'.

Softening our fear of death was a half-formed scheme to play with the devil until the last moment, and then, by a rapid repentance, slink through the Golden Gate before God could change his mind about pardon. In this respect, the thief on the Cross was an example to us. But the insinuating thought of sudden death could not be got rid of, and our playing with the devil was never a soul-free enjoyment.

The devil was sex.

My earliest memory of sex is a nursery incident when I was six and Clunie only five. We had stripped and were examining each other with great interest and considerable sexual excitement. The door opened, and Mother caught us. She gave us both a severe beating, then made us kneel down to ask God's forgiveness. Later, when Father came home, he took up the cudgels and spanked us again. I was then locked in the big dark dining-room. So I learned that of all sins, sex was the most heinous.

This incident affected my life for many years, not only forcing me to associate sex with sin but also giving me a fixation on Clunie, who was connected with the forbidden fruit. There were later sexual adventures with Clunie, but she always had a bad conscience afterward and told Mother, and I got thrashed every time. Only once did I escape a thrashing after Clunie's tale-telling, when Willie was in on it, too – indeed, had suggested our wrongdoing. As the oldest, Willie got all the blame. Being the favourite, however, he was never punished for anything.

A few years later, I went through a period of having hidden adventures with girls behind school doors. We were never discovered, though most of the other boys knew; in fact, they were jealous, because the girls said that I tickled them best. Another memory is my unsuccessful attempt at intercourse with a very sexy girl when I was about eleven.

Naturally, we never had any sexual instruction at home. My mother went on having babies, and we took it for granted that the doctor was bringing them, for Mother could not tell us lies. Other boys told us the truth, or rather, many half-truths; and by keeping rabbits and seeing farm animals, we knew that the young came out of their mothers. But we never applied this knowledge to Mother. I must have been about eight when I saw Father go into the water closet one day. At first, I stared at him in surprise; I knew he couldn't do dirty things; and finally concluded that he must be going to clean it out. So when we heard the man's part in making a baby, I simply did not believe that, either. My parents were pure and holy; they could never do a thing like that.

Willie went off to school in Edinburgh, and when he came home for holidays he regaled us with dirty stories of all kinds. We thought ourselves very sophisticated but still dared not face the application of sex to our own parents. They were over-modest always; nakedness was awful. Except for Clunie, I never saw my sisters naked; and if anyone came into my bedroom when I was dressing, I hastily covered my body with anything I could seize. Later, as a twenty-five-year-old student in Edinburgh, I got into the habit of having a cold bath each morning. On holidays, I got my mother to throw a bucket of cold water over me while I sat in a tub, because our home had no bathroom. Mother did this cheerfully but Clunie told me that my father strongly disapproved.

For any sexual offence in school, my father always gave a savage punishment. I remember his giving Jock Ross six with the belt, on his hand held down on the desk, for pretending to drop his slate pencil while taking the occasion to put his hand up a girl's petticoats.

I cannot recollect our ever mentioning masturbation or, for that matter, practising it. There are a few score slang terms for masturbation, but we did not know one of them. I know enough about psychology to realise that there may be some sort of repressive forgetting here, but to the best of my memory we did not masturbate either singly or mutually.

We did have a habit that we called 'looking' each other. We would lay a smaller boy on his back and open his fly, but that was always a collective practical joke. From the age of seven and a half, I slept in a bed with Willie and Neilie, who resented my presence strongly. This arrangment came about after my ejection from the bed I shared with Clunie, by an irate mother who again had discovered us doing things we shouldn't have. My brothers never let me forget my unwelcome intrusion or the circumstances which led to it.

Masturbation must have been known to me all the same, for I was chided one day by my father for making the dog Boulot jump on my arm. I also have a vague memory of Neilie and me being in a locked room, and Uncle Neil demanding entrance. When we let him in, he looked at us in a leering way and said: 'Aha, showing birdies!' We were most indignant, a circumstance that to any self-respecting psychoanalyst would have denoted our guilt.

Castration of sheep and cattle and horses was, of course, known to us all in a farming environment. The farmers called this 'libbing', and a threat to 'lib' us was a favourite joke of some of the ploughmen. To us, the laugh behind the threat possibly made it a pleasurable thrill, though I remember that Jeemie Barclay, the village softie, used to go into extreme panic at the threat of libbing.

I don't think that my schoolfellows suffered much from sexual repressions. Some came from homes where the parental language was obscene. The illegitimate ones did not seem to mind, for the bastard was no inferior in Kingsmuir. Fornication was common between ploughmen and servant lassies, and getting in the family way seemed just as common. But the most moral, condemning women in the village were always those who had had bastards themselves.

We all knew juicy verses of that delightfully obscene ballad *The Ball o' Kirriemuir*, which told of an occasion when some wag doped the liquor with an aphrodisiac. It was a strong ballad, Elizabethan in its honest bawdiness, redolent of the sex that springs from the soil. Obscene it may have been, but its ribaldry was of much higher essence than that of the sophisticated commercial-traveller story.

My position was a most difficult one. When I spoke dialect outside the house, I shared the villagers' open view of sex; when I spoke English and became respectable upon crossing the threshold of the schoolhouse, I had to put away all openness of mind concerning sex language and practice. At one and the same time, I strove to serve the God of the home and the Devil of the village. It simply could not be done. I fled from raw sex into the realm of idealistic sex.

49

EARNING A LIVING

When I was fourteen, my father decided to send Neilie and me out to work. Neilie was doing no good at the Academy, and I had been learning nothing at Kingsmuir School. When Father asked us what we wanted to be in life, Neilie replied, 'A sheep farmer', and I, 'an engine driver'. 'Ugh', said my father in disgust, 'you'll both go into offices.'

Father was what my mother called a 'flee-about'. He had changing enthusiasms about jobs, and his advice was nearly always bad. When Pat Craik came home on holiday from London, he was doing well in wholesale drapery. 'Trade is the thing', said my father, and planned to make us drapers. But a week later, Willie Adam came home on holiday, and he was flourishing in the Civil Service. Thereupon, Father forgot about the merits of trade and ordered us to prepare for the Boy Clerks' entrance examination. We always hated Willie Adam's visits, for they meant weeks of dull work, doing sums, reading unreadable manuscripts, and cramming geography. The Civil Service exams were competitive, and Father knew in his heart that Neilie and I could never get in. So he returned to the idea of our becoming trade clerks.

At that time, we did not know who or what lay behind Father's eagerness to get us out working. It was Willie throwing away money at St Andrews University – Willie dancing in hard-boiled shirts, going to special dinners, carousing with the other divinity students. Ever and again came wires saying simply: 'Send more tin – Willie', and as more tin vanished, my parents got grumpier and grumpier, working out their ill tempers on us.

I recall a Saturday when they took a cheap trip to St Andrews. Not expecting anyone, and with many things under foot, Willie spoke to them only a minute before rushing off. They came home in a tearing rage, and my mother gave Clunie a hiding for something of no importance. Since we understood the reason for the bad atmosphere, we hated Willie. Clunie, especially, was bitter about his extravagance: she saw things more incisively than the rest of us.

It now became evident that Neilie and I had to go away and earn a living. Neilie got a job as a clerk in a Leith flour-mill; three months later, I received a reply to one of my many letters replying to advertisements in *The Scotsman*. My handwriting was good at that time, and I had penned my applications in a slow hand that attempted to be copperplate.

The letter in answer to my application informed me that I had been appointed a very junior clerk in the office of W. & B. Cowan, Ltd, gas meter manufacturers in Edinburgh. My feelings were mixed.

I was now to be freed forever from studying Latin grammar, but against that weighed the knowledge that I also was to be freed from play and bird-nesting and catching minnows. However, I set off boldly enough. I was to lodge with Neilie in Leith. Neilie earned fifteen shillings a week, and I was to earn six. The landlady's son, a young man with a pessimistic view of life, shared our bedroom.

Cowan's works were two miles away – mostly uphill – in Buccleuch Street, on the other side of Edinburgh. I had to start off early in the morning, and was always late, so frequently had to take the tram. In those days, the trams were all drawn by horses. My difficulty was financial. I could afford threepence for lunch, but if I took the tram, that left me with only a penny for food. For a time, I solved the question by strategy. When the car left Pilrig, I noticed that the conductor went on top. If I jumped on while he was up there, I almost always got halfway up Leith Walk before the sight of his boots on the stair signalled me to leave the car. When I was too slow, I asked for a ticket to Leith. 'Wrong direction', he would say, and I would give a surprised: 'Oh,' hurriedly jump off, and wait for the next car with a conductor on top. Unfortunately, the conductors got to know me, and I had to give up this easy mode of travel.

Cowan's was one long misery to me. I did not labour in the

central office, but in a dark evil-smelling hole of an office in the middle of the works. There I lived in a stink of solder and paint and gas. My happiest moments were those in which I was sent to find someone in the works. I loitered with the workmen, and then got sworn at when I returned to the office. The only redeeming feature about it all was status: I was addressed as mister. The clerks always addressed each other as Mr So-and-So, and they all wore bowler hats. I wore a cap but it was disapproved of.

For the first time in my life, I experienced homesickness. I kept writing miserable letters to the family until finally my mother came to see me for two days. I clung to her in bitter tears and implored her to take me home with her. She told me that that was impossible, and when she left, my homesickness was almost unbearable; I addressed business envelopes and wet them with my tears. My senior clerk, a man called Wilson, was very sympathetic and kind to me, and on that occasion, took over the addressing chore for me.

Neilie lost his job. It proved too difficult for a boy of sixteen, and he went home, leaving me alone. After being in Edinburgh three months, I was allowed to go home at New Year's for four days. I could not enjoy a minute, however, because my thoughts kept turning to the misery that would lie before me when I got back to Edinburgh. After seven months, I was allowed to return home permanently. I still remember the embarrassment of that homecoming, a shame at not having been able to stick it out. When one farmer remarked in company that 'thae Neills canna bide at nithing,' Neilie and I blushed.

Why was I taken back? I do not know. No doubt my parents had tired of my despairing letters, though there might have been another reason, too. I had written to my father, telling him that the chances of promotion were very poor in Cowan's, and that my future would be much brighter if I came home and studied hard for the Civil Service. From the hell that was Edinburgh, sitting in Kingsmuir schoolhouse all day long seemed like paradise. And I think I truly believed that once home, I should study all the time.

Neilie and I were set down again to study for the Civil Service – Men Clerks this time. But history repeated itself; we could not concentrate. One night in despair, my father threw our textbooks at us and said he gave up. 'They're just fit for nothing, Mary'.

But Johnston the chemist needed an apprentice, and my father fixed things up that I should begin work there on the following Monday. During the week, however, another local firm advertised for an apprentice – Anderson and Sturrock, drapers – and my father's plans rapidly altered: Neilie would be the chemist, and I the draper. So early on the Monday morning we walked to Forfar to our new jobs.

My duty each morning was to get the shop key at the proprietor's house, and be down in time to open up at eight. Then, with another apprentice, I had to sweep the shop. We sprinkled it with a watering-can to keep down the dust, and I learned that a broom sweeps cleanest if the bristles are reversed. Most of my work was delivering parcels. One day, I had to walk a mile with a penny packet of pins that one of the upper-class ladies of the town would not carry. I learned never to expect a tip from the rich, but the poor always gave me a penny or tuppence for delivering their parcels. One of my jobs, to stand in the windows and clean them with whiting, touched the snobbish aspect of my upbringing. I really was ashamed of being in retail trade, and used to hide behind the whitened part of the windowpane if any of the better people were passing.

Snobbery also had its way in my idealisation of women, which commenced at this period. I did not idealise common girls; I aimed higher. The girl I loved was always quite unattainable, always in a rank of society far above mine. Forfar, like every other town in the world, had its social structure, with very definite lines of demarcation between classes. If a girl went to Miss Smith's private school she was a superior being, and naturally, at my stage of lowly occupation, I found my objects of worship among the Miss Smith clientèle. I say objects, for the admired one was never a constant. Today it might be Cis Craik; tomorrow, Jean Gray.

There was nothing consciously sexual about this. Even in imagination, I never thought of kissing them. I was satisfied to have seen them pass in the street; and if the adored one happened to glance in my direction, my joy was complete. Sometimes I made detours round by the Lour Road when delivering my parcels, hoping to get one glance at Jean Gray. One day when I met her, she looked absolutely beautiful in a large sun-hat, with her little tilted nose and her bright eyes. My face must have paled with excitement.

Of course, this idealisation was the result of the beatings I had received for what might be called sex in the raw; but even at this period, I was having quite earthly adventures with village girls whose feet did not turn the daisies into roses. The two interests never met; they existed in separate compartments, or rather, they were parallel lines that never met.

I hated the drapery business. I was on my feet from seven-thirty in the morning to eight in the evening, and then had the two-mile walk home. Since I wore heavy boots, my big toe joints got inflamed and gradually stiffened – their condition to this day. My toes got so bad in fact that I had to give up the job. This I did gladly, vowing to my father that now I had acquired sense, I would slave at the Civil Service exam. Poor Neilie had no excuse for giving up his chemist's apprenticeship; and for four long years he went back and forth, hating it all the time.

The old problem had arisen again. My concentration was no better than it had ever been, and for the third time my father despaired of me. This time he really gave me up, he said, and I stared gloomily into the future, seeing myself as a good-for-nothing tramp, wondering whether I would fail as an ordinary ploughman. My one ambition was to be a minister like Willie. I pictured myself in the pulpit delivering wonderful sermons in a kirk that was crowded to the doors, but preaching to only one: to Jean Gray of the great sun hat, which shaded the eyes fixed in holy admiration upon the handsome young minister. Violet Jacob's *Tam i' the Kirk* is a pure joy to me, because it so passionately sums up the Scots religion-sex constellation. The dream was there and the reality did not disturb it – the reality that the ministry could only be reached through long, hard study.

'The boy's just hopeless', said my father gloomily.

'He might be a teacher', ventured my mother.

'It's about all he's fit for', said my father grimly, and without a smile.

Now that Father had given me up, Mother stepped in. She pointed out that no other teacher had as many classes as he had, and 'Really, George, you need a pupil teacher'. I knew that my father wasn't keen about it, but somehow she got him to broach the subject to the school-board clerk, and in due time I was appointed PT, a student teacher, in Kingsmuir School. There I served an apprenticeship of four years. Though it is hard to recall my days in the school, I must have taken classes to relieve my father, for I do remember teaching small boys and girls to read by the look-and-say method. I found that the best way to learn anything is to teach it, and soon I could string off nearly every town, cape and river in the whole world, as well as the exports of Peru or the imports of China. I think I learned my profession well, for I copied my father, and he was a good teacher – good in the sense that he could draw out rather than stuff in. Father still disliked me apparently, and was inclined to treat me more like a pupil than a student teacher. Though he never ticked me off in front of my pupils, I was still afraid of him.

After his second year, according to student-teacher rules, the apprentice sat for his first examination – a small affair set by the school inspector. Then, at the end of his fourth year, came the King's Scholarship, or normal exam, that decided whether he would become a normal student or not. Passing with a First Class automatically made him a normal student, to be trained for two years in Glasgow or Edinburgh. If there were enough vacancies, a Second Class might get a student in; a Third completely disqualified him.

My exam by the inspector at the end of my second year was not encouraging. 'This candidate', said the report, 'is warned that his work all round is weak.' My father seemed more ashamed of than angry with me.

When I took the normal exam at the end of my apprenticeship, I came out Third Class, nearly bottom of the list. I was about nineteen then, and recall sitting in our conspicuous pew the next Sunday wondering if the congregation knew what a dunce I was. My father rather thoughtlessly nudged me and remarked that Nora Stewart was in the choir; Nora had taken the same exam and passed First Class.

In all my adversities Clunie comforted me, and on this occasion gave me a list of great men who had failed in examinations. She herself, clever in learning as she was, failed the normal exam a year later. When anyone failed to get into the Normal Training College, he became an 'ex-Pupil Teacher', but by passing two other exams, could get a teacher's certificate – again a class affair, First, Second, or Third. Then one became an authorised teacher but untrained, and therefore much inferior to a teacher who had gone through the Normal College. A man who managed to procure only a Third Class in the certificate exam ranked as the lowest worm in the educational garden; he had no chance of getting promotion, and was likely to remain an underpaid assistant all his days.

My student-teacher days are mostly a blank to me now, though photographs of school groups show me standing stiffly with a very high choker collar. I look back on my position as a difficult one, for I had to be on the side of authority before my own desire to play had been lived out. It was the role of a boy pretending to be a man.

PURSUING SOCIETY
AND CULTURE

When I was about seventeen, my social ambitions began to seek a tangible outlet. As children of a teacher, our social status was very poor, and the best families in Forfar did not 'know' us. Furthermore, we had no money and could not entertain or attend social functions. We realised we were outsiders. Willie and Neilie did not care, for they weren't snobs, and besides, Willie had his own society at the university. I aimed high. Neilie and I joined a small group calling itself the Graphic Arts Club, which suited Neilie, because he was a real artist, and me, as a possible door to society. I drew a little, mostly copies of Charles Dana Gibson women, but was never an artist, then or later. We drew in charcoal on brown paper, using models who generally came from the poorhouse. One club lady took an interest in me, and she and her sisters were very kind, inviting me to their house for croquet or supper. I was very ignorant of social behaviour, and had some difficult moments with, what seemed to me, an abnormal number of knives and forks. I hastily bought a book on etiquette, which hardly helped, for it concentrated too much on how to address bishops and princes. For many years after, an elaborate dinner table made me nervous. My first acquaintance with a finger-bowl was touch and go, but luckily I did not drink the water. A separate crescent plate for the salad proved another stumbling block. I thought it was for my bread and treated it accordingly; then discovered its true function, and sat very, very red throughout dinner.

56

Drawing-room behaviour meant nothing to me. I was unaware that one stood up when a lady entered or left a room; had no idea that during afternoon tea, you held your tiny bit of cake in your saucer and not on your knee. I learned my lessons well, however, and in a short time murmured a conventional thank-you after a lady had played a Chopin waltz on the piano.

Behind this social manoeuvring of mine there was a subtle plan: one day I might meet a girl I worshipped. Her name varied from time to time, but her class did not. Tennyson's 'Maud', which I read and reread at this time, became a symbol embracing the several ideals of beauty in the upper circles of the town. Unfortunately, the Mauds were not interested in books and music, and I did not meet them. But I did get myself introduced to the lovely Jean Gray. That was a sad happening, because her proximity deprived her of her golden glory, and I had to seek another really unattainable object.

I must have been a most objectionable prig and humbug during this period of my life. Still, something was gained from it. I heard good music for the first time in that pre-record, pre-radio era. In the beginning, I listened to Chopin and Schumann because it was the correct thing to do, but the time came when I listened because the music itself brought me joy. I cannot recall learning much of other cultural matters. When books were touched upon in conversation, I sat silent lest I should betray my ignorance. One day when someone asked me who my favourite author was, I answered 'Dumas', pronouncing the final 's'. 'You mean "Dumah",' said a superior man present, and I reddened and inwardly kicked myself because I had never read a word of Dumas anyway. Even so, I was slowly developing a certain literary taste at home. Willie brought us books of poetry – *modern* poetry, as we called it then. He introduced me to the majestic beauty of 'The Hound of Heaven' by Francis Thompson, and the queer, haunting rhythm of Meredith's 'Love in the Valley'.

Willie himself was a lad of varied talents, and had a great influence on my development. His style in drawing was original if somewhat stiff, and for years the St Andrews University magazine used his design with his pseudonym 'Nil' on its cover. He wrote neat triplets and sonnets, and his prose was good. But while he read voluminously, he never seemed to assimilate ideas. He showed no interest in politics or science, and avoided discussion and argument. I cannot remember his having a sense of humour. Yet I imitated Willie for years. If he was a minister, I would become a minister. If he edited his university magazine at

57

St Andrews, I would edit mine in Edinburgh. If he drew with pen and ink, I drew with pen and ink. Willie's only interest I didn't copy was writing poetry, for I never wrote a line of verse in my life.

My efforts to become a pianist reached their peak at the age of seventeen. All the other children had been sent to study music – Willie, the fiddle; the rest, piano. Neilie took piano lessons for about four years, and when they were ended, forsook the piano forever. Why I alone received no music teaching, I do not know. Every now and again, however, I would decide to learn by myself. For a few days, with the aid of something called *Hemy's Tutor*, which I bought or borrowed, my fingers would laboriously pick out the scale with one finger – 'Every Good Boy Deserves Favour'. By seventeen, I had beaten all my previous records; it took a whole week to convince me that anything more was hopeless. I have often wished half-heartedly that I had been taught to play, knowing that if music had been strong in me, I would have learned in spite of all difficulties; but knowing, too, that I could never have been anything more than a mediocre musician.

During my student-teaching days, I met a man who made mathematics live for me. He was Ben Thomson, the maths master at the Academy, and later its rector. When I went to him for private tuition, he gave me a genuine love for the subject, which explains why I belong to that rare breed of people able to while away a railway journey doing algebraic and geometrical problems. Ben was a staunch friend. He gave me most of the lessons free of charge, and years later would help me by post when I had difficulties with the subject. I regret that he never wrote a textbook, for his way of presenting maths was unique. I kept telling him he should do this, and my last request reached him shortly before his sudden death. Forfar Academy in his time turned out many brilliant mathematicians.

I have said that I was not a reader. Nevertheless, I must have read quite a lot in the practise-teaching period, and recall borrowing many books from the Meffan Library, mostly fiction. I revelled in the whimsical sentimentality of Barrie's novels, identifying myself with his Sentimental Tommy. Again and again I cycled to his Thrums (Kirriemuir, seven miles away), and sitting in the den, tried, not very successfully, to people it with his characters. Kirriemuir was on the way to Memus where the Craig family lived in the Free Kirk Manse. The Craig girls were an original, unconventional lot, gaily flirting but always keeping just out of reach. They kept sentiment at arm's length with a laugh, and were good companions rather than love objects. The oldest became a household word: every British housewife knows Elizabeth Craig as an authority on cooking. I haven't met her since those days.

Willie had taught us that there were two kinds of girls: the kind you had to be introduced to, and the kind you picked up. According to Willie, the latter were easily the more interesting. During the summer season, they could be seen in pairs, parading the beach at Carnoustie or the streets of Kirriemuir. Much experience was needed to know which pairs were pickupable and which were not. If our 'Good Evening' met no response except a haughty, withering glance, we concluded there was nothing doing, although we recognised a type who used the withering tactics to increase our effort. Almost invariably, one girl was pretty and the other plain. Whichever elder brother I was with, he naturally took it for granted that I should go off with the plain one, an assumption that did not appeal to me. Sometimes I would get in first, make off with the beauty, and then spend the cycling way home having bitter arguments about sportsmanship.

These flirtations were mostly superficial affairs, sitting on a bench in the dusk hugging and kissing. The truth is that we had very little success with pick-ups, either because we looked poor and country-bumpkinish, or, more likely, because the really attractive girls had plenty of followers and did not need to go looking for strays. Living two miles out of town and not being recognised by the town's social sets, we knew no girls, and our picking-up was as much the result of needing female companionship as it was of starving for sex.

About this time, I read an upsetting little book by Richard Le Gallienne – *The Quest of the Golden Girl* – whose heroine was a prostitute. The girls picked up were never golden; they were not even base metal. They simply played at love, and most of them feared that things would go too far. The average pick-up led one on for a certain length, then hastily said it was time she went home, and ran away. I suppose she was looking for a Golden Boy and was as disappointed with the reality as we were. We took our failures lightly, and rode home late at night feeling healthy and happy. Tomorrow was a new day. Tomorrow we'd try Montrose or Arbroath for a new romance. I was talking to Neilie about these days years later, and we agreed that the happiest memory of that period was the long ride up the hill to the Jubilee Arms at Cortachy, with the thirsty vision of the bottle of Bass we were to

59

have at the top. We did not smoke in those days. Where we got the money to buy even a bottle of beer, I cannot remember, though it was cheap in those days – threepence, I think. Whisky cost three shillings a bottle; and Gold Flake cigarettes, sixpence for twenty.

My ambitions seem to have been latent at this time. The future did not exist for me, possibly because I dared not contemplate a future as an unsuccessful teacher with no hope of promotion. What I daydreamed about is long forgotten. By this time, religion had become an empty, outside thing, and my churchgoing had only one object; to see the girls. I sang in the choir, but although I had a good ear and could sing anything in tune, my voice lacked strength, and I never became a permanent member. I enjoyed choir practice once a week and sang lustily the bass of the anthems, but always timidly, a tenth of a tone behind the leader: one of my phobias was to be singing an anthem to a full congregation and coming in at the wrong time. Excellent orchestral performers have told me that this is a frequent nightmare.

A YOUNG DOMINIE

When my apprenticeship ended, I applied for jobs, and finally got one in Bonnyrigg near Edinburgh at fifty pounds a year. The school was run by an old lady called Miss MacKinley, who looked like an eagle and was a very stern disciplinarian. After the laxity of my father's school, it was a great shock to find myself suddenly in a school where the children were not allowed to talk in class. I was ordered to thrash any child who even whispered, and did so because I was really scared of the old woman. I stood it for two months and then got a better job at sixty pounds a year in Kingskettle in Fife.

If anything, the discipline of Kettle school was worse than that of Bonnyrigg. For three years, I had to be the sternest of taskmasters. The room used by Calder, the headmaster, was separated from mine by a glass partition, and his sharp eye could see everything that went on. For three years, I did my work with fear in my heart. Calder never relaxed; he kept me at arm's length, and all my attempts to approach the human side of him were frozen by his stony stare. Yet, in a queer sort of way, I felt that he liked me; and also in a queer sort of way, I liked him in spite of my fear. Calder's teaching methods were surprising to me. When he gave his class a test in arithmetic, he slowly worked out every problem on the blackboard first; then the children worked out the same problems in their books. Only the very stupid ones got the answers wrong under such a system, and God help them when they did, for the headmaster wielded a fierce strap and laid on heavily. The HMI gave Calder excellent reports – because he kept excellent whisky, the cynics said.

Kingskettle remained a horror to me. There must have been times during those three years when I was happy, but the main memory is one of fear; fear of being late in the mornings, fear of having my class examined by Calder, fear of him when he leathered the poor ones who could not learn. I realised that if I had been his pupil, I would have been strapped every day. My father had never been that strict. True, he had strapped often and sometimes hard, but there was in his school a certain freedom, freedom to laugh and chat and carve your name on the desk. We never had to march in or out like soldiers.

Kettle school was like a new world to me. There was no laughter in the school save when Calder made one of his oft-repeated jokes at the expense of a pupil. All pupils moved in military style; and everyone, including myself, was insincere, inhuman, fearful. Calder was my first contact with a real army disciplinarian. I had heard of the type – a few notorious ones existed in Forfar – and they all had a common characteristic: they were all men of small stature.

One interesting point about Calder was his habit of always writing very slowly in copperplate. Even if he made a pencil note, it was beautifully written. Practically every pupil in the school could write well, too.

Once I took Calder's senior drawing class in his room, while he stood doing his registers at the desk. The lesson was given in dead silence, but when he went over to his house, hell broke loose, and I could hardly keep the pretence of discipline. But I never reported the ringleaders to Calder when he returned. I tried to teach designing, with flowers and leaves as bases, and some pupils brought forth rather good, balanced patterns of the wallpaper type. These designs were the only original work ever allowed in the school, for even an essay was first written on the blackboard by Calder and then copied by the class.

Calder was unhealthy, kept having painful boils on the back of his neck, and was quite unable to carry on his work for weeks at a time. During such periods, I was in complete charge of the school. I enjoyed these times, even though it was not an easy matter to keep order; not that I tried very much, knowing well that the moment Calder came back, his army discipline would grip the pupils automatically.

My farm lodging cost me fourteen shillings a week, and the wife of the farmer, Mrs Tod, gave me more than my money's worth. The food was excellent – I can still remember the cream, so thick that it had to be raked out with a teaspoon. I was treated like a member of the family, which included a daughter and two sons. Will, the elder, had been to sea; at that time, indeed, was an unemployed ship's engineer. I called him Sir Oracle, for he laid down the law about everything and everybody. He believed that no conversation was of any value unless it contained a sequence of what he called 'smart things', and I thought him a witty lad. Will made me feel like a very unsophisticated person when he talked about what he had seen on his voyages, and what sins he had committed in foreign ports. Looking back now, I am inclined to think he exaggerated more than a little.

He had a lovely bass voice, and I liked to hear him sing 'Out on the Deep' while his sister Aggie, who also had a fine voice, accompanied him on the piano. But he always broke down with coughing after the first verse, for he had been thrown down by an express train when a schoolboy, and his heart had been affected. He did not live long, nor did his younger brother Walter, who was a simpler soul than man-of-the-world Will. I liked Wattie. He tried to sing in a small croaky voice, but always broke off, and laughed at himself. He was a dear laddie, and when he died not long after I left Kettle, I suffered genuine grief.

Wattie belonged to the volunteers and persuaded me to join. That was good fun. Once a week we put on our khaki uniforms and were driven in a wagonette to headquarters some miles away, or to the rifle range up on the Falkland Hills. Our usual driver, Geordie Henderson, was landlord of the local hotel and a real character. We laughed at his efforts to talk like an educated man. When Kettle Farm caught fire and Geordie had to take charge as captain of the fire brigade, he wanted volunteers to come and man the pump. 'Come away, Gentlemen', he cried, 'come away and call the pimp.'

My first visit to the rifle range was thrilling. When I lay down at a hundred yards, never having fired a rifle in my life, and I had four bull's-eyes in succession, the officer in charge got much excited. 'At last', he cried, 'I've got a marksman in my company. Come back to the five-hundred-yards and have a shot there.' Proud as Punch, I went to the five-hundred-yards' stance – or was it *butt!* – and took a long and steady aim. I missed the target completely, and went on missing it completely, till the disappointed captain gruffly told me not to waste any more good ammunition.

Volunteering was a picnic until we went to camp for a fort-

63

night in August. Then they put us through the paces with a will, and at night we turned into our tents dead beat. Camp was a social kind of life for us, a jolly lot who did not take our military duties too seriously. Some of the more independent Fifers in our battalion refused to salute officers, and once I saw our colonel, Sir Ralph Anstruther, stop a miner, demanding to know why he did not salute. 'Can't you see I'm an officer?' he said sharply. The miner shrugged his shoulders and spat. 'I doan't give a dawm what ye are', he said, 'I never saluted anybody in my life.' So speaking, he walked leisurely away while the impotent colonel stood and fumed. The officer got his own back, however, by ordering a special saluting drill after supper, and we had to march up and down saluting a lamp-post when we should have been swaggering along the streets of Carnoustie with the girls.

Eager to be a soldier, I got the infantry training manual – a new edition had been issued after the Boer War – and studied it well. But I never won my sergeant's stripes, though passing the exam with flying colours, because of my departure from Kettle and resignation from the corps. While with the volunteers, I won a prize – for shooting, *mirabile dictu*. When asked what I wanted, I chose books: one of them *The Right Line and Circle*, and the other a trigonometry text. The captain's sister made me very proud when she raised her eyebrows in presenting them, and said: 'Ah, a student!' God knows my reasons for selecting these books; I certainly never used them.

Another great memory of that period is King Edward VII's review of forty thousand volunteers in the Queen's Park in Edinburgh. What a day! We left Kettle at two in the morning, marched to the park, and stood about for hours. As we marched by the King, he was heard to say: 'And a damn fine regiment, too'. We were proud of this until learning that the remark had been meant for the regiment that had passed before ours. All I recollect about the King was his yellowish face and how unhappy he looked.

It was during my stay in Kettle that I became ambitious, again, to enter the ministry. The man who encouraged this desire was the local minister, the Reverend Aeneas Gunn Gordon. He was a Canadian, tall, straight, distinguished, with a strong beard and a nose like an eagle's beak. He took me under his wing, and I told him of my wish. 'You need Greek', he said. 'Come down to the manse every morning at eight and I'll teach you.'

He knew his Homer, almost by heart, and taught me so well that I could read the first two books of the *Odyssey* and a part of

Herodotus. (Today I cannot read a word of Greek.) Gordon had one failing – which never affected my admiration; sometimes he drank too much, and I recall seeing him of a morning holding Homer upside down, while quoting it correctly. He was a man who read everything but appeared to absorb little and gave out less. Though liberal in the way of charity and human kindness, he delivered dull sermons, and his conversation seemed commonplace. Yet he gave me a certain interest in literature. He used to read aloud from *Paradise Lost*, and I learned to appreciate 'the organ music of Milton'. On his advice I read Dante and Tasso, and then the essays of Macaulay. The latter gripped me, making me conscious of literary style for the first time in my life; I was then in love with a girl in Glasgow, and used our correspondence to improve my own style. How far beyond her those purple passages and that noble diction must have been. My present attitude toward style, with few exceptions, can be stated simply: the important thing is *what* is said, not *how*.

When Gordon got married, I was his best man. It had been arranged that I should wear my father's frock coat and striped trousers, which fitted me well. But getting ready for the morning train – my holiday had been spent in Kingsmuir – I could not find my black shoes. I searched in vain, keeping one eye on the clock; sister Ada had taken them to be repaired. My only other boots were yellow as a dandelion. There was no way out; I set off in my frock coat and tall hat and those dreadful boots. In Dundee, as I crossed from station to station, I met all the Newport folks coming off their train; their amused stares still haunt me. In the southbound train, I tried to hide my feet under the seat.

My functions as best man worried me. I knew that my chief job would be to scatter sweets and pennies to the children around the kirk, but all I had in my pocket was ninepence. After the wedding, when I had to send an announcement of the ceremony to *The Scotsman*, I was obliged to do so without payment, and of course it did not appear next morning. The bride was furious with me, scorning my explanation. She never liked me after that, which made me resentful, because I really felt responsible for the match. Certainly I had been the go-between during the courting days. Looking back now, I think she disliked me because Gordon liked me so much. Thirteen years later, she gave me quite a cool reception when I dropped in to see them on my motorcycle. After the wedding, I believe, Gordon never touched drink again.

It was in Kettle that I began, briefly, to shoot rabbits and crows with Tod's gun. One Saturday morning, I killed a few crows.

Walking through the field the following night, I heard a faint squawk and saw on the ground a poor bird with half its guts blown away. Almost sick, I killed it with my heel, and from that day in 1903 to this, have never shot another bird or beast.

I never got to know the people of Kingskettle. East Fife people have a difficult reserve that will not break down: they never allow anyone to enter their private lives. The people of East Suffolk, where I now live, seem very similar. The people of Glasgow are much friendlier than those farther east in Edinburgh. But why there should be this difference between east and west, I cannot say. The breeziness of the west may be only superficial and meaningless, but it is easier to live with. In Kettle, I always remained an outsider. It was a village with much musical talent; as a singer, I might have been more welcome, but my only accomplishment was reciting, and they did not care much for that.

My elocution days were a painful, ludicrous interlude. I must have been about eighteen when they started. It was usual then for people to contribute something to the common entertainment when invited out; some sang, some played piano, one man did card tricks. My line casually became known as reciting. I began with an American fragment called 'Oh, My!' but soon progressed to more ambitious stuff. Books on public speaking always gave extracts for recitation, and a common one was *Rubinstein's Playing* as described by a backwoodsman or cowboy. Once memorised, this was a gem for the amateur who fancied his histrionic powers. I can still look back with shame to an evening when I 'did' Rubinstein, tearing my hair and letting my fingers run up and down an imaginary piano. The audience was rural, had never heard of Rubinstein, and had seldom, if ever, heard a piano played; naturally they wondered what this was all about. Resolving to stick to the obviously comic, I had some success with a *Strand Magazine* story called 'The Presentation to Lamb', in which I was supposed to make up a speech for the bashful Lamb when his club gave him a wedding present. Lamb got drunk and muddled my speech in glorious fashion.

My first political efforts occured in Kingskettle. My landlord Mr Tod, a Tory, was thick in the fight against Asquith, whose constituency included East Fife. Tod used to read me A. J. Balfour's speeches from *The Scotsman*, and I was full of zeal for the Tory Party. When Asquith came round, arrogant and rather bored, I joined in the hooting against him. On election day, I sailed about with a blue ribbon on my lapel, which delighted Gordon, another Tory sympathiser.

At this time, too, I recall going to the theatre. I had seen my first play, *A Night of Pleasure*, at the age of twelve in Edinburgh's Theatre Royal. For me it certainly was a night of bliss, for I had never seen such visions of radiant loveliness in my life. I had never imagined any woman could be so beautiful as the heroine. What the story was about I do not remember, save that the lovely damsel was wronged in some way. But it all came right in the end.

My next visit to the theatre occurred during Neilie's medical studies in Edinburgh. We waited for two hours in the gallery queue before the doors opened, then scrambled for a front seat and got one. After another half-hour's wait – at nineteen I fidgeted like a small boy – we saw the great Sir Henry Irving in *The Bells* and *Waterloo*. I sat through these performances in open-minded ecstasy. But now, after all these years, I see Irving as an actor in the worst sense of the word. He strutted, made wild gestures, and overplayed both the false passion of Matthias in *The Bells* and the sentimentality of dotage in *Waterloo*. Of course, I may be blaming the actor for the faults of the dramatists. In either event, I had no criticism in my soul during the first years of the century: life had not tarnished my boyish wonder.

Having reached by stages a teaching salary of seventy-five pounds a year, I applied for a job in Newport at a hundred pounds. About four o'clock one day, two strange men called at the Kettle school to take me to tea. One of them was H. M. Willsher, the Newport headmaster. They offered me the job, and I packed my little trunk. Willsher could not have been more unlike Calder. His discipline was easygoing – he did not care how much the children talked – and from the first day I loved the school. My two years in that southern suburb of Dundee were perhaps the happiest of my life thus far.

Newport could be reached via the Tay Bridge or the Tay Ferries. It was residential, and the only proletariat consisted of people who did the necessary work in the suburb – tradesmen, street cleaners, etc. So the pupils were socially mixed. The highest class sent their boys to the public schools and their daughters to other private schools. Our school got the lower-middle and working classes.

For me, Newport was an opportunity to realise my more snobbish dreams. In Forfar and elsewhere, my class status had been fixed; but here in Newport, I saw that Willsher and the other teachers were hail-fellow-well-met with the goodly citizens and, even as an ex-student teacher without a university degree, I also might be in good society. Actually, I had passed my final exam and was now the possessor of an Acting Teacher's Certificate. That, of course, explains why I now earned a hundred pounds a year.

Anyway, I was determined to go to the university by hook or by crook. During my time in Kettle, I had worked hard, and one morning cycled over to St Andrews for the first part of my preliminary exams – two subjects, English and Maths. I made a bad mess of the first maths paper; it was far too difficult for me, even though Ben Thomson had been coaching me by post. I came out in despair, half thinking that I should give the whole thing up, without attempting the second paper in the afternoon. At lunch I ran into a lecturer, an old pal of Willie's, and told him of my failure. He patted me on the back cheerfully. 'What you want is a brandy and soda', he said, and led me to the Cross Keys. I had never tasted brandy before but liked the taste and had another double. If not singing as I entered the exam hall, no doubt I felt like it. My memory of the paper is nil, but I did pass in both subjects. Thus, when I went to Newport, I was already a semi-matriculated student. Now I studied Latin and Physics for the second portion of the exam.

The first thing that happened to me in Newport was romantic; I fell violently in love with a pupil. Margaret was about sixteen; I, twenty-four. Her voice struck me as the essence of sweetness. To me, she was all that was lovely. Her long lashes almost hid her beautiful eyes, and I found that I could not look at her when she looked at me. She personified the whole school for me: if she happened to be absent, the day was dark, long, and dreary; when she was present, the day was always far too short. Years later, when I told her how much she had meant to me, she seemed much surprised. Wiser now in human motive and behaviour, however, I think she must have known, and no doubt used her dangerous eyes to torment the bashful, half-baked youth who trembled at her glance. Her beauty was not real to me, but something on which to build fantasies. So, of course, I made no advances. Wooing her did not seem to be so important as worshipping her.

The remarkable thing about Margaret was her persistence in my mind. While other girls faded from memory, she continued to haunt my dreams for years. I have found other grown men whose dream-Margarets ever and again came back into their lives as dream-pictures, and I have known women who had their dream-men. This puzzles me still. I have had long periods of psycho-analysis with different specialists, but the Margaret image baffled them all. They guessed she was my mother as I first knew her, young and desirable; then they said she must be a substitute for Clunie. Neither explanation gave me any emotional response. I do have a strong feeling that her indifference was her chief attraction. She obviously did not admire me; yet, on the evening before I left the school, she suddenly threw her arms round my neck and said: 'Mr Neill, you are a dear'. Damn the girl. That should have broken the spell. But it only made her more desirable than ever.

For years I heard nothing more of Margaret. Then, when she was a widow past seventy, I wrote to her and later went to see her. The beautiful eyes were dim, the long eyelashes had gone. I often wrote and phoned her thereafter; she was lonely living by herself, also lame and in pain. She had had a slight stroke and dreaded another. All her life, the lass had remained lower-middle-class, outside the mainstream of new ideas. I laughed at her shock when I used a four-letter word. As time went on, however, the ageing Margaret began to change. 'You have opened up a new world for me,' she would say. And she was a sweet old woman, though too set in her ways to accept modern ideas. One Sunday night, when I phoned her, there was no reply. Neighbours found her in a coma.

Poor Margaret. We agreed that marriage between us would have been a mistake, and I doubt if she ever could have overcome her conventional life in a Scottish suburb. But what is the use of guessing anyway? She was a youthful dream. A young man's fantasy assumes that if a girl is pretty, she has a pretty nature as well. And Margaret was doubly blessed. She had true manners, being considerate of others and hating to offend.

Adoration of Margaret did not prevent my having decided interests in other girls, and I gradually achieved a socially satisfying life through the Leng family. Sir John Leng had founded the big newspaper industry in Dundee. Lady Leng was a kind old lady, and I became tutor to one of the young Leng boys. I was invited to a dance they gave. Thus, at last, I had reached my long-wished-for ambition – to move in the best society.

Alas, I had never learned dancing and had no evening clothes. With only a hundred pounds a year, I could not afford to go to a good tailor. So I went to the Kingsmuir tailor and asked him if he could make me an evening suit. He scratched his head doubtfully, but thought he might have a try if he could find an illustration in *The Tailor*. I got my suit by post, and stupidly enough did not try it on. When entering the ballroom for my first dance, I found the trousers had been cut about two inches too long.

The cloth my tailor suggested was far too heavy; and for years

I sweated much more than I should have done at dances, which were mostly waltzes then. Stoutish men had to take three collars with them. I would guess that the eightsome reel accounted for turning one collar into a soaking rag, and the waltzes and lancers accounted for the other two.

But even before the problem of costume was solved, I had to learn to dance. A young teacher in Dundee gave me three lessons in waltzing – one, two, three – turn – four, five, six – and I picked up the step easily. Quickly, too, I learned the intricacies of the eightsome reel and lancers, soon being able to take my position at the head of a lancer set.

In the fashion of that era, the girls stood with programmes in hand, while the men moved among them like farmers buying cattle at the mart. One youth would pretend not to see Mary because she had almost broken his arm in the waltz, and looked the other way when he saw Jean, who had no rhythm at all. This tactic could backfire, however; frequently all the best girls had booked up their programmes in advance. One entire evening, disgusted by the whole custom, I danced only with plain wall-flowers. At the time it seemed the most heroic thing I had ever done; now I am inclined to question my motive.

Socially, I was fairly well pleased with my life. But culturally I had progressed, too. Harry Willsher, the school's headmaster, became my musical mentor. Apart from his personal talents, he was a music critic for the Dundee paper. One evening, hearing me remark that I liked Elgar's 'Salut d'Amour', he sat down and played it. Then, without a word, he repeated the composition. 'Shall I play it again?' he asked, but I said no. He smiled. 'The lesson is this, Neill. Good music you can hear again and again: inferior music bores you stiff if you get it more than once.' I was much impressed; yet today, if I had to listen ten times in succession to something I really like – the trio from *Der Rosenkavalier*, for instance – I should feel like drawing a gun on the singers.

For the first time in my life, I was within distance of drama and opera. It wasn't first-class opera, but good enough for someone who was not a first-class appraiser of music. I heard *Faust, Tannhäuser, Lohengrin, Carmen*. Because of someone's organising genius, I also heard Saturday concerts for a shilling, thus coming to know the artistry of Pachmann, Paderewski, Siloti, Elman, and our own Scottish Lamond. I was more impressed by their names than by their music, and feel certain today that if someone put three famous pianists behind a screen and had each play a Chopin polonaise I could not tell which one was playing. That may be an overstatement: I can tell when a waltz is played by Pachmann, but that is only because he had so individual a style. Of orchestral music I was equally ignorant, and still question whether anyone lacking a musical education senses the real difference between one conductor and another; though a non-musical person may be able to distinguish between a good and a bad rendering of a favourite piece. I like the polonaise from *Eugene Onegin*, for instance, but have heard it played well only once or twice; loving it, I can detect a bad performance.

In those days, Dundee had a theatre. Touring companies came every week, and I had the joy of becoming a regular theatre-goer. Musical-comedy successes came from London, and we saw Martin Harvey, a popular actor of the period, in *The Only Way*, *The Breed of the Treshams*, even *Hamlet*. His *Hamlet* played one week; that of Sir Johnston Forbes-Robertson the next. To me, both were surpassing fine. My cultural standards those days may be better understood, too, if I say that *The Only Way* seemed a much better play than *Hamlet*.

During this period, I discovered my dislike of seeing or hearing anything alone. The same desire to share with others comes over me today when I listen by myself to a good concert or opera on the radio. Sometimes, in Dundee, I took Clunie to my favourite plays. She was just as ignorant of the theatre as I, but my slight advancement made me laugh in a very superior way when the curtain fell on the first act of *The Only Way*, and she, with memories of local shows in the village school, remarked: 'Martin Harvey will be helping to shift the furniture, won't he?'

Newport was well off then, but Dundee was mostly a dirty slum. Yet I remained incredibly unaware of social disparities, with no feeling at all about riches and poverty. Indeed, there were no signs of my being a potential rebel. When Winston Churchill came to contest Dundee as a Liberal, I rejoiced at a Tory handbill: 'What is the use of a WC without a seat?' and threw things at young Winston when he spoke at an open-air meeting, mainly because a girl called Ella Robertson dared me to.

My brother Neilie, about to qualify as a doctor, did his obstetrical cases in Dundee. He would be called out at dead of night, and I sometimes gave him company through the long streets. We entered houses that were hovels, where women laboured in beds swarming with lice. Sometimes a woman would be having a baby in a room full of sleeping children. Such sights should have made me conscious of social evils, but apparently they didn't. I must have been emotionally and intellectually asleep.

71

Newport is one of the few places I still return to with strong feelings. It gave me peace, and helped me to carry on my teaching work without fear. I shall always have a tender spot in my heart for Harry Willsher, who was a companion rather than a master.

In Newport, as mentioned earlier, I came into contact with a higher class of society. There I learned how to behave like a gentleman, picking up all the futile little tricks comprising the term *good manners*. My frock coat and tall hat saw me through evening affairs; on Sundays, I went to church all dressed up, with white slip showing bravely under my waistcoat to indicate a non-existent one beneath. But here an eccentricity began to edge its way in. I recall finding a highly coloured waistcoat that had belonged to my maternal grandfather, and wearing it with my frock coat. I have always had a definite complex about dress, and wore open-necked coloured shirts long before they became fashionable. Unusual dress is one means of drawing attention to oneself, and in the beginning no doubt that was the reason for my perversity in dress. But now, when I have other ways of being an exhibitionist – lecturing, for example – I still dress unconventionally. There is a protest in the habit, a sort of 'why the hell should I be limited because everyone else wears this or that?' Fashion has always made me resentful; uniformity pains me. I associate proper dress with social usage, and never wear collar and tie to go to London except when I have to meet diehard prospective Summerhill parents.

But in Newport days, my dress reform was timid and hardly perceptible. I was too much afraid of alienating the little circle I had entered, for status was the one thing that mattered to me then. I was interested in society only as an external thing, rather than as a means toward gaining artistic or intellectual culture. I enjoyed hearing Willsher and his friends talk about books or music, but I did not expect men and women in society to do so. They talked of tennis and dances, as healthy young people ought to. Possibly, in my superior way, I tried to educate some of them. I remember lending H. G. Wells's *Marriage* to a girl of sixteen. Her father read it, wrote me a note calling me a dangerous seducer of innocence, and said I should never darken his door again. That, no doubt, put a stop to my attempts to uplift.

Meanwhile I had gone to St Andrews and passed the second half of my entrance exam, feeling very much pleased with myself. The door to the university was now open, and I said a sad farewell to Newport in the summer of 1908. Since the university did not open until October, I went back to Kingsmuir. I had saved enough to carry me over a year, or maybe two – heaven knows how. My main difficulty was choosing a profession. I had long given up any wish to enter the church, and had no definite ambition to enter anything else. The return of an old pupil to see my father settled the matter. He had worked toward a BSc in Agriculture and spoke of big jobs in the colonies. 'The very career for you,' said my father with enthusiasm, and I accepted the suggestion.

It was because of this degree, ostensibly, that I went to Edinburgh instead of St Andrews. My dreams of a university had always attached themselves to St Andrews. In visits to Willie, I had been enraptured by the romance of the 'grey city' with the scarlet gowns of the students and the happy atmosphere of Willie's tales. The social life there appealed to me strongly. It had a happy, family air about it; almost dangerous in a way, because St Andrews' men had a backward longing for their Alma Mater resembling the maudlin drunkard's rhapsodical desire to weep on the village pump. I chose Edinburgh because it was easier to get a degree in agriculture there, really because it seemed likely I should get a more cosmopolitan education. In St Andrews, I knew I should meet men from Perth and Stirling, whereas in Edinburgh I might meet men from all over the world. My acceptance of the plan to study agriculture shows how much of a drifter I was. I had no interest in agriculture, and knew that I never could have. For me, accepting it as a career meant as much as accepting an invitation to play tennis because I had no wish to do anything else at the moment.

UNIVERSITY LIFE

Neilie was in his final year of medical study, and I went to lodge with him. It was a cheap place off Clerk Street. The better-off students all lived over Marchmont way. Mrs Sutherland, our landlady, was a gem; a dear, kind woman who looked after me for four years. I was now really hard up and had to look twice at every penny spent, for there was no means of earning more. Luckily, I came under the Carnegie Trust and had my university fees paid by that grant, although matriculation and exam payments were not included. Neilie and I could only allow ourselves threepence a day for lunch. The Students' Union had a restaurant; also a lunch counter, where every day we each had a glass of milk and two penny buns. Other students had the same but they dined well at night. We could only afford high tea in our lodgings, and our only good meal of the week was the Sunday midday dinner. We always quarrelled about the division of it until we evolved a sound plan: Neilie divided the main dish between two plates, and then I chose one.

Though my approach to higher education may have been casual, I took seriously my first-year classses in chemistry and natural philosophy – at least in the beginning. Every morning we had a lecture by Sir James Walker, the chemistry professor, and I took voluminous notes. I thought it a waste of talent, however, for Walker to spend his precious time teaching raw students the elements of this subject; and in 1936, when I dined with the principal of Johannesburg University, I made such a remark at

74

table. The professors present were up in arms at once. They defended the lecture system by saying that this very contact with a man like Walker was the best education a student could have. I still don't believe it. Any assistant could teach a class what happens if you put sulphuric acid on zinc, and why should a good chemist like Walker not spend all his time doing research at the expense of the university or state? I liked chemistry with its practical lab work and passed it easily. But my work must have cost the university something, for I used up all the chloroform cleaning my pipes.

Natural philosophy was double Dutch to me. Professor MacGregor was the worst lecturer I ever encountered, mumbling into his beard as he wrote mysterious formulae on the blackboard, while we passed the time cat-calling and tramping tunes with our feet. MacGregor never seemed to mind: I wonder if he ever heard us. Our greatest day occurred when the lab assistant, Lindsay, had to turn the handle of an instrument to show the workings of sound waves. Then we all threw pennies at him; but like his master, he stood there quite unperturbed. He had had many years of this, and possibly his only interest was the amount of the collection he would sweep up when class was over.

Lab work in Nat. Phil. was a farce to me. I remember being given some apparatus concerning an inclined plane, and repeatedly timing something, so I could write down each result. After getting about fifty of these results, I added them up and took the average. I disliked the dullness of this work and hated my inability to do it quickly. Another man would finish his experiment in about half an hour, and looked to be the class medallist. One day I asked him how he managed to get through his experiments so quickly. 'Take three readings and fake the rest,' he said shortly. After that, my experiments took about twenty minutes each.

I can honestly say that I hardly understood anything about sound, light, and heat – not to mention electricity. When the final exam came round, I stared at a paper that was far beyond my comprehension, and went home for the summer vacation feeling depressed. I passed. Still wondering how and why, I can only conclude that old MacGregor was as absentminded in correcting papers as he was in the lecture hall, and muddled my paper with someone else's. For all I know, he mixed up mine with that of his medallist, whom he may have failed.

By the end of the first year, I had discovered that science was not in my line, and made up my mind to take a degree in Honours English. Probably one of my father's old pupils had come home

75

and was doing well as an MA in Hon. Eng. Honours English meant that, with the exception of history, I could spend all of my time taking English classes. I duly entered for history and first-year English.

We had Sir Richard Lodge for English History, and I enjoyed his lectures thoroughly. There was no cat-calling in *his* room; one look from him and we all became diligent little boys and girls who were seen and not heard. One youth tried cat-calling one day. He sat behind me, and I looked round in annoyance. Suddenly I heard Lodge shout: 'You, sir!' He was looking, I thought, at the bad man behind me. 'You, you, you, sir,' came the persistent, hard voice of the professor, and he pointed at me. I rose from my seat and silently asked a vital question by indicating myself with my forefinger. 'Yes, you,' thundered Lodge. 'Get out of this classroom, sir.'

Very white, I marched from the room with my head up. After class, I knocked at the door of his private room. 'I thought you would come to apologise,' he said. 'I didn't, sir. I came to tell you I had nothing to do with the noise.'

He eyed me with some suspicion. 'Of course, if you say so . . .' He shrugged his shoulders as if to show he didn't believe me.

Then suddenly I lost all my fear of authority and my temper as well. 'Look here, sir,' I said. 'I had to work for years to save up enough money to come to the university. I am years older than the average student. Do you think, in these circumstances, I came to Edinburgh to behave like a raw schoolboy?'

His eyebrows went up in surprise. Then he smiled, held out his hand, and apologised. My honour was satisfied, but I could have sunk through the floor next day when Lodge began his lecture by offering a public apology, for it wasn't so much an apology as a panegyric. His word-portrait made me not only a scholar but a super-gentleman – and a prig.

My English professor was George Saintsbury, the renowned English author and critic. I sat under him for three years, but he did not know my name or know me by sight except on one occasion. His lectures were soliloquies: he spoke them like a parrot, and did not seem to care whether we listened or not. That suited us all right, for we did not listen. At least I personally did not, knowing that I could find it all in his voluminous writings a week before the exam. He had a high, squeaky voice, and amused us by his gentlemanly attitude toward his contemporaries: 'Er – I do not quite agree with my friend – er – (then quickly) Mr Bridges when he says – but I must be just and take into considera-

76

tion what Professor Raleigh, who by the way in his attitude towards Dryden . . .' We had great sport trying to stick to the main road through all his parentheses.

Our course of study was not a creative one. We were supposed to 'know' literature from Beowulf to Pater. We had to learn Anglo-Saxon and Middle English. We used set books and studied set periods – my final exam covered Elizabethan drama. In effect, we read books about books. For an exam, it was necessary to know what Coleridge and Hazlitt had said about Shakespeare; in any question on style, we were supposed to know exactly what Longinus had said about the subject. By that time I had discovered Ibsen and was full of enthusiasm for his plays. When my class-work demanded from me an essay on *Much Ado*, I quite foolishly wrote a damning criticism of the play, comparing its theatre with the contemporary theatre of Ibsen. That is, I criticised Shakespeare for not writing a realistic play – a stupid thing to do, but putting forward the point of view I held then. Saintsbury was very angry with me – the one time he must have recognised my name.

I held then, and do now, that it is better to write a bad limerick than be able to recite *Paradise Lost*. That is a fundamental thing in education. But the university never asked us to compose even a limerick; it did not ask from us any original opinions about Shakespeare or about anyone else. In those years, I read Spenser, Chaucer, Pope, Dryden, most of Shakespeare and much of his contemporaries; practically all of the Restoration Drama, Coleridge, Tennyson, Dr Johnson, Keats . . . . But why go on? I was compelled to concentrate on whether a blank-verse line had elision or not, or whether one could trace the rhythm of 'Christabel' in 'The Lotus Eaters'. It was all piddling stuff, like taking Milan Cathedral to pieces stone by stone to discover where the beauty lay. I had to read so glorious a thing as *The Tempest* with annotations, painfully looking up the etymological meaning of some phrase that did not matter a scrap.

Saintsbury gave me a feeling for prose style, and that's about all. He knew the beauty of literature, but he could not get it across to us. I spent three years with him in dreary swamps of prose rhythm and poetic diction, seeing the trees but never the woods beyond. He held that his work had to deal with manner and not matter; otherwise, he said, English Literature would bring in every study under the sun. I can see that, but it simply isn't possible to treat Macaulay's *Essay on Clive* as a piece of literature without giving – or having any opinion on – the historical and

77

political aspects of Clive's life. Saintsbury found it so easy to separate subject from style that he praised Blake as a great technical poet, and Nietzsche as one of the greatest prose writers, while dismissing the subject matter of both with the words: 'They were, of course, mad.'

Whatever I actually gained from Saintsbury, it was certainly not an appreciation of literature. To this day I cannot read poetry for pleasure, cannot touch the Classics. One year I went over to Norway – an MA in Honours English – and my literature for reading on the voyage was a bundle of *Black Mask* magazines – American crook yarns. True they were shoved into my hand by a friend as I left, but if I'd had Keats and Shelley in my bag, I still would have read the *Black Mask*s. I hasten to add that it would be grossly unfair to name Edinburgh University for any bad taste acquired: I am merely suggesting that if my years there had been spent in studying matter instead of manner, I might have had a better taste in literature today. I know that anything I could say about Chaucer and Keats would be unimportant and uninformed.

When Professor Chrystal, the celebrated mathematician, died, I went to see Saintsbury about giving me an obituary on the Professor for our university magazine, *The Student*.

'I am just going into my Honours Class', he said. 'If you are quick at taking notes, I shall allow you to come in, for I mean to say something about my old friend.'

'But, sir, I have been in your Honours Class for three years.'

He looked up quickly and asked my name. When I replied, he said, 'Good heavens, how you have grown.'

I had been six feet years before I entered the university, and there weren't a dozen of us in that class. Saintsbury recognised books but not students. Lecturing to a bunch of raw undergraduates must have been hell for him.

On the whole, social life at Edinburgh was pleasant. Being a member of the Union, I always had a meeting place and an armchair of an evening. The difficulty was the shortage of cash. Most of my friends were well off. They wore the same sort of golfing jacket and flannel bags as I did, but they had money to spend; and when drinks went round it was awkward, because I never had more than a few coppers in my pockets.

I could not afford to play any games or even go to see matches. I had to pretend I hated music-halls in order to avoid joining parties going to the Kings or the Empire. Nowadays I should tell them the truth, that I was poor. Mainly from my mother, who feared that we might revert to her working-class mother's status, I had the Shavian idea that poverty was a crime, a thing to be ashamed of, to hide as skilfully as one could. I must have played my part well, for years afterwards a fellow-student, who had been a pal, remarked: 'Yes, it was all very well for you, Neill. You had money and I hadn't.'

During my second year I had a stroke of fortune. My landlady gave me her paper to read one Sunday, and I idly tried a competition therein. A week later, seeing a placard on Nicholson Street: EDINBURGH MAN WINS FORTY POUNDS, I did not make a connection. Only later, back at my digs, did I learn of my luck from the excited landlady. 'You've won first prize!'

A pal of mine at that time received a similar amount from an uncle; and though just as hard up, he gave a champagne supper, blowing his money in one night. I put mine in the bank and lived on it for a very long time, drawing on it sparingly for necessities only. I mention the other man, not because I considered him a damned fool then, but because humanity is roughly divided into two classes, represented by him and by me. In my own family, Willie would have squandered his forty pounds at once; Neilie would have kept it as I did. I never saw the pleasure in eating all your cake at one bite, because temperamentally I am not entirely forgetful of the morrow. Or to put it in the fashionable way, I like to lay up treasure in heaven. But apart from that, I still think the other man was a fool. We argued the point later, when he was lunching on fourpence but kept persisting that the fun he got out of his champagne splash had been worth a year of fourpenny lunches. It would not have been so for me.

This diversity of character makes me think of the prodigal son story. Ask yourself: what side am I on – the son who went away and had a good time, or the dull brother who stayed at home? Most men say they are with the prodigal son. I never do, and I know why: I think of Willie getting all the jam when he went away, while the brothers who stayed at home got the dry bread. And I never admired the prodigal son for having his champagne supper and then in cowardly manner coming back to beg for forgiveness and a meal.

The whole question of my attitude towards money is important. Because of the poverty suffered in my young years, I have a queer meanness about money. I grudge paying out small sums, yet can sign a cheque for a large amount without a moment's hesitation. Many other men regard cheques in a similar way: to us, a cheque isn't real money. It is fantasy money, and therefore of no emotional value. When motoring, I pay for petrol without quibbling; but if I have to take a taxi, I sit and watch the meter painfully whenever there is a traffic jam in the street. If I suddenly became a millionaire, I should still travel third-class and buy a secondhand car. I dislike borrowing money and dislike more lending it. Only once was a lent fiver paid back to me – by a Scot, of course.

In still another way, money was a problem on occasion. My editorship of *The Student* gave me free dress-circle tickets to all the city theatres on Monday nights, and luckily, evening dress was not obligatory. But there was a whole week of opera once – *Die Meistersinger, Orpheus, Elektra*, some others – and I went every night to these more formal events. Towards the end of the week, I had to doctor my one dress-shirt meticulously with white chalk to make it look decent.

Of all the week's opera, *Die Meistersinger* knocked me over. I had never heard such music. To me it was the purest of gold; but instead of inspiring me to noble thoughts and deeds, it made me a swindler. Another performance was scheduled during the week, and of course there were no more press tickets. Determined to hear the opera again, however, I dressed myself in my chalked boiled shirt and went down to the theatre just before the end of the first act. During the interval I sneaked in, pretending I had lost my pass-out, and with good luck found a fine, empty seat.

As editor of *The Student*, I also had the privilege of being invited *ex officio* to an inter-university conference in St Andrews. It was a great affair. Champagne flowed like water, and most of us got canned, gloriously canned. We all thought Walter Elliott, one of the delegates from Glasgow, the most brilliant speaker of the conference. But why so good and likable a man ever became a Conservative, and cabinet minister in such a government, is a riddle to me.

I was allowed a small grant from the SRC (Students' Representative Council) towards my expenses at the conference. It was not enough, and I drew about a pound more. But Walker, the secretary, stood me on the mat and gave me a thorough dressing-down. 'No other editor ever used more than the allotted amount', he said, and I stood silent, ashamed of my poverty, hating the man. He was comfortably off, and looked at me as if I were something the cat had dragged into the house. My predecessors in the editorial chair had been gentlemen; that seemed to be what he was trying to tell me. I felt both angry and guilty.

As an editor without money, I had to spend more than I could afford. I was invited to all university dinners, and although these cost me nothing, the small outlays on cloakroom tips, dress-shirt laundry, etc., were beyond me. Matters became easier when an ex-editor told me I should sell the books sent in for review. I did so, getting half the published price; but there again there were difficulties, because my medical student friends kept asking for the privilege of reviewing costly books. Often I put them off and wrote the reviews myself; by studying the indexes, I managed to write passable reviews, though knowing nothing of medicine. When a book came out that I wanted, I wrote to the publishers, telling them tall stories about the circulation and influence of *The Student*, and in nine cases out of ten they sent the book.

I cannot recall exactly when I began to write, but it must have been some time before becoming editor. I began by submitting drawings and cartoons – awful things that make me blush to remember; my drawing, then as now, was atrocious. At that time, a student advised me to try a comic literary sketch for the *Glasgow Herald*. I sent one in, and a few mornings later found it in the paper. Possibly that was one of the most ecstatic moments of my life, the first time in print. It seemed incredible, wonderful, glorious; I trod on air all that day. Later, I sent in other sketches and received fourteen shillings for each one that was published.

About then, I became friendly with a girl in my English class. It was a platonic friendship that lasted a long time. During long walks, May and I talked mainly about ourselves; in vacations, we wrote long letters to each other – again, I fear, mostly on the same subjects. She was a clever lassie, who encouraged me to write prose and helped me to gain a self-confidence that was lacking. I see now that I abused her friendship, using it to flatter my own ego, for her belief in me supplied much that I needed. I look back on that friendship now with a feeling of tenderness.

We were both snobs, but strangely enough, it was our snobbery that ultimately parted us. She had friends among the aristocracy and used to stay at their country houses. To me she brought some of the glamour of the best people; yet at the same time, I found my resentment against them growing. May had strong opinions about what was 'done' and what wasn't; and I rebelled when she expected me to have manners like her rich friends. Fundamentally, she was what we might call fascist today, while I was fundamentally socialist. She remained a positive snob, while I became a negative one. She was critical of individuals but accepted society without question: I was critical of society and apt to accept individuals for what they were. I liked her humour,

81

and we laughed at the same things (manners excluded). We made no pretence about the fact that she was my Lady Bountiful, patronising a very raw youth who, with some encouragement, might do something in life. I was slightly afraid of her, I remember, but she was a good scout and someone I could meet again with real pleasure.

It might be interesting here to contrast my growth with Willie's, since he had been so strong an influence on my early life. Later he veered to the right, while I gradually assumed a more leftist attitude towards politics and other matters. There was one great difference between us as boys. He developed very young, reading the Bible at three, and entered the university when sixteen. My own advancement seemed incredibly slow. Though I was twenty-eight when editing *The Student*, my editorials might have been written by a boy of fourteen. Their puerility is lamentable and their arrogance – comical is perhaps the best term. As editor, I suffered badly from being the sole authority. There was no need to ask anyone's opinion, and I published my own geese, believing they were swans. Some of my friends called certain articles tripe; alas, that happened after their publication. But editing the magazine was a liberal education in its way. I got to know about spacing, proof-reading, and technical production matters. My position gave me a certain standing among students, and I met interesting men at public functions. After one big dinner, I half-carried home one of Edinburgh's best surgeons. On his doorstep, he drew himself up and said thickly, 'Young man, I'm tight, absolutely bunged up, but if someone came now and told me I had to go to the operating theatre, I'd cut out an appendix with a hand as steady as a rock.' I never had any doubt that he spoke the truth.

During one of the summer vacations, I fell in love with Beatrice. We went through heaven and then hell, and I know that the hell was on account of Clunie. Unconsciously, I compared every girl with Clunie; unconsciously, she hated every girl I loved. While praising them, she subtly made me see their shortcomings. I lost Beatrice, warm and dear as she was, because – without knowing it – I was looking for the ideal that my mother's sinful notion of sex had compelled me to form. There was, of course, more to it than that. Half of me wanted to marry Beatrice on the spot; the other half cried: 'Wait, don't tie yourself up before you have made your career'. There was a definite pull – women versus ambition – that may have come from hearing my mother say: 'Marriage hinders a man, because it forces him to think of bread and butter'. While I thought and hesitated, the practical Beatrice went off and married someone else.

I cannot honestly say that my four years in Edinburgh were very happy. I always return to the city unwillingly and without any interest. It is beautiful – more beautiful perhaps than any other city I have seen – but for me, Edinburgh remains a dead city, parochial and pompous. Its university life had little or no group spirit. We all lived in digs. The only meeting-place was the Union, and thousands were not even members of that. A man could take a degree in Edinburgh without speaking to a single student during the time he was there. And some students seemed to do just that, too.

Union life itself was narrow. Many students were medicals from the colonies, bringing with them their beastly colonial attitude towards the 'nigger'. Many coloured students studied at Edinburgh; and because fo the colonial men, they were all classified thus. One day when I lunch edwith an Egyptian – supposed to be a prince – two South Africans hastily moved away from the table. When the exploited native populations finally rise to smash their chains, not a few of their leaders will have received their impetus from the abominable treatment of the 'nigger' in the English and Scottish universities.

My finals were at hand. During my last year, I had given up my time and interest to editing *The Student*, and anticipated a very poor degree – in fact, the poorest possible, a Third-Class pass. But in the finals I did not do as badly as expected; indeed, at the end of the week, I almost dared hope for a First in spite of my frankly bad Anglo-Saxon and Middle English. I got a Second and was quite pleased. In due course, I was capped MA; but by then, sad to recall, I did not feel unduly proud or pleased. Everything in life comes too late, we hear. Whether that is so or not, it was certainly true of my degree. As Robert Louis Stevenson said: 'To travel hopefully is a better thing than to arrive'. The degree, once a glittering peak, had become a minor hill, from the top of which I could look far out and see distant peaks, high and perhaps inaccessible – work, fame, perhaps death. More bluntly stated: I had got my degree and didn't know how to use it. All I knew was that *I didn't want to teach*: to think of going on all my life as English master in some provincial secondary school or academy, made me shiver. No, teaching would be the last resort, if every other line failed.

83

LONDON

Journalism was my future, and I studied the ads in the papers, I applied for a few jobs but got no answers. Then R. Scott Stevenson, later an ear, nose and throat man in the West End, said he could get me some work at T.C. & E.C. Jacks, the Edinburgh publishers. The job was sub-editing a one-volume encylopaedia planned to contain something more perhaps than the Britannica. Its chief editor was H. C. O'Neill. It turned out to be a lousy job. Half the contributions came from clergymen with unreadable penmanship. When the copy was readable, it ran too long. We often had to throw the stuff into the waste-paper basket and rewrite it ourselves. I recall writing up the Panama Canal in this way, cribbing of course from other encyclopaedias. The work was extremely useful in one way: it gave me a dread of superfluous words.

I had been about a year at this work when O'Neill persuaded the firm to transfer its editorial office to London. Having reached the age of twenty-nine without crossing the border, I found the idea of going to London both wonderful and inevitable; had not Barrie and lesser Scots writers gone south to find wealth and a name? I counted the days before I should set off, but as often occurs in life, something happened to dampen my enthusiasm and hopes at the last moment; my mother became very ill. Now having a small but regular income, I arranged for her to go to a nursing-home and have the offending gallstones removed. My hopes went south; my fears stayed behind in that nursing home. I stayed just long

84

enough to see her after the operation – she was down but not out – and then set off with definite relief.

I don't recall how I looked, arriving in King's Cross station on a Sunday morning late in 1912, but I felt much as Keats's baffled Cortez: 'Silent, upon a peak in Darien'. Here was London, the centre of life and everything valuable to life. I made for the Strand and Fleet Street. With a thrill I looked round, trying hard to keep from realising a slight disappointment. They were meaner streets than I had pictured, less picturesque than the Strand that appeared so colourfully on the jacket of *Strand Magazine*. Still, these were but names; wait till I saw the great men who ran the British press. During the next few weeks, I would wander at lunch time from Long Acre to Fleet Street to look at the great men. But never did I see anyone who looked more important than a messenger boy, and this made me wonder.

Dorothy, an actress friend I had met in Edinburgh, lived in Hammersmith, where I went to find lodgings. Dorothy was the only soul I knew in London, but even she left in a week's time, to go on tour again, so living in Hammersmith did not help me much, although her mother was good to me. For the first time in my life, I learned the truth of the platitude that a man can be loneliest in a crowd. When my work was over, I had no one to speak to. Weekends were the worst. Visiting places like Harrow and Windsor, I saw cheerful groups playing tennis on inviting lawns, and heard pianos played in the evenings within suburban houses, while I stood on the road feeling lonely. Sometimes I had the mad impulse to walk up to a group on a lawn and say: 'Let me sit and watch you play. I'm as lonely as hell', but was inhibited by Scots caution. I got into the habit of hiring a skiff at Richmond and rowing upstream. Never having handled an oar in my life, I learned painfully, blushing at the insults hurled at me by occupants of nicely varnished boats I scratched. Many a time on a grey and windy day, mine was the only skiff on the river. But I wasn't afraid, though unable to swim – except for one occasion, when Neilie, visiting in town, came with me and did the rowing. While nervous sometimes when sitting beside certain drivers – what motorist isn't! – I have never been afraid while driving a car myself. Fear, converted into action, ceases to be fear. On sunny days up the river, I hated myself for coming; the sight of merry boatloads of parties, of punts with pretty girls lying under parasols while young men poled them along, these made my loneliness almost unbearable. Sometimes I went for long walks, hoping for something to happen – a miracle of some kind – but always returned to my lodgings disappointed. God, they were dull, too!

One Sunday night in Uxbridge, while feeling especially miserable, I saw an attractive-looking girl sitting on a bench reading a novel. Quite nervously I sat down beside her, knowing that I would speak to her and dreading a rebuff. For some time, I remained there, glancing sideways at her. She seemed to bury herself more deeply in her book. 'Let's talk', I said suddenly, 'I'm damn lonely.'

She gave me a cold glance of fear, murmured something about not knowing me, and buried herself still more deeply in the novel. Suddenly, I felt a wave of anger come over me. 'Christ, woman', I shouted, 'you sit here reading a foolish story and when a chance for real romance comes along, you escape it with a look that says, "We haven't been introduced!"'

'It's the way I was brought up', she answered wretchedly. I didn't know what to say next, for I saw then that the poor kid must have been just as lonely as I. We talked a little in an awkward way, but she hadn't much to say and was, I thought, not well-educated. Our 'romance' lasted about five minutes, and then she said she had to go.

There were pleasant interludes, however, in this lonely time. When Dorothy came home from her tour, her boyfriend took us out in his car – oh, wasn't he proud of its being able to touch forty on the Windsor Road! Sometimes we boated up river, and they always wanted me around, as the welcome third gooseberry. We made a jolly party. I can still hear Dorothy's silvery laugh when I overbalanced with the pole and nearly fell in. Sometimes she would bring one of her musical-comedy friends. I learned that a touring company consisted mainly of very conventional, ambitious middle-class girls, many of whom sent money home to help the family. They were easy folk to get on with, but so narrow in their interests – 'the show', and what Bert said, and how wild the stage manager was. Dorothy, in her waggish way, kept telling her friends that I was a very clever fellow – an MA. I don't know what lay behind her joke, possibly delight in seeing them stare at me as if I were inhuman. The magic letters did seem to scare them, however. They began to apologise to me for their lack of education.

During the working day, I divided my time between Long Acre and the British Museum. The encyclopaedia having been finished and published, I had been asked to write the English Language-and-Literature portion of a popular-educator reference work that Jacks were then preparing. After completing it, and fearful of losing my job, I took on the Mathematics section. Then I did Drawing, with my illustrations that fortunately never saw the light of a bookseller's shop, for O'Neill wisely decided to cut out that subject. At last, nothing remained for me to write, and I found myself unemployed. I was worried. The one thing I did not want to do was to return to Scotland and – the only possible job there – teaching.

By this time, Neilie had come to town, and we set up house with J. B. Salmond, later editor of *Scots Magazine*. He worked in Fleetway House then, and our studio flat was always full of carefree lads from the Northcliffe Press. They kept telling me that if I could write a washerwoman's weekly serial, they could guarantee me five hundred pounds a year. Unfortunately, all my attempts to write such a serial ended in obscene laughter when Salmond read the results aloud.

When our lease of the studio ended, Neilie and I tried several lodgings and hated them all. Meanwhile, my health had gone bad and I was far from fit. Poor feeding at the university, followed by bad feeding in London digs with ill-nourishing lunches outside, and, finally, the sardine and tinned salmon lazy table of our studio flat – all these affected me, and lack of exercise didn't help. Also, I was very much worried over the threat of being summoned as co-respondent in a divorce case. This I escaped, possibly because the irate husband, a well-known musician, knew that I hadn't got a bean.

One night, I woke up with a sharp pain in my leg. Neilie, being a doctor, diagnosed it as phlebitis – inflammation of a vein. I was alarmed because I knew that such inflammation caused a clot, and if even a tiny fragment of this clot broke away, there was a chance of very sudden death. Neilie exaggerated this danger, I fancy, in order to keep me from going out to work next day. I went to King Edward Hospital in Windsor, where an old university pal of mine named D. G. Watson was house surgeon. I had been out there often and knew the staff well. The surgeon ligatured my vein, so that the clot could not move, and I lay in bed for about a fortnight, having the time of my life.

After my recovery I returned to town and answered various ads. One ran: 'Art Editor wanted for new magazine in Fleet Street', and gave a box number for reply. Obviously, this was no job for me, but having nothing to lose, I sat down and wrote an application letter, frivolous in tone. My surprise a few mornings later, when I got a reply asking me to come and see the editor of *Piccadilly Magazine*, 40 Fleet Street, was mixed with trepidation; I knew nothing about art. I went, however, and was interviewed.

Vincent, the editor, took up two letters. 'That one', he said, 'is from a man who has been on —— Magazine for ten years as art editor. This one is from the art editor of ——— Magazine where he has been for twelve years.'

I swallowed hard.

'I am going to offer you the job', he went on.

I gasped and said, 'In God's name, why?'

'Because', he said, 'your letter was the only one that amused me. When can you start?'

I accepted his offer of one hundred and fifty pounds a year.

I really liked working on that newly formed magazine, even though, because of my leg, I spent my weekly salary on taxis. My job was to read short stories and hand on my choices to Vincent. If he approved, I had to find the right illustrator for the story: Balliol Salmond, if it was a yarn about a girl in a boat; someone else for a story with shooting; Harry Rountree for animals. When returning a serial to H. G. Wells's agent as unsuitable, I felt myself grow inches higher.

As part of my duties, I also interviewed people. Once, when we were running an article on the human behaviour of horses, I went to the great jockey, Steve Donaghue, to get his opinions. He gave them in a friendly way, and as I was going, offered me a tip for the next race. When I got back to No. 40, the whole staff was on the doorstep. 'Did he give you a tip?' somebody asked. I thought for a moment, and passed along the horse's name – whatever it was. They all rushed out to bet their shirts on it. This amused me, for I knew nothing about betting or horses. The horse came in either last or second to last.

My interview with a fighter known as Bombardier Wells was difficult. For the magazine's first issue, a symposium had been planned on the question: *Should the knockout be abolished?* I set out cheerfully enough to ask Billy Wells what he thought about it, but suddenly, on the street, I realised that Billy himself had been knocked out the previous night. Finally, when a man in a dirty sweater led me into his presence, I never felt so small in my life – literally. Billy towered above me, and his hand crushed mine so tightly that I almost squeaked. Asking the embarrassing question made me tremble, but he took it quite well and we had an interesting chat.

WORLD WAR I

The *Piccadilly Magazine*'s first issue had been scheduled for the end of August, 1914. One of the articles, well illustrated with photographs, was entitled 'The Real German Danger – The Crown Prince'. But the shot at Sarajevo killed, among other things, the budding *Piccadilly Magazine*. It never appeared.

I was staying with Watson, my doctor friend in Windsor, when war was declared, and still remember how the two of us – both Socialists – sat up talking about it while the Life Guards nearby cheered all night long. He said tensely: 'Oh, the fools, the bloody damn fools. Can't they see it means their death and the death of most things we love?'

During that period, I had joined the Westminster Labour Party, which met in a small room somewhere in St James's, to talk and plan a new world. Among the speakers who stood on a soapbox in the Park, along with me, were two men I had known at the university. One later became a metropolitan police surgeon, and the other a Harley Street doctor – both probably lifelong Tories.

There are moments in every man's life which he looks back on with sudden embarrassment, saying to himself: 'What a bloody fool I was then!' Today I feel like that about my soapbox oratory. My ignorance of politics and economics was profound, so I can only conjecture that my self-confidence was robust. On one occasion, I foolishly mentioned the GPO as an example of socialism. A postman knocked me down, propped me up again, and then beat me into political impotence and death – his battering ram a thorough, shattering knowledge of the inner workings of the post office.

Neither Watson nor I had any grasp of the realities behind the war. In our previous meetings, we had sometimes talked about the chances of war being stopped at the start by the refusal of international labour to load a ship or move a shell. Like most other people, we were quite vague about the whole question, and the only thing we strongly agreed upon was that Germany had asked for it and was going to get it, too. We talked about what we should do. He would volunteer at once as a doctor, and I said, unenthusiastically, that with my university degree I could easily get a commission. 'No go', said Watson. 'They wouldn't have you with your leg as it is at present. You need six months' rest, old man, and of course the war will be over by then.'

Watson went to a base hospital in France but got tired of the monotony, volunteered to serve with a regiment, and died of wounds. He was one of the nicest fellows I have ever known – bright, keen, with a jolly sense of humour. We had been friends for a long time before discovering that our fathers had taught in the same school as apprentice teachers.

I went home to Kingsmuir perturbed in mind. I felt that I really should join up, preferring the artillery because of my bad feet. On the other hand, supporting my cowardice, was the statement of Watson and another doctor that I wasn't fit. After a few weeks, I applied for and got the job of temporary headmaster at Gretna Green school. When I arrived there, I found that the permanent head, a hefty he-man, was serving with the KOSB (King's Own Scottish Borderers), but I did not feel too bad about the situation. My bad leg was swollen and numb, rather than painful, and I think now that the condition must have been, in modern parlance, psychological – my protection against joining the army.

The story of my stay in Gretna Green was told, more or less truly, in my first book *A Dominie's Log*. But its sequel, *A Dominie Dismissed*, was pure fiction, written during my army service later.

Coming from Fleet Street to a slow village required some adaptation. I had lodgings in a small cottage, and when my landlady brought in the paraffin lamp of an evening and drew the blind of the small window, I felt that I was separated from the whole world. It was characteristic of this gulf separating Gretna from London that she frowned on the use of typewriters on

90

Sundays. I think I began to write books to keep myself from going barmy.

It seems ludicrous that a man who is known as an educational heretic should have taken to this profession merely because journalism and his military courage failed him. Yet I began to think about education for the first time in Gretna. My predecessor had been a disciplinarian, and I arrived to find a silent, obedient school; but I knew that the bigger lads were watching me carefully to see how far they could go. I put on my severest look and glared at them; and on the second day, when the biggest of them tried me out with a semi-insolent answer, I gave him a leathering with the strap. I was still governed by the old dictum of the teaching profession: show you are master at once.

To say I could have gone on as a disciplinarian if I had tried, would be a silly thing to say, for I couldn't will myself to do that. Gradually, the children discovered that my discipline was a bluff, that I really didn't care if they learned or not. The silent school became a beer garden, full of noise and laughter. But we carried on the usual lessons, and I suppose they learned as much as they would have if afraid of me. Either way, it seemed to me such futile waste to teach the geography of India to children who were going out to the farms.

The school board did not care very much what I was doing. Some of its members, as individuals, became friends of mine; Stafford the minister, Dick MacDougall the board clerk, and their wives, were kind to me. According to general opinion among the villagers, I was quite a nice chap but, of course, half daft. To my horror, I found myself fast becoming countrified – narrow, interested in local gossip, craning my neck to see where the doctor was going. I tried to keep in touch with larger affairs by having the *Nation* and the *New Age* sent weekly by post.

One sunny May morning, a terrible troop-train disaster took place a field's breadth from my lodgings. When my landlady woke me and told me there had been a smash, I jumped on my cycle and went off. The scene resembled a silent film. The only sounds were the hissing of engines and the pops of cartridges as fire crept along the wreckage. Men were lying dead or dying; one soldier with both legs torn off asked me for a cigarette, and he grinned as I lit it for him. 'May as well lose them here as in France', he said lightly. He died before the cigarette was half smoked.

To me, the whole affair seemed unreal, like a dream. I joined a party that was trying to free a man from under an engine. As we worked, another man said to me: 'They expect the engine to

91

explode any second'. But after an uneasy glance at the hissing steam, I thought no more about it. The quietness of that morning was unbelievable. Hardly a man groaned, and when the dying men called aloud, it was always for their mothers. Women and children were among the injured, but no cries or sobbing seemed to come from them. It was said that the officers shot some of the men who were hopelessly pinned under the blazing wreckage. I never knew if the story was true, but hoped it was.

What impressed me so strongly that morning was my lack of any emotion at all, even pity. To be fair to myself, of course, I was busy all the time doing things for the wounded. I felt uncomfortable about this, however, and late at night, sitting in the manse, I said to the minister: 'I must be the greatest egoist God ever made: nothing to give anyone, selfish to the core. This morning in that field I had not the tiniest suspicion of any feeling. I was just a stone of indifference.'

Stafford stared at me with open eyes. 'I was just about to say the same thing to you. I thought I was a monster because I felt nothing.' We apparently had assumed the attitude that doctors and nurses have. Just as a person's fear changes into positive energy when rowing a boat in a bad swell, so he can absorb terror and pity whilst assisting others in pain. And one cannot feel deeply for complete strangers.

Contrariwise, I recall how one of my pupils – a boy – was killed that morning, run down by a motor cycle on his way to the disaster. His mother asked me to go and see his body that night, and I felt a real grief. I also felt keenly the plight of the signalman whose mistake had caused the accident: I had his sons in school and liked them, as well as their father. To me, imprisoning him was only one of the many signs of barbarity in our legal code.

I went off one Saturday to Dumfries to join the army. I know that I had no real wish to be a soldier, but something must have influenced me; either a bad conscience after a friend had been killed or, just as likely, an order that all men should be examined under the Derby Scheme. I was rejected because of my leg, and given a certificate stating that I was permanently unfit for service. Just as I left the building, however, a sergeant asked me if I had joined the Derby Scheme. I told him that I did not need to, because I had been rejected. 'But', he said, 'you get half-a-crown if you join.' When I asked him how, he took me to an officer, before whom I swore that I would serve 'my King and Country' when called upon to do so. The sergeant got a half-crown from me for his pains. Later, when all rejected men were ordered to be re-examined and I was passed as fit, I should have had the disgrace of being drafted, if that sergeant hadn't had a thirst on him and an eye to the main chance.

It is difficult to return even in fantasy to my Gretna days. I have motored through the village at least once a year but have stopped there only once – and regretted it. Dimly I recall pleasant tea parties with my assistants, May and Christine and Bell; the bustle and chaos of the building of the great munition works, and the transformation of a dull hamlet into a township with cinema and shops. There was also a love story – wrecked again on the Clunie fixation.

Later, in the Army, I made a good friend, and we were always together. A year after the war, we ran into each other in the Strand, delighted to meet again. We made a date to have dinner, and for half an hour we talked about old times: 'Remember Tubby? That morning when he hadn't shaved and the sergeant . . .' We laughed a bit. Then the conversation ceased, and we both realised that we had nothing more to say to each other. Army life had drawn us together because we had to concentrate on military things; in civilian life we hadn't an interest in common. It was a sad dinner party, and although we tried to make an artificial cheerfulness, and promised to meet again, we both knew in our hearts that we never could. I know now that if someone long dead – someone I loved (say Clunie) came back to me, we could not pick up where we left off.

In the early spring of 1917, all medically rejected men were ordered to report for re-examination. I was passed A-1 by a doctor I had known at the university. This was in Dumfries, and the recruits were sent off the same night to Berwick-upon-Tweed. There we were asked what regiment we wanted to go into. Thinking of my feet, I said the artillery. The sergeant gave me a look.

'Artillery' – he laughed nastily – 'hi, youse blokes, here's a guy as wants to join the artillery!' Then, to me, he snapped: 'You have two choices, King's Own Scottish Borderers or the Royal Scots Fusiliers'.

I asked where the training camps were situated.

'KOSB, Catterick; RSF, Greenock'.

I chose the RSF simply because Glasgow was nearer to the people I knew. I was given a pass and set off for Ayr, the RSF recruiting base. One other recruit had chosen the RSF, and he advised me to take two days' French leave before I reported. I was afraid to, but when I got to the barracks in Ayr and found

93

that nobody expected me – the sergeant in fact was annoyed at my turning up on a Saturday night – I much regretted not having taken the man's advice. By this time, my heart was in my boots: I was a walking misery. The incivility and arrogance of the NCOs with whom I had come in contact, together with the prison appearance of the barracks, gave me a hate of the army that has never left me. I was given a mattress, told to fill it with straw, and then, with other recruits, had to do some fatigue – carrying beds. Next day I got my uniform, along with my first instruction from an absent-minded corporal whose interests were apparently elsewhere. In a few days we left by train for the training camp at Fort Matilda, between Greenock and Gourock. After vaccination and inoculation – a sickening business to me – our training began in earnest.

My chief associations with the RSF are two; feet and fear. My feet have always been tender, and even today, when I have my shoes specially made, my toes blister if I walk far on a hot day. For years I had worn only shoes, and after an hour's drill in army boots, my ankles were raw flesh. I reported sick again and again, and usually had some dressing put on, but the doctors never seemed to think rest was necessary. I had to go on parade again every time. One lance-corporal said to me: 'Hi you, big fellow, if you don't be careful you'll be up for swinging the lead (malingering). You've reported sick for three mornings and got MD each time.' MD meant Medicine on Duty.

I cannot recollect any fear of going to France. I knew that we were supposed to have a few months' training and then go out automatically in drafts, to replace casualties. Strangely enough, that didn't worry me; my fear was attached to the lance-corporal who made my life a hell for weeks. For some reason, he disliked me at sight, and after parades, when there was any fatigue to do, he always chose me, usually addressing me as 'youse big bastard'. He was a cab-driver in civilian life, they said.

One day, while giving out our letters, he stopped and peered at an envelope. 'Jesus Christ, who the hell's this?' he asked. 'A. S. Neill, Esq., MA, author of *A Dominie's Log*. What the hell . . . ?' I modestly held up my hand. His mouth opened. 'You an MA?' He gasped. 'My Christ!' The sequel was astonishing. He never gave me fatigue again, never bullied me. On the contrary, he treated me as if I were the colonel himself. Later, I was to find other NCOs who confessed to a great feeling of inferiority when I was in their squads: they were ashamed of their lack of grammar.

We slept twenty men and an NCO to an army hut. Many of the

94

men, who came mostly from Glasgow, were Glesga keelies, rough diamonds of the slums. They were fine, friendly lads, always kind to each other, usually cheerful. To them, the army food I found almost uneatable was the best food they had ever had; to them, army discipline seemed not much worse than the discipline of the factory. Their language was almost completely sexual, everything – food, parades, sergeants – described as 'fucking'. They discussed openly the most intimate details of the anatomies of their wives and sweethearts. They told very dirty stories, mostly without any point, and looked a little nervously at me while doing so. They knew I was a teacher and always addressed me as mister.

One night, when the stories were particularly lurid, every man had told one except myself.

'What about a story from you, Mester Neill?' said one.

I smiled.

'All right, boys. A sparrow was sitting on a treetop one morning. A horse went by and left some droppings. The sparrow flew down and made an excellent breakfast, and then it flew back to its tree-top and opened its throat and sang to its maker in joy. A hawk came along. It seized that sparrow in its talons and bore it off.'

'But here', said one, 'what's the point o' the story?'

'That', I said, 'is a story without a point. But it is a story with a moral, and the moral is: if you've eaten shit, don't make a song about it.'

Dead silence followed, and I realised that I had told the wrong story. They were taking it as censure, feeling themselves to be reproved by teacher. Hastily I told them a dirty story that out-classed anything they had told, and their loud laughter showed me that they accepted me as one of themselves.

Life in the army seemed like one continuous rush: we never had time to do anything properly, even shaving. Worst of all was the duty of mess orderly for the day. One waited in a queue for meals to be carried to the huts. Then one had to wash up after the meal and be spotless for the next parade, with rifle clean, buttons and boots shining. Behind all this rush was the dread of being late for parade; that was a crime. But one could be 'crimed' for many things – being unshaved, having dirty buttons, unpolished buckles, unwhitened braid. To be crimed was to be given pack drill with full equipment, doubling up and down the square till exhausted.

I managed to avoid being crimed except once. My rifle, a

95

modern one that I cared for as tenderly as a child, had been taken from me; and I was given an old-fashioned Lee Enfield instead. At rifle inspection, the officer crimed me for having a dirty rifle. I went to my sergeant and told him I had spent an hour trying to clean the thing, but the dirt was ingrained. He took me to see the sergeant in charge of musketry, who examined the rifle. 'Nobody can ever clean the thing', he pronounced. I don't know what went on behind the scenes, but my name was taken off the crime list.

This incident was exceptional. Generally, one had no redress, and it was this feeling of absolute powerlessness that kept me in the depths. Any corporal could crime you, and you dared not say a word. Theoretically you could, but we all knew that any complaint about a superior officer made you a marked man, and you would get it in the neck ever after. Old soldiers always pleaded guilty without defence, whether justly charged or not.

Hated duties could not be evaded. As a system, the discipline was mistake-proof. You had to be somewhere. If you went sick, your name appeared on the sick list; if you were doing fatigues, your squad sergeant had a note of it. The only man I knew who dodged the system effectively for six weeks was a youth who had been transferred from one squad to another. When he joined his new squad, he found that his name wasn't on the roll; they had forgotten to transfer it. He gave up going on parade. Every morning, he walked out of camp with belt and cane, a large envelope in his hand marked OHMS. When he was finally found out, nothing happened to him, because the NCOs who had left his name off the roll knew that they were 'for it' if they reported him.

My feet were giving me hell. Every night I soaked them in cold water, and every morning I soaped my socks, but the blisters came as before. I was limping during square drill when a major came along. He told me to fall out and asked what was wrong. I told him. He said I should report sick, and I told him it was useless, for they would only send me on parade again. He then ordered me to take off my boots and show him my feet. 'You go back to your hut and rest', he said. 'By the way, what are you in civil life?'

Two nights later, while I sat tending my feet in the hut as usual, the orderly sergeant came round.

'Neill here? Wanted at the Company bunk.'

I trembled. Wanted at Company headquarters generally meant being put on the mat. I thought of all my crimes – dodging church parade every Sunday, overstaying my leave – there were enough of them – and reported in trepidation. The major who had ordered me to rest sat writing at a table. I saluted and waited at attention. By this time, I was certain that because of my bad feet he would offer me a job clerking in the office. Finally he looked up.

'Know anything about mathematics?' he barked.

'Yes, sir, I wrote a book on mathematics.'

'Oh! You seem to be the very man we want.' He lifted a document. 'I have here a form from the War Office saying they need men of mathematical knowledge as officers in the artillery. I shall put your name forward.'

I was then transferred to the Cadet Corps. All sixteen of us had special drill. We were supposed to show the regiment how the best soldiers perform, and our training was modelled on that of the Guards. When slapping our rifle butts in presenting arms, we almost made our hands bleed. We had lectures in huts and out on the hill, and my feet got a chance to recover. My pet aversion was bayonet fighting. We were told to regard the sacks as Huns who had just raped our sisters, and were instructed to stab them with fitting fierceness. Unsuccessfully, I thought of ways and means to get out of a form of fighting that would be useless to me in the artillery. But fate again found a way. I had gone to visit Clunie and found that her landlord knew our gym sergeant-major; they had been pals in the Scots Greys. The landlord told me to give him his regards when I got back.

The sergeant-major looked forbidding, but I pulled myself together and went up to him. 'Well?' he demanded. When I gingerly gave him the message from his old pal, he thawed at once, insisting on taking me into his hut for a drink. When he asked what I was doing, I told him of the artillery commission in the offing. Next morning, while I was stabbing clumsily at a Hun sack, he came up. 'Here', he said, 'this is to be no good to you. Buzz off. You don't need to come to bayonet fighting or, for that matter, early-morning PT.'

I was delighted. Luck had rid me not only of the hated bayonet drill but of the almost hated gymnastics besides. There was another danger, however, when I stopped going on first parade. At any moment, an officer might buttonhole me and ask why I wasn't there. And I knew that on no account must I ever give away the kind gym sergeant-major. Also, if I were caught 'dodging parades', I might lose my chance for the commission. I solved the question by joining the signallers. Signalling would be useful to me as an artillery officer, I thought, but what appealed to me more was the fact that signallers had little footwork to do. I learned to like reading morse by telegraphy or light flashes, but never

97

became proficient enough to read the lamp messages that passed between vessels of the fleet in the Clyde every night.

By this time, I had become a good soldier – that is, I knew my way about, and knew how to get on with my immediate superiors. Bribery could be hazardous, but without it weekend leave wasn't always easy to get. It could be highly dangerous to offer money to a sergeant-major, yet there were ways and means. At one time, our sergeant-major was most sparing with weekend passes, and for three weekends in succession, he refused to give me one. So I sat down and wrote to Walter Martin, the cigar merchant in Piccadilly (his wife had admired my *Dominie's Log*, and Martin had sent me cigarettes at times): 'For God's sake, make me a present of a barrel of panatellas.'

The cigars came. I sauntered out and saw the sergeant-major tending his little garden. I lit a cigar, took up a position with my back to his garden fence, and waited as if expecting someone. I puffed hard, and with the tail of my eye, saw him sniff.

'Evening, sir', I said with deference.

'Evening. That cigar smells good', he said.

I took out the small case that went with the barrel. 'Try one, sir.'

He invited me into his hut for a drink, and we had a few whiskys. As I was going, I said, 'Look here, sir, I'm in a difficulty'.

'If I can help . . .' he began.

'It's like this, sir. A friend has sent me a box of cigars and really they are useless to me, for I don't like cigars (this was and is true). I thought of giving them to the lads in the hut, but . . .'

'Nonsense', he interrupted hastily, 'that would be waste.'

'I'll bring them round to you sir,' I said, and duly did so. Though weekend passes came easily after that, I felt rather mean and small; the other poor devils had no rich friends to help them.

Shortly afterward, however, I did a real Boy Scout deed. In the train compartment, while off to Glasgow on a weekend pass, I saw Pat, an Irishman graded C3, whose job was to clean out latrines. Sick of the army, he was running away.

'But, Pat,' I said, 'at Glasgow station the military police will look at all passes, and they'll pinch you for being without one'. He was cast down at this, but I cheered him up by saying I thought I had a plan. When we got out at the Central Station, I saw two redcaps approaching us. I gave them one scared look and legged it down the platform as hard as I could, ignoring their cries to stop. When they caught me at the barrier, I handed them my pass, trying to explain that my haste was to catch my train at Buchanan Street. I looked round and saw that Pat had got off safely. He must have returned to Ireland, for I never heard of his being captured.

One day, in company orders there arrived a command that 32703 Private Neill report to Trowbridge Cadet School, Wiltshire.

After Fort Matilda, Trowbridge seemed like heaven. Discipline was easy and polished buttons did not seem to matter much. The whole section, including the officer in charge, burst into laughter when I marched with the Guards' swing-of-arm, up to the shoulder; and I was ordered to cut out that swank stuff. Then the section laughed at my cleaning my boots before afternoon parade. Tut, tut, I thought, a pleasant place, but, oh, what soldiers!

For the first time in my army career, the work was interesting to me. We studied map-reading, maths, laying out lines of fire, and had gun drill with six-inch howitzers. We did much with an instrument called a No. 5 Director, and all of us used the prismatic compass. The other fellows were nearer my level than those of the RSF, many having been clerks and teachers, and we had some jolly times together.

Sometimes our study excursions would be made on army bicycles. For some queer reason, we were always about half a dozen cycles short, and six unfortunates had to go on foot, perhaps six miles. The lucky ones knew that the pedestrians would make sure of getting a cycle to ride home, so they took out their tyre valves and hid their saddles and pumps; one man took his front wheel off and carried it about all day. I was one of the outward walkers once, but sneaked off early to the cycle park and found, as I expected, an assortment of valveless, saddleless, handle-barless bikes. All I had to do was to collect several items from several bikes and make a finished article – easily done, because they were all standard makes and their parts interchangeable.

One of these excursions was utilised as our exam in map-reading. We all received a map and a small table, and were placed at different points. I stood alone in the middle of a large field. While bending over my map, I heard a sniff, and thinking it was the inspecting officer, I tried to look as busy as I should. On hearing a second, louder sniff, I looked round into the face of an enormous bull with a ring through his nose. Edging round the table, I wondered if a jab of the map on his horns would blind the animal long enough for me to leg it to the distant fence. I spoke to the bull in a friendly way, hoping to convince him that I knew I had no right to be there in his field. After a time, he quietly began to eat grass. Probably because of the bull incident, I missed the carping criticism the other fellows had taken from the inspecting officer that day.

I had one degrading experience at Trowbridge, involving a major who lectured on bracketing, a most complicated study of range distances in firing practice. He was not a good lecturer, and his voice must have put me on the verge of sleep. Suddenly I started, for he was looking at me and, in an angry voice, was ordering me to the blackboard to explain what bracketing was. I had not the faintest idea but of course could not say so, proving my complete ignorance by standing there like an ass with a bit of chalk in my hand. By this time he was livid and red.

'Why brainless idiots like you get to cadet schools is more than I can understand. I don't blame you – you can't help your stupidity; I blame the system that sends you up here. Have you had no education?'

I hung my head.

'Answer me. Where were you educated?'

'Edinburgh University,' I said humbly. A titter round the room was nipped off by the glare of the officer. He never spoke to me again.

Our term ended, we passed our exit exams, and in front of us was Lydd – the real thing, the nightmare lying ahead of a pleasant dream. Trowbridge had been like a university, easy and academic. But Lydd was officered by men just back from the front with no sympathy for the academic in anything. Our three weeks in Lydd were one continuous grind, and we discovered that anything we had learned at Trowbridge was of no value there. Laying out a line of fire no longer suggested a leisurely problem in maths; it was a thing to be done in ten seconds with a slide rule. The men at Lydd knew their jobs and put the wind up us all, for failure meant not only the disgrace of being returned to Trowbridge for a month or two, but also being put into a section of new men. No, that probability we dared not face, so we slaved.

The major at Lydd who taught the bracketing was a fearful man, and we had been warned about him long before we came up. When we were using real shells for the first time, he took us one by one to the observation post. There we all watched the burst of a shell, and had to know at once which directions to telephone to the gunner for his next shot. The major kept firing questions at us, and when we made mistakes – as we did, mainly through fear of him – he called us everything he knew.

We all passed, however, and were duly notified that we had received commissions in the Royal Regiment of Artillery. After

100

our ten days' leave to collect uniforms and kits, I was posted to an officers' 'pool' in Aldershot, saddened to find that most of my pals had been posted to Farnborough. Our pool consisted of about sixty officers waiting to be sent to France. The life was pleasant enough. I remember clearly the night I arrived and being saluted by the sergeant-major. How hard to believe that I would never again fear an NCO! I had a bitter feeling when I thought of our good food and comforts, and compared them with the food and lack of privacy I had as a non-com. Officers and privates lived poles apart in every way; the old distinction was still there – Eton at one end, the slums at the other. The officer planned; the private had no need to think, only to clean with spit and polish.

I had a batman, an independent sort of fellow from Lancashire. He was an active socialist, he said, and to hell with it anyway – what was a bloody officer but the servant of capitalism? So my orderly lay on my bed, smoking my cigarettes, while I polished my leggings and boots for the morrow. He kept assuring me that he bore me no personal grudge because I was an officer. He seemed a nice chap but a born pessimist, who swore that every league football match was faked – sold to the highest bidder – and offered to bring me written evidence if I liked.

Aldershot was a lazy life. We had lectures and sometimes slow exercises, but we all felt that these were just to keep us from getting too discontented. Every few days, a list of officers for the next draft would go up, but my name never appeared among them. Instead, I was told to attach myself to a training battery where my duties included lectures on lines of fire.

One day, I saw a gunner obviously paying no attention as I laboriously, and badly, tried to explain the mathematics of laying out a line of fire. To me, he seemed a stupid sort of a fellow.

'Here you', I said, 'you don't seem to be taking any interest in what I am teaching. What are you in civil life?'

'I am maths master at —— Secondary School,' he said.

Rising to the occasion, I held out my chalk. 'For the Lord's sake then, show them how this damn thing is done.'

And he showed them.

I kept hoping to be sent to France on a draft; not because I had miraculously acquired more courage, but simply because the other men were all out, or going out, and I felt left behind, like the lame boy in the Pied Piper story. Then an epidemic of influenza ran through the camp, and I went down with it. Mine was a bad attack, ending in neurasthenia. At Gretna Green, I had once been off work for a month with the same trouble, but this became worse – a complete nervous breakdown, with insomnia, and nightmares when I did fall asleep. In short, I was a dud as a soldier or anything else. The MO worried about me – probably suspected me of being a mental case – and said he would send me up to a nerve specialist in town when I was fit to travel.

The specialist turned out to be Dr William H. Rivers, the famous anthropologist. I did not know anything about him, nor did I know anything about psychology. I recall being mildly surprised when he asked me to tell him a dream, and being more and more surprised at his evident interest while I told it. It was a dream about a snake I had killed that kept coming to life again. I had never heard of Freud then, but apparently Rivers had. Finally he said to me: 'If you go to France you will either win the VC or be shot for running away. We won't risk it. I'll recommend that you give up your commission on grounds of ill health.'

So ended my inglorious career as a soldier. I must have cost the nation quite a lot of money, giving back little in duty or work. I realise now that my nervous breakdown was the method used by my unconscious to keep me from danger. On a conscious level, I seemed ready to go to the fighting front without any abnormal fear. In fact, I felt that as an officer it would be easier because I would be leading men and would have to show them how to face danger.

Years after the war, Walter Martin, my cigar-king friend, said something to me that was unbelievable.

'Neill, I saved your life.'

'How?'

'I had a pull at the War Office and arranged that you would not be sent to the front.'

I can scarcely believe this, but if it were so, it would explain why my name never appeared on the draft notices in the officers' pool. Walter died before I could ask him to tell me more, and I still doubt very much if any such influence could have exempted an individual soldier.

After a long convalescence, I began to think of a job. Back in the Gretna Green period, a lady who was much involved with King Alfred's School in Hampstead had written me, after having read my *Dominie's Log*, and when I went to see her she told me about Homer Lane, who founded the unique Little Commonwealth reform camp for juvenile delinquents. She gave me a report of one of his lectures. She also introduced me to John Russell, the headmaster of King Alfred's.

While at the cadet school, I learned that Lane's Little Commonwealth was in Dorset, not very far from Trowbridge. I wrote him asking if I could come to see him, and, when he said I could, got weekend leave. Homer Lane was easily the most impressive personality I had met up to then. He told of his cases as I listened, entranced. His young delinquents charmed me, and I got Lane to promise to let me work at Little Commonwealth when I had finished army service.

My first act, when I felt fit enough, was to write Lane, saying I could come. I got a reply telling me that the Commonwealth had been closed, and that Lane himself was in bad health in London. Disappointed, I thought I should try second-best. I wrote to John Russell about a job, got one, and joined the staff of KAS.

J.R., as we called Russell, was a dear old man, I liked him from the first moment I saw him, and he liked me. Since Russell's beginning as a pioneer thirty years before, KAS had been regarded as the most advanced school of its kind. While perhaps not the first to practise co-education, it did more to force the issue upon English opinion than any other school. Long before my time, it had done away with prizes and marks and corporal punishment.

I entered this famous school rather timidly with my very Scottish accent. My reputation as a mad Scots dominie had preceded me, and some of the pupils later told me that they had stared at me the first day, wondering if I were really mad or only a crank.

I liked the *Stimmung* of the school at once; its free and easy discipline took my heart. But I disliked the staffroom, and often have wondered why it was not a happier place than it was. It did not have the congenial atmosphere of the classrooms; and although the staff members were friendly as individuals, they were collectively – what I called them then – bloody. J.R. got me to ask Homer Lane to come and give the staff a few talks on psychology. Lane sat with a face like vinegar, and after the first talk, said to me; 'My God, Neill, what is wrong with that staff? It gives me the absolute jim-jams. It's full of hate.' In a way, I think that I may have been a fly in the ointment – the young whipper-snapper who had come to tell them how to run their school. Very properly, they put me in my place.

Fundamentally, the problem was J.R. himself. He was God, a lovable old God, but nevertheless God – and a moralist of great force. I first realised this when Patrick, aged eight, kissed Clare, aged seven. J.R. had a 'call over' about it and spoke for nearly an hour. I came away feeling that kissing must be the main sin against the Holy Ghost.

103

There was something dead about the pupils; they lacked an interest in life. This seemed most obvious at meetings of former Alfredians, when the 'old boys' sat at the feet of J.R. or George Earle, an English master who served as second-in-command, and listened as if their one-time teachers had all the wisdom in the world. Their attitudes towards the old school resembled a St Andrews student's toward his old alma mater – a regressive looking-back to Elysium. They were not quite of this world.

I learned with mixed feelings that some of the big lads in the school had never heard the word *shit*, and did not know the ordinary swear words, but that one or two of the girls knew them all. Dimly, I began to sense that I had come to a school whose life attitudes were fundamentally and essentially those which had damned my own life in Scotland – moral standards from without. KAS was far from being free, and very soon I found myself 'agin the government.'

I had begun to be analysed by Lane and became a frequent visitor to his home. What he said about freedom was the gospel I had been looking for; a scientific foundation for the vague yearnings shown forth in my *Dominie's Log*. Thus it came about that I began to try to 'improve' KAS in staff meetings. The school wasn't moving with the times, I complained. It should have self-government. Dear old J.R. spread his hands and said, with his usual smile: 'Go on, Neill. Try it. Try it.'

I tried it. The classes changed from one room to another at the ringing of the lessons bell. Thus the Betas would have maths the first period, say, and then come to me for geography when the bell rang. Naturally, all self-government meant to them was a chance to let off steam in my room for an hour. They made a hell of a row, and the teachers in neighbouring rooms got annoyed. At the next staff meeting, they all said it was obvious, of course, that self-government didn't work. It didn't, but it certainly 'played'. The day came when J.R. came to me very perplexed and very sad, and said: 'One of us has to resign, Neill.' Once more I was unemployed.

HELLERAU AND
THE FOUNDING OF
SUMMERHILL

It was while I was at KAS that Clunie died. A wire sent me north to find her ill with pneumonia. For years she had had some obscure disease of the throat, and for years she had been treated by x-rays. I think I knew that she would not recover. I sat for hours by her bedside, trying to appear hopeful and cheerful. God, it was a week of a kind of hell that I had never known then and have not known since. I did not dream: I woke up each morning feeling that I had been in the deepest pit in Dante's Inferno and that I had been there for a thousand years. Most men know what it is to have someone who will always understand, someone you naturally turn to in joy or sorrow. To me Clunie was that one: I knew exactly what her reactions would be to anything I said, knew what would make her laugh, what would pain her. I knew also that she was always on my side: I was her hero, and I could do no wrong. The Peter Pan in me loved Clunie because she appreciated me. When something amusing happened my first thought had always been: 'I must tell Clunie this: how she'll laugh!' At her funeral some small thing happened – I forget what, maybe only a top hat falling off some dignified mourner – and my first thought was: 'Clunie will laugh at this when I tell her.'

My grief was made more harrowing by remorse – the remorse that is always a component of grief. If only I had done more for her.

*

That is the most painful cry in every grief. I remembered the times when I had neglected her. She had wanted me to come home for the previous Easter holiday but I went to Dorset. That seemed to me, in my despair, unforgivable. I kept remembering what I did not want to remember. My mother, on the other hand, kept forgetting what she did not want to remember: as her wet eyes followed the coffin to the hearse she said: 'She was the perfect daughter: I never had to lift my hand to her in all her life.' It struck me then that that was one of the things I should have liked to tell Clunie, for my mother had given her many a spanking. Clunie had often laughed at my mother's ability to deceive herself: she had the extrovert's trick of forgetting what was unpleasant, and although my father was an introvert he had a similar ability to put things behind him. Clunie and I at one time called them the ostriches.

Nearly all children go through a stage when they become very critical of their parents. This happens when the psychological urge to break free from the apron strings becomes strong. I went through this stage from the age of about eighteen to twenty-four. At one time I was ashamed of them. I was ashamed because my father had no 'manners': if we had a guest to dinner Clunie and I implored my mother not to have soup because of Father's method of supping it loudly. I was ashamed of Mother because she talked too much, and too often talked irrelevantly. She was really a very bad listener, and was always trying to edge her word in even when the conversation dealt with things she knew nothing about. I recall one occasion when I was furious. A visitor was telling us about his adventures in China, and she kept interrupting him with silly remarks about her brother Sandy once having known a man who was in China. I was an impatient, arrogant person then. My father had the patience of Job. He read his *Scotsman* every morning. My mother always took up the paper about bedtime. 'Listen to this, George', she would say and she would read out a whole column of news that he had already read. Not once did he dare to say: 'I've read it, Mary'.

My rather hateful critical attitude to my parents seemed to disappear after Clunie's death. It was only then that I began to have tender feelings towards my father. I was no longer the Cinderella of the family. My father had by this time accepted me as someone who had made good, a son to be proud of, but he still tried to look out for good jobs for me. An old friend of my mother came on a visit from Australia where he had been successful. My father spoke to him about prospects out there for me, and he said that he was a bosom friend of the Prime Minister and would get me a job as inspector of schools if I said the word. I didn't say the word, and have sometimes wondered what would have become of me if I had gone out to Australia.

When I had to leave KAS I was genuinely anxious. I saw no future for myself. True, I might get a job as English teacher in a Scots school, but London had gripped me, and I didn't want to leave it. Mrs Beatrice Ensor stepped in and offered me the job of jointly editing *The New Era* with her. I took up my duties in Tavistock Square, sharing a room with her husband, a non-smoker, who hated my smoking all day at work. The Ensors were theosophists.

It was good fun having a paper to edit. Mrs Ensor gave me a free hand to say anything I liked, and I soon saw that the more outrageously I attacked pedants and schools the more delighted she was. Some people found her rather a forbidding person, but I liked her and ragged her most of the time. She was about the only theosophist I ever met who could laugh at theosophy and herself. One or two books about me have said that Beatrice and I were at loggerheads over education, but I have no memory of rows between us. All I can recollect is my ragging her about her theosophical higher life complex. She was a born organiser, and it was through her that I went to Holland to meet the Austrian children who came to England after the war.

It was my first trip abroad, and my ten days in Holland were full of interest to me. Everything was a thrill, and today I would give all I possess to recover that feeling of adventure that accompanies the first trip abroad. Later I went abroad reluctantly, hating the waits at customs offices, the examination of passports, the tiresomeness of hotels and porters, worst of all the long train journeys. An experience is always a death: it can never live again. I drive a car automatically but when I was learning every mile was a delightful mastering of a difficulty. When I come to think of it, although it may sound platitudinous, surmounting difficulties is the dearest part of life.

The New Era was no abiding city: I knew that I must move on. Luck brought me an invitation to take part in a New Educational Fellowship Conference in Calais, and another to go on from there to Salzburg to lecture to an international conference of women.

Salzburg bowled me over. Its beauty and warmth made me want to stay there until the day I died. I still have vague longings to go there again, but I know now that I never shall.

107

From Salzburg, I went on to Hellerau, a suburb of Dresden, to stay with Dr Otto Neustätter and Frau Doktor who later became my first wife. Her sister Henry Handel Richardson was the brilliant Australian novelist who wrote *Maurice Guest* and *The Fortunes of Richard Mahoney*. Together with Karl Baer, an architect, and his American wife Christine we founded the Internationalschule, Hellerau. Otto was the dear old man in my *A Dominie Abroad*.

Living in Germany gave me much that living at home could not give me. For one thing I lived for nearly three years in an atmosphere of rhythm and dance, of great opera and orchestral music. The only thing that taught me nothing new was the German educational system. To me it was barren and bare: it was pedantry masquerading as progress. The simile comes to my mind of the Meistersingers with their rules and foot measures, hating and fearing the new young Walther with his *Preislied* of freedom. The Germans did not really want freedom: they were afraid of it and their more honest and enlightened teachers confessed that they were.

My stay in Hellerau was the most exciting period of my life. For the first time I mixed with European nationals. I knew not a word of German. When I took out my first English pupil, Derrick, aged eight, I was trying to learn German from *Hugo's Tutor*. In three weeks Derrick was not only talking German; he was speaking Saxon dialect. (I notice that today my German pupils are talking English in a few weeks and if I speak to one in German he or she replies in English.)

Our International School had three divisions – Eurythmics, my *Ausländer* (foreign) division, and the German school, which was part day and part boarding. I have told in earlier books of my quarrels with the German teachers over education. They were benevolent moulders of character while I was the opposite. My period in Hellerau gave me a *Weltanschauung* – a world view – and in a way it killed any tendency I had towards nationalism. And it humbled me. Here was I with my Hons English Degree, having to sit silent when the talk was of art and music and philosophy. I felt uneducated and, indeed, would feel the same today, for my ignorance of many subjects is abysmal; meaning that a specialised university education is no education at all.

How blind I was; how blind we all were. We did not see that the terrible poverty of Germany would lead to a Hitler. I expect that the Valuta made me smug, for I was a millionaire; I travelled first-class from Munich to Vienna for half-a-crown and had a stock of benedictine, curacao, brandy etc., no bottle costing me more than eightpence. I changed ten pounds into marks in Dresden, got a wire asking me to go to Vienna, took my marks with me and ten days later they were not enough to pay my train fare out to Hellerau.

I gave psychological talks to the Eurythmics girls. One day one of them, a Russian, came into my office. She threw her arms around me and said 'Herr Neill, ich liebe Sie'. I did not know her name and it was a bit of a shock to get a declaration of love from one I did not know personally. My shock became alarm when she went on: 'I wrote and told my husband and he is coming to shoot you.' Two mornings later, as I walked over to the school, I saw her approaching with a man who looked six feet four. She introduced us and he shook my hand warmly if painfully. The poor lassie had got a transference to me and had built a fantasy around me.

It is odd that in thinking back to these days I dwell on what is trivial, meaningless – *unbedeutend* is the excellent German word for it. Another incident involving fear comes to mind. The French had put black soldiers in the Ruhr and the Germans were furious. In the tram one day four tough-looking youths came in. I saw them eyeing me, and heard one say the word Frenchman. They came towards me and I hastily got out my passport. 'Ach, an Englishman?' 'Nay', I said, 'a Scot'. They insisted that I got out at the next stop to have a drink with them, and I discovered that they were full of pity for me, because they thought that Scotland was a slave state held down by the English.

I was never a brave man and my account of my Calvinist boyhood suggests why I had no courage. I have already told that my father and his father were afraid of the dark. I also feared the dark but went one better than my father . . . I always faced it. I can recall only one occasion in my life when I showed some bravery. Around 1936 I had to wait two hours for a train in Hanover. It was a lovely Sunday morning and I took a walk through the town. Suddenly I heard the sound of a band and a troop of SS men came marching down the street. Everyone stood still on the pavement and gave the Heil Hitler salute. I could not bring myself to raise my hand. Two troopers came toward me and I trembled, for not long previously my friend Geoffrey Cox, now Sir Geoffrey, had had a similar experience in Berlin and his passport did not save him from a beating up. Hastily I showed my passport and they hesitated and passed on. I sought the safety of the Hauptbahnhof waiting room.

109

I was not allowed by the Ministry to teach Germans and my division consisted of English, Norwegians, Belgians and Yugoslavs. I wasn't even allowed to teach English to the German division because I had not taken my degree in a German university. I had to appoint a German woman whose pronunciation was terrible. She kept arguing with me about accent, and when an Irish visitor came with a brogue you could cut with a knife, she cried: 'Wunderbar; das is the proper Oxford accent.'

Our staff of teachers were a mixed lot. Some were Communists and demanded that the school be ruled communally. I bought a bicycle for about a million marks, fifteen shillings in English money. It was never there when I wanted it: 'It should be common to the whole staff'. How earnest the Germans were. I made a gift of a cinema projector to the whole school, and a programme committee was elected to choose the films. When I gave priority to Charlie Chaplin they were shocked . . . 'That is not education.' So we had the children sit and watch boring films about travel and shell-fish. If a film did not have a pedagogic message it was considered useless. The leader of the German department began his speech to parents with the words: 'Here we work'. He was annoyed when I asked him why his opening words were not: 'Here we play'. He and I shared the hostel, the *Schulheim*. I had the upper storey and he the lower one. Of an evening my lot would dance to gram records while below he was reading aloud Goethe or Nietzsche. One by one his pupils would sneak up the back stairs to join in the dance. There was bad feeling about that.

Many of our pupils were Jews and I am sure that they all ended in Belsen or Auschwitz. Even in 1921 Dresden shops had notices saying that no Jews would be served. I played a futile trick on one of these shops, a bookseller's. I asked to see editions of Ibsen, Strindberg, Nietzsche, and the counter was soon covered with beautiful volumes. The staff fussed around the rich *Englander*. I said there was a book in the window I wanted to see. I went out and then said: 'I see you don't serve Jews.'

'But, mein Herr, you aren't a Jew.'

'No,' I said, 'I am no Jew but in my country we do not bar Jews from shops.'

I had had no intention of buying anything. Later I saw that I was most likely only adding anglophobia to anti-Semitism.

One of the pleasures of those days was the presence of Edwin and Willa Muir. Willa was on our teaching staff and Edwin wrote his poems and prose. I cannot go into all the arguments and difficulties we had, our fights with the authorities, our internal differences about policy. I came across the German prolixity. We printed a syllabus and they asked me to translate it into English so that we could get English and American pupils. It was about ten pages long. My translation ran to a page. They were annoyed.

'But,' I said, 'that's all you have said,' and it sure was. Brevity is not a feature of German writing.

We had taken a lease on the school building. At that time Gurdjieff was looking for a house for his school of thought. He fell in love with our *Anstalt* and persuaded the owner, Harold Dohrn, to hand it over to him. We said we would fight the case in court and Dohrn suddenly changed over to our side. I heard afterwards that Gurdjieff made a case of it and Dohrn said in court that he had hypnotised him. Gurdjieff lost the case and later, with Ouspensky, set up in Fontainebleau. I could not read Gurdjieff after that incident. I never got over his saying: 'They don't matter; my work is of infinitely more importance.'

He and all my Hellerau associates are long dead. Christine Baer died of cancer. Karl Baer was shot by the Russians in Vienna when he was trying to protect his housekeeper from being raped. Harold Dohrn, a Russian, was also shot by the Russians. I should say here that in this book I shall seldom mention the living. Suppose one of my brothers had been a prison lag, or one of my sisters a prostitute. I could not tell of them in a book for their children, who most probably would still be alive.

In 1923 revolution broke out in Saxony. Shots were fired on the Dresden streets. Our school was emptying. The dance division went to Schloss Laxenburg near Vienna and I took my division to the top of a mountain at the edge of the Tyrol, four hours' train time from Vienna. It was an old monastery and beside it was a church of pilgrimage, Wallfahrtskirche. The story was that a pilgrimage docked four hundred years off purgatory.

The church had stone saints all around and when the pilgrims came from all over Catholic Europe our English pupils used to give the saints haloes by shining broken mirrors at them. There was much crossing of themselves by visitors and, when the children's trick was discovered, I wondered why we were not lynched, for the peasants were the most hateful people I ever came across. Few had ever seen a foreigner and the fact that we were heathens was enough to kindle their hatred of us. A German girl of nine sunbathed in a bathing costume, and we had a policeman up next day saying the village was shocked and angry.

Farmers and their wives threw broken bottles into the pond we

111

bathed in. The climax came when I was summoned to the Education Ministry in Vienna.

'Herr Neill, do you teach religion?'

'No.'

The official took down a hefty volume and read out a law: every Austrian school must teach religion. I explained that I had no Austrian children, but that was no excuse; the law must be obeyed. So in late 1924 I took my little group to England.

But we had fun too in Sonntagberg. When we arrived the snow was deep and we had to buy skis (we pronounced the word the Norwegian and German way – 'shees'). Our postman used to take nearly an hour to climb the mountain but he took about ten minutes to return. None of us reached that stage of proficiency. We danced a lot, foxtrots, tangoes, and I loved dancing. Today I cannot dance, not because of age – I could still dance a tango – but because the new rhythm is too quick for me, and the skill seems to me to have fled, for I can see none in wagging knees and bottoms.

I had a sentimental attachment to anything Austrian. The first German book I ever read was *Das Tagebuch eines halbwüchigen Mädchens*, which was translated later into English as *A Young Girl's Diary*. It was the diary of a middle-class girl from the age of eleven to fourteen, and, written in child's language, it was easy for me to read. Indeed I learned many Viennese words that even Germans do not know. Freud wrote a short preface to this book, calling it a jewel. In a way it explains much of Freudian theory about sex; he cannot have escaped being influenced by the ignorant sex repression of the late nineties. In fact he could have founded his sexual philosophy on the book. It is a wonderful story of a girl's sex repressions and sex ignorance. Cyril Burt thought it was a fake story composed by an adult but I am convinced that he was wrong; no adult could have pictured the misery alternating with joy of a young girl.

It also gave me a glamorous, really romantic view of Viennese society with its afterglow from the days of the Strauss waltzes, the *Rosenkavalier*, and the gaiety of the city with its *Gemütlichkeit*, its *Schlag Sahne* (coffee with whipped cream) and its *Wiener Schnitzels*. My love for Austria gave me a fantasy I held for years, that when I retired I would settle down in Salzburg in spite of its heavy rainfall.

In late 1924 I rented a house in Lyme Regis, Dorset. It was called Summerhill and stood on the hill going to Charmouth. Lyme was and is a place mostly for retired people, a class-conscious little town. We were outsiders; our dirty little youngsters were looked at down upper-class noses. Till one day a Rolls Royce with a crest on it drove up. The Earl of Sandwich, one of the founders of the Little Commonwealth, had come to visit us for a few days. Then people bowed to us. It reminds me of Bertrand Russell's story in his autobiography. During an anti-war protest he was being roughly handled by a policeman. A woman cried: 'That is Bertrand Russell, the writer and philosopher'. The cop paid no attention and went on hustling Russell. 'He is the brother of an earl', cried the woman. 'What?' The hustling ceased. Good old English snobbery.

We had only five pupils, three paying half fees, two paying nothing. My first wife and I (by this time I had married Frau Doktor Neustätter) would stand looking at an ironmonger's window wondering if we could afford a spade. Because Lyme was a holiday resort we turned the school into a boarding house in the vacations and managed to make ends meet. Then, as now, we got too many problem children, misfits that other schools did not want. Fifty years later we get the same trouble. An American father will write: 'My boy is a normal kid but he hates lessons'. He arrives, his face is full of hate; he bullies, steals, destroys. Obviously the father knew he was dumping his failure on to us. In fact the school's whole life has been handicapped by too big a proportion of problem kids. None of our academic successes, our professors, doctors, lawyers, scientists came as problem children.

Bertrand Russell was thinking of setting up his own school with his wife Dora. He came and spent a week with us and we all liked his wit and humour. One starry night he and I went for a walk. 'Russell', I said, 'the difference between us is this; if we had a boy with us now you would want to tell him about the stars while I would leave him to his own thoughts.' He laughed when I added: 'I maybe say that because I know damn all about the stars anyway.'

I was not happy in Lyme. The air was so relaxing that walking up the hilly streets was an effort. When we moved to Suffolk the kids' appetite doubled. Our staff was small: George Corkhill taught science, 'Jonesie' who had joined us in Austria taught maths, and my wife was matron. It was a stirring time, and because they were so interesting the problem children gave us more joy than sorrow. One girl, who later became the golf champion of half a dozen countries, had been accustomed to making her parents and teachers angry at her defiance. She decided to take me on. She kicked me for an hour but, in spite of

113

the pain, I refused to react. Finally, she burst into tears, and I expect learned the hard way that her attempts to take the micky out of adults did not always succeed.

At that stage I was a proper fool. I thought that psychology could cure everything barring a broken leg, and I took on children injured at birth, sleepy sickness cases, mentally deficient boys and girls. Of course I soon found that I could do nothing to cure them.

When the three-year lease was up we had twenty-seven pupils and could not house them. I bought an old Morris car and set off along the south coast to find a house. I saw some beauties at £50,000 each. Then I went up the east coast and the last house on my list was Newhaven in the small town of Leiston, Suffolk. It was only £3,250, a sum I had not got, but I bought it on a mortgage. I brought the name Summerhill with me and in forty-five years not one visitor has asked me why the name when the place is dead flat.

When World War Two broke out we stayed on in Summerhill during the first phoney war period, but after Dunkirk, when we expected invasion, we had to move. We found a big house in Festiniog in North Wales; it was dilapidated and local boys had smashed all the lavatories and most of the windows. We were there for five years, the longest years of my life. It rained and rained. I had to give up my car and queue for buses. All around us were Welsh-speaking people; some of the aged knew no English. I had returned to the atmosphere of my native Scottish village. Chapels and hymns were everywhere, with their accompanying hypocrisy. One shopkeeper said to me: 'I don't believe in any God but if I didn't go to the bloody chapel every Sunday I wouldn't get any custom.' The villagers were shocked by our pagan behaviour, but one by one they began to sneak into our Sunday night dances. Shortly after we arrived there one of our bright boys was accidentally drowned, and later my wife had a stroke – her speech went and her mind became confused. She died in a hospital in 1944. No wonder Festiniog was a misery to me.

We lived in gorgeous scenery, just as we had done in our Austrian mountain, but after a week I never saw it. I have never been observant: I was in the same lodgings for four years as a student, and when at the end of my student days my mother asked me the colour of my bedroom walls I had not the faintest idea. So with people; I never know what they are wearing, a handicap sometimes, as when I praised my mother's new hat: 'I have worn it for four years', she said indignantly.

114

Wales was hell for me, and I have few memories of our time there. I cannot even recall the rooms in the house or the names of most of the staff there; corroborating, I suppose, the Freudian theory that we forget what we want to forget.

In vacations the children had a long weary train journey to London from Wales. We were lucky; not once did our pupils get blitzed. But the school was not really Summerhill. Parents sent their children, not to be free, but to be safe, and when peace came those parents withdrew their kids. We were overcrowded. Food was rationed and tobacco was difficult to buy. The pubs closed at 9 p.m. as against 10.30 p.m. in England. Our boys had a perpetual war with the village boys, who were most aggressive, in spite of, or perhaps because of all the chapel-going.

I had also returned to the joys of the Scottish Sabbath. One dared not dig the garden on a Sunday. Once, after a spell of rain that had flattened the corn, we had a bright windy Sunday, but not a farmer would reap on that day.

But Wales had its advantages. I discovered a deep resentment against England and its war laws. The school was registered with a coal merchant for fuel, which was stiffly rationed. Another coal merchant came to me and asked if I needed coal. I said I did but could not deal with him because I was registered with Jones Brothers.

He laughed. 'That's okay', he said, 'how many tons do you want?'

'But,' I said, 'what about the law?'

'Bugger the law', he said. 'In any case I have just supplied two tons of coke to the leading magistrate and he also is registered with Jones Brothers.'

After that we never ran out of coal or coke.

We heard Welsh spoken for five years and never learned even a phrase. I must have spent, in all, a year in Norway and never learned to speak a word of Norwegian. In both cases there was no motive to learn; the residence was temporary.

115

Part Two

ON AUTOBIOGRAPHY,
FAME AND
SELF-ANALYSIS

        I wrote my autobiography in Norway in 1939. My then publishers did not think it would sell so I dumped the MS in a drawer and forgot about it until my good friend and translator Shimoda asked if he could translate it into Japanese. He did. I see the volume on my shelves, but, so far as I know, it could be *Lady Chatterley's Lover*. It was only when my American publisher suggested my writing my life that I remembered the hidden pages. Difficulties arose. Could I go back to the stage in my life I had left behind in 1939? There was a real problem here; I found that I wasn't really interested in myself and my life, found it a bore to look back. This may have been caused partly by my years of being analysed, when I spent many hours talking about myself and my problems, meaning that I had got fed up with myself as a private person as opposed to myself as a worker and writer. So the remainder of my book is not a chronological account of my later life so much as a series of reflections on my life and beliefs, written at intervals over the past few years.

        Every autobiography is, if not a lie, an evader of the truth. Indeed I wonder what value an autobiography has. To know that J. M. Barrie and Ruskin and Carlyle were impotent, to know that Freud, when catching a train, had to be in the station an hour beforehand (Erich Fromm), to know that Reich was over-jealous or that Wilde was homosexual: I cannot see how such knowledge affects our judgement of their work. Luckily we know almost nothing of Shakespeare. Wagner was a nasty man, anti-Semitic, mean to his friends, mean about money – but knowing this does not take away from the delight I have when listening to *Die Meistersinger* or *Tristan und Isolde*.

The only good a life can do is to explain or try to explain what made a man take the road that he did, and I really cannot see how much that helps. Take Ernest Jones' theory of Hamlet and his Oedipus Complex, his unconscious wish to kill his father and marry his mother. His wicked uncle had done that in reality. Hamlet's indecision was thus due to his ambivalence . . . Uncle has done what unconsciously I wanted to do myself, so how can I condemn him? Suppose Shakespeare had written his own life and told how, in his early youth, his stern father had terrified him and his mother. Would the knowledge make a scrap of difference to our enjoyment of the play? Ibsen, like myself, was a physical coward but when one sees *An Enemy of the People* one does not long for a big he-man when the morally brave doctor challenges the whole iniquity of the town Establishment. A man's writing is not himself. Dickens was not David Copperfield nor Mr Pickwick.

Not my life, but only what I have done seems to me cogent, and what have I done anyway? The great ones, the Freuds, the Einsteins, made new discoveries: I discovered nothing. The new dynamic psychology showed that the emotions are the driving force in life, not the intellect, so I founded a school in which the emotions would come first. For years I have wondered why a million teachers did not grasp the simple truth and leave kids to grow up in their own way and at their own speed. Maybe they could not because they had to bring their own personalities into their work.

If I have any special talent it is that of staying in the background. Often I sit through our school parliament assembly without saying a word. Without boasting I think that here I go one better than Homer Lane, whose strong personality coloured the Little Commonwealth. I was never a strong man and I don't like strong men who sway crowds or families or classrooms. When I watch boxing on TV I am always on the side of the smaller man – though I confess that this does not apply to Muhammad Ali whose style is almost poetic. I know that many deprecate boxing as a cruel sport. I loathe sports like bull-fighting where the poor animal has no choice, but if two men want to bash each other up in the ring I am all for it, maybe because I lodged with a fellow student who was a champion and I had to be his sparring partner. (Of psychological interest is the fact that when he went out boxing I had to go with him and bring him home because he was scared to walk the London streets at night. For all I know Muhammad Ali may be afraid of mice. In a TV interview he confessed to a dread of flying.)

I ask myself: what sort of a guy am I? Folks call me amiable and it may be so, for I am pretty equitable and placid, never flying off the handle as Reich used to do. I am not suggesting that I am a Pharisee, thanking God that I am not as other men, yet in some ways don't we all at times? To say that Smith is a dull bore means that I am a much better, wiser chap than he is. Every criticism is Pharisaical.

I have no idea how I look. I can't recall looking into a mirror since I took to an electric razor some years ago. It takes a long time to realise that no one cares a damn how one looks. The lovelorn swain of twenty really thinks that the desired one will be impressed by his having socks and tie that match in colour, just as the simple fellow believes that if a girl is beautiful she has a beautiful character. I have often wondered why beauty in a girl's face is so important, why graceful carriage or lovely figure take second place. Most questions in life are never answered. H. G. Wells said something like this: 'One is just beginning to understand a little about life when Nurse Death comes along and says: Come on, little boy, put away your toys; it is time to go to bed.' At 89 I understand what he meant.

I have had fame, or maybe I should call it publicity, with two thousand visitors to Summerhill each year. My large fanmail is pleasing even if it means hours answering folks I do not know. There is some satisfaction in appearing on TV, also a lot of irritation, for the popular speakers on TV seem to me to have nothing to say, while I like to think that I have a hell of a lot to say. It has always been so; millions who know of Bob Hope never heard of Freud or Milton or Summerhill.

In a way fame has had a negative reaction in my case. I never expect to be recognised on a street, and would be surprised and no doubt pleased if a stranger asked me if I were A. S. Neill. And it is not false modesty. It may be the result of my youthful experience of being the dunce of the family: 'Mary, that boy will come to nothing', said more than once by my father. Perhaps I 'came to something' as a compensation for my inferiority then.

Along with this humility goes the opposite. When one is old praise is sweet to be sure but blame has no special emotional impact. A recent rather nasty article in a Sunday paper about the Summerhill fiftieth anniversary party in London did not make me

angry or even concerned. Perhaps because I have not been accustomed to enmity. I know of no one who is my enemy, though there must be a few thousand parents in the USA, Germany, Brazil etc. who hate my guts. I hear of some from their children . . . 'When I quote your *Summerhill* to my parents they go haywire. Daddy has forbidden me to read it.' It may be just as well that I am too old to go back to the USA, lecturing in that Christian land, where anyone can carry a gun, or, to be topical, should I say a Betsy or a John Roscoe?

I am often spoken of as the man who loves children. Love is hardly the word to use when a problem boy is breaking my school windows. One cannot love masses, only individuals, and all individuals are not lovable. No, I reject the word love; I prefer Homer Lane's being on the side of the child which means approval, sympathy, kindness plus a complete absence of adult authority. It is of more value to understand children than to love them; indeed, if in every school the teachers were Charlie and Maggie I guess that many discipline difficulties would disappear.

I read recently that a coward is always an introvert, that is a solitary person. The hero is brave because is he one of a crowd feeling unconsciously that its strength and courage is behind him – the regiment, the Party. An interesting theory. It may be that while the brave extrovert is courageous physically, the introvert is brave morally. But then who is wholly introverted or extroverted? We are all a combination of both make-ups, but I fancy that most people lean towards the extrovert side. They are the ones who are influenced by public opinion, by speeches, by TV advertisements. Myself, if I go into a drug store to buy a shaving stick and see a row of well-known brands plus one labelled John Jones, I buy that one. Maybe Ibsen exaggerated when he said that the majority is always wrong, but the introvert is convinced that he is always right. If taking sides is a question of emotion, why do I not, as a Scot, automatically want a Scot to win when boxing an Englishman? Possibly a true Freudian would make it all simple. The extrovert is he who accepted father and followed his ways, while the introvert rebelled against father, and there must be much truth in this. I rejected my father because in my childhood he rejected me, made me frightened, inferior, obedient. But why my brothers did not react as I did I cannot guess, for one of them was more scared of Father than I was, and he did not challenge anything later. My sisters never challenged; they accepted the mores and talk of the home and only Clunie was a rebel.

But yet, doubts again. Clunie and I had the same anti-life Calvinistic environment. I became an atheist later in life than she did and I doubt very much that on my death-bed I'll mutter the prayers of long ago. It is so difficult to know whether a belief has both intellect and emotion behind it. Is the rabid radical marching with his red flag because he loves the poor, or because he hates the rich? Alas, to look for motives is as useless as to look for a life plan.

I have a strong belief in justice, and children when free have this belief. I have never shown favouritism in my school, not that I didn't like some kids better than others, but I hope I never betrayed any preference. Once I heard some kids discuss the staff and their favourites. One girl said: 'Who are Neill's favourites?' Two names were given – the two pupils I liked least. I should have been an actor.

Fame is a mirage. A few millions, mostly in the USA and Germany, have read one or two of my books. Many schools in the USA have been inspired by Summerhill, yet I know that after a few obituary notices I shall be forgotten just as Bertrand Russell was forgotten a few months after his death.

I recall a day when I was a student, looking at *Who's Who* with a fellow student. 'Wouldn't it be marvellous to get your name into *Who's Who*', I said. My name has been in it for a long time but if it were taken out in the next edition I would not care a jot. So with a university degree. How wonderful to get a degree! But when it comes the glory has departed in the long bookish struggle to attain it.

And yet there is sadness in the knowledge that Keats did not live to realise his fame, which he said was writ in water. George Douglas Brown died just after his great novel *The House with the Green Shutters* was published and never knew that he had written a masterpiece. Maybe it is better to die.

The word fame like the word genius can mean anything. Wagner is famous, but in the popular mind so is Elvis Presley. Posterity decides. Only a little man will have the nerve to think of himself as a famous man. I feel sure that neither Freud nor Einstein felt that they were famous. A man's dream life should show him how small he is. In the daydream we are in control and we dream of success, courage, conquest; but the night dream is beyond control. I doubt if Freud was right in claiming that every dream expresses a wish, however complicated the symbolism. Having had hundreds of my dreams analysed in therapy, having analysed hundreds of children's dreams, I cannot believe that all are wish fulfilments. In any case, I give the opinion that I don't think the analysis of any of my dreams helped me one bit.

I mention dreams because they get behind the image a man has made for himself, behind what Reich called his armour. Big men can be little men in their dreams. I knew a high churchman who often dreamt that he stood in his pulpit naked. I have dreamt that I was shitting in a pot in a crowded ballroom . . . an odd kind of wishful thinking. In our dreams we all do daft things, infantile things, idiotic things, but not, in my own experience, cruel things, backing up the belief in original virtue. So I am not trying to say that a man is a combination of Dr Jekyll and Mr Hyde; nay, he is a combination of an adult and a baby. The irrationality of the dream is that of a baby; its pictorialism is that of the nursery and the children's books. A professor can dream of flying elephants. Maybe the motive of the dream is to prick the conceit bubble, to show one that one is emotional, primitive, undeveloped.

My own dreams I cannot analyse. They have no connection with people I know. I never dream of my family, my school, my early life. I did when younger. For years after the death of my dear sister Clunie and after Homer Lane's death I dreamt of them again and again. They were unpleasant dreams; the sun did not shine in them. Vaguely I knew they were dead and the contact with them was not a happy one. Twice since Reich died I have talked with him in dreams, again with no happiness. In these cases the wish fulfilment was not disguised by symbolism.

Dreams of course depend on the glands. Octogenarians do not have sex dreams or prowess dreams – they don't run races, don't drive fast cars. My anxiety dreams have gone with the years. I used to dream of standing before a large audience unable to say a word. I had distressing travel dreams. The train was moving out of the platform but my feet would not take me up the stairs. For many years I dreamt about travelling to my childhood home in Scotland. My parents were expecting me on a certain day by a certain train. I never got there. Everything seemed to stand in my way . . . the taxi was late or the train was late or I couldn't go because of a forgotten lecture date. It was all misery and frustration. I must have had a very bad conscience about my parents, although consciously I did not neglect them. I wrote them regularly every week, with difficulty to be sure, for their interests and mine were different. They were weather letters. In my time the gulf between parents and children was a very wide one; contact about real and deep matters was impossible.

Here I am gropingly trying to say that I am a split personality.

I am the pioneer educationist and I am a child still bound emotionally to my parents, to my environment. I made images and never could destroy them. In my dreams, Newport, Fife, for instance, where I taught for the first time in a school with easy discipline and where I fell in love with Margaret, became a heaven to which I kept returning. Possibly my situation is that of millions, a conscious busy life in the daytime and a regression at night to a past life romanticised in fantasy. Many men and women have long-lost loves that have lived on unconsciously, and it is likely that many a marriage has been wrecked by this romantic fixation on the past.

So when one writes about one's life what side of one's personality is being described? Usually the conscious one, too often the name-dropping snob one often sees in the lives of actors and showmen – 'Dined with the Duchess of Theberton last night'. And we cannot sniff and be superior about this kind of snobbery. I have written about 'my old friend Bertrand Russell' but apart from his spending a week in Summerhill nearly fifty years ago I saw him only once again, although we corresponded.

Self-analysis is impossible. You cannot psychoanalyse yourself because you cannot face the factors that would offend your own opinion of your ego. He would be a brave man who declared that behind his outer image of a stalwart citizen lay a mean character, envious, narrow-minded, cruel.

HOMER LANE AND
WILHELM REICH

Homer Lane was an American, but his work is much more widely known in England than in America. After working in the George Junior Republic he was invited by a few well-known social reformers – the Earl of Sandwich and Lord Lytton among them – to open a home for delinquent children in Dorset: the Little Commonwealth. It was that remarkable experiment that I had tried unsuccessfully to join after leaving the army. Lane never wrote, but after his death in 1925 his pupils who had taken notes at his lectures allowed an editor to make a book out of them, *Talks to Parents and Teachers*. The man who did most of the work was John Layard. A few years ago there was an American edition for which I wrote the preface. David Wills wrote Lane's biography and the matron at the Little Commonwealth wrote a book called *The Little Commonwealth*.

This is not the place to describe Lane's philosophy of education. I only want to tell what Lane did for me, for he was the most influential factor in my life. After the Commonwealth was closed, Lane set up in London as an analyst. I knew nothing then about analysis and had hardly heard of Freud: I had no thought of being analysed until Lane told me that he thought every teacher should be, and offered to take me on without my paying any fees. I had a daily session. It was not a Freudian style of analysis; I did not lie on a couch; we sat and talked. And like my later analysis by Stekel it did not touch my emotions, and I wonder if I got anything positive from it. I did get something negative. In inter-

preting a dream one day Lane said: 'This shows a fear of heights.'
And I laughed.

'Good heavens, Lane, in my student days I used to climb a
tower and sit with my legs dangling over the side while I read a
book.'

He wouldn't have it. Dreams don't lie, he said.

'Okay, Lane, I'll prove you are wrong', and next day I climbed
the Wren Monument. I looked down and was terrified. The usual
explanation of a height phobia is that one has an unconscious
wish to jump, and that may be, but what puzzled me then was
that I could look down a deep well easily, but once on the top of a
mountain in Bavaria I had had a sudden attack of anxiety. In that
case there was no temptation to jump, for it was a gradual slope
downwards. So Lane did not cure my complexes; he gave me one.
His role was dealing with wayward children, not with neurotic
adults. His practice ruined him in the end when he stupidly took
money gifts from a female patient, and her relations put the
police on to him.

What Lane did for me positively did not come from analysis;
it came from his treatment of children. His immortal phrase was
'You must be on the side of the child'. His humour pleased me.
He took up a word from my dream – 'lime'.

'Lime, the stuff that binds. I am the lime. I am helping you to
rebuild yourself . . . lime – Lane, see the connection?'

'But, Lane, I dreamt about a line, a railway line.'

He roared with laughter. His dream analysis was just a game to
him, a sort of crossword puzzle before crosswords were invented.

He was charming, always immaculately dressed, genial . . . and
a dreadful romancer. He told us stories of his youth, how he had
run away to the Indians, how he had knocked out a gang leader
and taken his place as foreman on the job. David Wills discovered
that he had done neither. Lane was a great admirer of Barrie and
hated Shaw. He loved *Peter Pan* and *Dear Brutus*; like Barrie he
never really grew up, and all the stupid things he did in his life
were infantile things. Yet it was this Peter Panism that made him
the creator of a new way of treating sick people. When he built a
wall with his Commonwealth boys and his part of the wall was perfect while theirs was bad, the boys began to knock the place down.

Lane joined in. His rationalisation was that he had to show
them that children were more important than bricks, but I have
an idea that he enjoyed the destruction because he also was a mis-
chievous little boy.

Every Sunday night of my 'analysis' I supped with his family, his wife, children and a few ex-delinquents from the Common-wealth. Often Lane was the merry soul of the party; often he sat silent in deep gloom.

His influence was limited. Since his death in 1925 the State institutions for problem children have not been changed in favour of freedom and understanding. They treat young delinquents with all the evils that made them delinquent – punishment, obedience, hard discipline, moral talks. I wonder how many teachers in Britain know his name. To me he was a revelation. I recall my first visit to the Little Commonwealth, arriving in the middle of a stormy self-government meeting. Then Lane and I sat up into the early hours talking . . . no, he talked while I listened. I had never heard of child psychology or for that matter of dynamic psychology of any sort. I had written two books before I met Lane – groping books, groping for freedom. Lane showed me the way and I have always acknowledged it. I don't think I am being smug when I say that many have been in-fluenced by Summerhill and have not acknowledged it in books and articles. It is always the case. Recently an English doctor published an article on the connection between neurosis and the stiffening of the muscles, Reich's discovery, but the article did not mention Reich. I grant that it does not matter in the long run, but I think that honesty should admit sources.

We, his disciples, accepted Lane as the Oracle. We never queried his dicta. He would say something like 'every footballer has a castration complex', and we would nod our heads in agreement. It never occurred to ask how he came to that con-clusion, yet we were not all young fools; in his group were Lord Lytton who later became Viceroy of India, Dr David, the Rugby headmaster who became Bishop of Liverpool, doctors, teachers, students. David Wills says in his biography, that of all his disciples Neill was the only one who later could view him ob-jectively. That may be because I am a hard-headed Scot, or more likely that I had not a transference so strong that time could not break it.

I had a quarrel with him in the middle of my analysis. He accused me of misrepresenting his idea when I went lecturing. We had a proper set-to and I stopped going to his sessions. For a few months I went to a doctor who then was the leading Jungian in London. Again I got no reaction emotionally. I cannot recall anything about the analysis save that when I dreamt of a black dog the analyst said it represented free-floating libido, whatever that meant.

One Sunday night in his home Lane asked how my analysis was going and I told him. 'You come back to me', he said and back I went again to listen to his elaborate analysis of my dreams.

I never believed the story of his seducing delinquent girls in the Commonwealth. Later when the law accused him of seducing his patients on the analytical couch I had my doubts, but no feelings of shock. Maybe some female patients got more out of seduction than I got out of his dream analysis. Professionally of course it is wrong, for when a woman becomes the analyst's lover the analysis stops dead. My old friend, the late Professor J. C. Flugel, a well-known Freudian, told me that on a visit to the States a New York analyst said to him: 'Flugel, I am not one of those analysts who fuck *every* patient.' Jack was one of the few analysts I met who could laugh at himself and others.

The tragedy of Lane's life was that he was associated with social scandal and not with the great work he did with problem children. In my early youth we knew Oscar Wilde as a bugger and not as a wit and dramatist. Scandal cannot kill a man's work for ever, but it can during his lifetime.

I have called Lane a romancer and took with a pinch of salt his story about sitting next to Barrie at a dinner party.

'I asked Barrie if he knew the symbolism of Peter Pan and he gave me a look of alarm, said "Good God, no", turned to the lady on his other hand and never spoke to me again.'

When I read of Lane's death in the papers I found myself smiling. I thought it hard-heartedness but later I think I got the true explanation: I was free at last. Up to then I had relied on him . . . what would Homer say? Now I had to stand on my own feet.

Later in Vienna, I became a patient of Dr Wilhelm Stekel, one of the Freudian school who, like Jung and Adler, broke away from it. I had reviewed a book of his that claimed that analysis was too expensive and too long: Stekel said that an analysis should not take longer than three months, a statement that appealed to my Scottish thrift. Stekel was a brilliant symbolist. He hardly ever asked for an association to a dream. 'Ach, Neill, this dream shows that you are still in lof with your sister.' I cannot recall having had any emotional response to anything Stekel said, it touched my head but never my emotions. I don't think I got a transference to him. Maybe because he was boyish in some ways.

'Neill, your dream shows that you are in lof with my wife.'

'But Stekel, I like your wife but she has no sexual attraction for me.'

126

He flared up angrily.

'Vot, you do not admire my vife? That is to her an insult. She is admired by many men.'

Another time I asked him if I could use his WC. When I returned he looked at me in an arch fashion and pointed a finger.

'Ach so! Der Neill wants to be Wilhelm Stekel, the king; he vants to sit on his throne! Naughty Neill.'

My explanation that I had diarrhoea he brushed aside with a laugh. One of his favourite sayings about Freud was: 'A dwarf sitting on a tall man's shoulder sees farther than he does', a doubtful assertion.

I have no intention of describing Reich's work; I shall simply tell how he affected and influenced me. I met him first in 1937. I was lecturing in Oslo University and after my lecture the chairman said: 'You had a distinguished man in your audience tonight: Wilhelm Reich.'

'Good God', I said, 'I was reading his *Mass Psychology of Fascism* on the ship.'

I phoned Reich and he invited me to dinner. We sat talking till late and I was fascinated.

'Reich,' I said, 'you are the man I have been searching for for years, the man to link up the soma and the psyche. Can I come and study under you?'

So for two years I went to Oslo in the three vacations I had each year. He said I could learn only by undergoing his Vegetotherapy, which meant lying naked on a sofa while he attacked my stiff muscles. He refused to touch dreams. It was a hard therapy and often a painful one, but I got more emotional release in a few weeks than I had ever had with Lane, Maurice Nicoll, Stekel. It seemed to me the best kind of therapy and I still think so, even having seen patients after Reichian therapy remain apparently neurotic.

Reich often said: 'Bend the tree when it is twig and it will be bent when it is fully grown.' I doubt if any therapy ever gets down to the roots of neurosis. In the early twenties we were all searching for the famous trauma that caused the sickness. We never found it because there was no trauma, only a plethora of traumatic experiences, from the moment of birth. Reich realised that therapy was not the answer, only prophylaxis, and kept up his practice of therapy mainly to raise money for his scientific studies.

127

When the war came in 1939 I trembled for his fate, for he was a Jew on the Nazi list for destruction. An American patient, Dr Theodore Wolfe, who later became the translator of his books, managed to get him into the States. His history there is well known up to his death in prison. His widow Ilse's *Wilhelm Reich: A Personal Biography* is a brave and sincere description of a brilliant and complicated man.

Reich, as Ilse points out, was deficient in humour and my friendship with him was marred by the fact that we could not laugh at the same things. No one would have dared to tell a sex story in his presence. The word fuck infuriated him . . . 'The sick sex, the aggressive male, fucks but women do not fuck. The word is embrace.'

He had no liking for ordinary conversation about cars or books and gossip was anathema to him. His talk was always about his work, and the only time I saw him relax was during his weekly trip to the movies in Rangeley, Maine, near his clinic in the US where I visited him after the war. He was completely un-critical of films. Once I said a film was kitsch and he was angry with me: 'I enjoyed every minute of it'.

I stood in a special relation to Reich. Around him were all his disciples, his doctor trainees, and all was formal. I was the only one who addressed him as Reich. True I had also been his patient, his trainee, but, maybe owing to my age, I was in a category by myself, along with Dr Ola Raknes from Oslo. We had seminars. Reich filled the blackboard with hieroglyphics, equations that meant nothing to me, and I doubt if they meant anything to the others present.

I could not understand Reich's theory of Orgone Energy. It may exist, but what can one do about it? Reich said it was visible but I had a blind eye to it. He had a small motor which was charged by an orgone accumulator. It ran slowly but when gingered up by volts from a battery it seemed to revolve at a great speed. Reich was in ecstasies: 'The motive force of the future!' he exclaimed. I never heard of its being developed. I did not know enough about his rain-making to form an opinion. What one might call psychic orgone energy cannot be used in any way I can imagine. But here I admit my ignorance of science of any kind. I was never interested in Reich's later work. To me he was the great man of his earlier books, *Sexual Revolution*, *Character Analysis*, *The Function of the Orgasm* and *The Mass Psychology of Fascism*, which I still think is a masterpiece of crowd analysis.

I wish our conversations in Maine could have been taped. We

talked and talked and consumed a lot of Scotch and Rye and, oddly enough, had no hangovers. In general Reich never relaxed but his lower jaw was so loose that it worked as a well-oiled joint on a machine. His muscles relaxed but his brain never did. Often he tried to persuade me to bring Summerhill to Maine.

'No, Reich, I had my school in a foreign country once and I would never do it again. I don't know the customs, the habits of the USA, and anyway my school would come to be regarded as a Reich school, and that I would never have.'

Reich was impossible to work with. He was an all or nothing man. One had to go his way, and any dissenter went out on his neck. I knew I could never work with him. I had a feeling that he was not a fearful man, not for himself anyway, but when being driven by car he was on edge, just as I am if the driver is not good. He was anxious for others: when Ilse drove their small son, Peter, to school it was: 'Be careful, Ilse. Don't drive fast.' When he was having his observatory built I climbed a high ladder to get a view from the top . . . I don't know where my height phobia had got to then. He stood at the bottom in much concern. 'Be careful, Neill. Look out. Come down.'

Reich and I loved each other. When I parted from him in Maine for the last time in 1948 he threw his arms around me. 'Neill, I wish you could stay. You are the only one I can talk to. The others are all patients or disciples.' Then I knew how lonely he was.

Once I said to him: 'Why are you so formal? Why do you address Wolfe as Dr Wolfe? Why aren't you just Reich to them all?'

'Because they would use the familiarity to destroy me as they did in Norway when I was Willy to them all.'

'But Reich, I am Neill to my staff, pupils, domestics and no one ever takes advantage of the familiarity.'

'Yes, but you aren't dealing with dynamite as I am', was his cryptic answer.

Reich had no effect on my school. I had been running it for twenty-six years before I met him. But he had a big effect on me personally. He widened my perspective, my knowledge of self; he uprooted remnants of Scots Calvinism about sex matters, showing that my approval of children's sex-play had been an intellectual one and not an emotional one.

It is obvious from Ilse's book that Reich in the end lost his reason. That never worried me; many great men went mad – Swift, Nietzsche, Schumann, Ruskin, lots of others, (I know I am

129

not a genuis because I haven't). It is an odd world in which a Reich is mad while a Reagan, a Nixon, a Franco are sane. I saw symptoms of paranoia in Reich. He kept a loaded gun in every hut on his estate. 'I have many enemies. I might have the Ku Klux Klan up here any night.' He was an excellent shot and he and I often had revolver practice. He was much better than I was. I recall one day he stood in front of me with a loaded gun in his hand. His look frightened me.

'Neill, am I crazy?'

'Crazy as a coot', said I and he laughed.

Ilse has told about his jealousies, his tempers. I saw the tempers often when he would fly off the handle about what seemed to me trifles. One morning at the breakfast table when he had been raging at Ilse he turned to me. 'Neill, why do I do it?'

'Because of the reconciliation', I said, 'you want a second honeymoon.' He burst into laughter and cried: 'That is a profound and true explanation.'

I wish I could recall his sayings. I remember one. 'What is wrong with psychoanalysis is that it deals with words, while all the damage is done to a child before it can speak.'

We corresponded from the time he went to America until he went to prison. Ilse tells of the time when Reich rejected me. When he was being tried I was in Oslo and with Ola Raknes and a few of his old friends sent him a telegram of sympathy. The reply came back: 'Don't trust Neill'.

I knew why. His boy, Peter, had visited me in Summerhill and when American planes went over he said that they had been sent to protect him. I knew he was quoting his father. I told him it was nonsense and when he went home he must have told Reich. But Reich and I made it up and there was no break in our friendship.

He gave me the German MS of his *Listen, Little Man* to read and asked my opinion about publishing it in English.

'No, Reich. It will make your enemies cry that you are a conceited fellow who sees all the others as inferior or sick.'

He agreed with me but shortly afterwards, when a woman wrote a poisonous article about him, he rushed the book into print as a counter-blast. I often told him he was a fool to react to every ignorant or spiteful journalist who attacked him. Ignore them as I do, I said. But no, he had to fight.

Like all men Reich was also a little man, but unlike most men he was conscious of the fact. Not that he could laugh at himself; he had not humour enough, but I am sure he was conscious of his extreme jealousies and suspicions. Yet, as Ilse said, he had no

130

Menschenkentnis – knowledge of people. More than once I saw him taken in by people I suspected as phoneys. His instinct was to trust people and when it turned out to be wrong, his fury was terrible.

I am sure that unconsciously he was seeking martyrdom. His *Murder of Christ* is almost autobiographical. Again and again he said to me: 'They will kill me'. He had been a martyr before I met him. He fled from Hitler, was thrown out of Denmark and then Sweden, and his enemies were plotting to have him thrown out of Norway.

Ilse tells of the shattering thing that happened to Reich when he was a boy. He found his mother in bed with his tutor and told his father. His mother killed herself. This incident accounts for his life-long jealousy, his distrust of all his womenfolk – they would betray him.

I felt his death more acutely than I felt the death of Lane. A bright light had gone out; a great man had died in vile captivity. I think that Reich will not come into his own as a genius until at least the second generation. I was most lucky to know him and learn from him and love him.

On Summerhill

THE SCHOOL

Maybe the most joyous day of my life was the day when I returned to Leiston in 1945 after the disastrous interlude in Wales. The school was in a bad way. The army had had it for five years and had done more damage in that time than my kids had done in twenty-five years, but it did not seem to matter. We were home to dear old Summerhill. We gladly sat and slept on mattresses on the floor until our furniture began to come from Wales about ten days later. I had visited the old place once a year during the war, and it was annoying to see soldiers at every window and to be ticked off by young officers.

'Sir, what are you doing on government property? Who are you anyway?'

'Nobody of any importance; I just happen to own the house.'

'Can you prove that?'

'Oh', I said wearily, 'arrest me and take me out to the road and ask the first passer-by who I am.'

But at one time the Scottish Fusiliers were occupying the school and when I told them it was my old regiment they let me go anywhere I liked. Only once did I have the courage to say to a blustering young power-struck subaltern: 'I want your name for I mean to report you to your commander for fatuous insolence', but then when he climbed down I felt sorry for him.

I have written so much about Summerhill that I have no desire to describe it now. Today it is not well known in Britain. Many Americans say to me: 'We talked of Summerhill to people in

London and they had never heard of it, whereas in New York or Los Angeles many know of it.' I do not know the answer. Not claiming to be a seer I hesitate to quote the Bible saying that a prophet is not without honour save in his own country. Maybe the answer lies in Britain's old class system. Most of the gentry have had to sell their old castles and mansions, partly because domestics are few and far between, but the gentry tradition lingers, with its Eton and Harrow for the upper class, its grammar schools for the middle class, and its secondary modern schools for those who will never work with a white collar. But I guess the system is extant in all countries, even communist ones.

Summerhill was never patronised by the élite – the rich, the stage, the TV folks. I doubt if Princess Anne would have fitted in, not after her first vacation when Buckingham Palace would have learned a few four-letter words. Ethel Mannin, the popular novelist, sent her daughter, Professor Bernal his two sons, but on the whole famous parents eschewed us. We get many Americans but I know not who is famous there, only a few are notorious; no names no pack drill. Two years ago I met a woman in New York who runs a day school and charges $3,000 a year, but I am sure that none of her parents would send their kids to a school like Summerhill.

Interestingly enough, children have no class feeling at all. If one of our pupils were driven to school in a Rolls Royce the others would have no reaction whatever. So with colour. When we get black pupils even the smallest child does not notice their colour. We have Jewish pupils and no one knows or cares – though it would be a different matter with children of Orthodox parents. I had one forty years ago. He had to tell some beads every morning and wrote home saying he had lost them. His father drove up in a chauffeur-driven Rolls, said nothing to me, took his boy by the collar, shoved him into the car and drove off. I was concerned for he had paid a term's fees.

So with a Catholic boy I took on. I had to send him home because the poor kid was living in a school that did not believe in sin and in vacations he had to go to a priest and confess his sins. The conflict was more than any kid could bear.

I never regretted coming to Leiston. The air is bracing and the eleven acres are a paradise for kids. I am often asked what the town thinks of us and never know the answer. My staff and I frequent the local pubs – I have never seen a State teacher there, or for that matter a doctor or a lawyer, but Summerhill, having no class, belongs to all classes. I don't think the town understands what it is all about, but the people are friendly. One youth of about seventeen hung about our gates for a time, and when I asked him what he wanted he replied: 'A free fuck'. I don't say he was typical of Leiston inhabitants.

I am 'Neill' without any mister to some of the workmen as I am to staff, domestics, pupils. No one touches his hat to me and some locals may wonder what the crowds of world visitors come to see. I was a member of a local golf club for twenty-five years and I think that only one member knew who I was . . . my school doctor.

I have always had the ability to laugh at myself, even when being capped for an honorary degree. Years ago a friend wanted a copy of my first book, written in 1915. I went into a bookseller's shop in Ipswich.

'Have you ever heard of a book called *A Dominie's Log* by A. S. Neill?'

'Heard of it? Why, I've got it, saw it on the shelf the other day.'

He could not find it.

'That's the worst of insignificant writers; their books go astray. If you leave your name and address . . .'

'Thanks, I'll look in again.'

Some years ago I went for a walk in the woods above Oslo. I lost my way. I saw a man coming up through the trees, and, not knowing any Norwegian, I pointed and said: 'Oslo?'

'I'm buggered if I ken', he said. We talked for a bit about Scotland. 'Now that we have met', he said, 'we may as well exchange names. My name is McDonald.'

'My name is Neill.'

He looked up at me quickly. 'You aren't *the* Neill?'

I made a fitting gesture of modesty.

'What do you mean by *the* Neill?'

'Bobby Neill, the footballer.'

I think that what was wrong with Stalin and Hitler was that they could not laugh at themselves, and maybe that is what is wrong with our cabinet ministers. The first requirement of any man is to recognise his absurdities.

SUMMERHILL STAFF

I sometimes think that I have had more trouble with staff than I have had with pupils. I have had some odd bods in my time, the science man who let a boy of eight handle a bottle of cyanide and a girl of the same age pour fuming nitric acid into a tube so that she burned herself. So many reacted to freedom in the same way as unfree children do. There are no duties for our teachers barring being in their classrooms at teaching periods. Neurotic ones have taught their classes all morning and slept or read all the rest of the day. Good teachers have always used their free time mixing with the kids.

Summerhill attracts neurotics and I hear that the new schools in the USA are having the same experience as we had. It simply is not easy to get a good staff and, in spite of Summerhill's fame, I find it hard to get new teachers. If I advertise I get letters like this: 'I am not a teacher, I am a bank clerk (or a librarian or what not) but I know I can teach'. Many think that teaching is an unskilled job. Why so few apply I do not know. It may be a question of money; yet we pay as near the State standard as we can. Today (1972) the salary is £800 p.a. including board, lodging, laundry. It may be that teachers fear to teach in a school where lessons are voluntary. One has to be a good teacher or else the class is not attended, and my worst job is to say to a teacher: 'The kids say your lessons are so dull that they won't go to them, so you'll have to leave.' If such a system obtained in State schools our city streets would be full of unemployed teachers.

135

By law I have to have qualified teachers, not that training makes much difference; I have had trained and untrained teachers with good and bad in both categories. Teaching is an art, not a science. But the law is there, and a Picasso could not get a job as an art teacher in England because he has not been trained. Of course I want a teacher to put his or her lessons across, but that is not the main consideration in Summerhill. I want teachers with some humour, with no dignity; they must not inspire fear and they must not be moralists. I am inclined to get more introverts than extroverts, but I do not want he-men with strong personalities. My pupils reject such. When we had an ex-Scout master with his: 'Come on, lads, we'll build a boat', they turned away in scorn. Free children will not follow a suggesting leader.

One feature has appeared again and again – the teacher who seeks popularity by being on the side of the child for the wrong reason. Children soon see through such a teacher. Too many new teachers and housemothers have difficulty in discriminating between freedom and licence. One housemother let her crowd smash a lot of furniture because: 'I thought I wasn't ever supposed to say no.' But I have had some excellent teachers – no, not teachers but community-minded people. George Corkhill (Corkie), our science master for nearly thirty years, good stolid old George, never ruffled, always the centre of a group of little ones whose criterion of chemistry was making lemonade and fireworks. George followed their interests. He was a great loss to the school when he retired. He died this year.

Since this book is about me I must tell what reaction I had to the staff and its reaction to me. Never once have I told a teacher what to do, how to teach – one or two complained that I did not come to their classrooms often enough. But my chief difficulty was when there was a disagreement between a teacher and a pupil.

Once a boy wanted to make a banjo. The woodwork teacher refused to let him, saying that it was too difficult a task. Both came to me to arbitrate. I said: 'If he wants to make a banjo that is his affair, his wish; if he makes a mess of it it is his affair. Give him the wood.' The teacher was furious, accusing me of siding with a pupil against the staff. He resigned on the spot. I thought too late that it should have been a matter for the general meeting to decide.

I have a complex about being a boss that is almost morbid. I hate telling anyone what to do, rationalising perhaps . . . If he does it only because I tell him to he isn't original enough. I hate being God, and when I have to send a kid away, say, for making small kids terrified, I am always miserable and slightly guilty. But I never feel guilty when I tell an unsuccessful teacher to leave, not guilty, just embarrassed.

I may demand too much from my staff. I mean in my own mind. I want gay people, full of fun, active in school life, balanced people. I get a few but not as many as I should like.

Once a big stone was knocked off a wall by some kids. It lay on the path. I stopped to lift it and then paused . . . leave it and see what happens. Staff and pupils walked round it for six weeks and then I lifted it back to its place. But here a factor comes in. I have a feeling of possession about the house and grounds. They are my property. My staff do not have this feeling that the place is theirs, and I understand.

Generally speaking Summerhill staff have been a contented lot, with few of the bickerings and jealousies so often found in staff rooms: 'Jones has six periods for English while I have only four for maths'. Now and again we have had a bad *Stimmung* in the staff. Once a young man thought he could run the school better than I could. He agitated among the staff and made some converts so that the atmosphere was one you could cut with a knife. I should give up being the boss; the staff should handle everything, finance, enrolment of pupils, salaries. Naturally I got rid of the rebels as soon as I could, reluctantly, for they were good teachers. I fancy that, instead of challenging father at fourteen, they delayed the challenge until they found a father substitute, even a non-authoritarian one.

My second wife Ena gets much more hate than I do because she is the mother figure. I got our needlework teacher to make dolls for my play therapy in the days when I used therapy: father, mother, son, daughter, all with sexual organs of course. I left them around on the floor, and children up to the age of twelve played with them. In six weeks poor mother was kicked to bits but father remained untouched. Made me wonder if Freud's Oedipus complex was all wrong. Father is out all day; mother has to live with the children, feed them, say no to them: she is the real authoritarian in the house, so that resentment against mother is greater than that against father. The hate is most evident when Ena is serving our meals, when the Me First element enters with a vengeance. Maybe Freud should have made food the driving interest in life, not sex.

The men on my staff and I seem to get less hate than the women staff from the disturbed pupils. In my own case the explanation is obvious . . . my neutrality. The English teacher can complain at a general meeting about the savagery of a problem boy but I dare not, for, if I have to take a PL (private lesson, seldom given today) I cannot be an accuser and a therapist. Here I am modestly soft-pedalling my natural charm.

Sad that old pupils do not become teachers and return as members of the staff. Perhaps they are too well-balanced to teach, but I have had housemothers who were ex-pupils and they did this work well – partly because they did not require a period of living out their complexes when coming to a non-authoritarian atmosphere. One old girl of 19, when I offered her a job as housemother, said: 'I'd love to, but no, I'd feel I was making Summerhill a funk hole instead of facing the outer world.'

I hasten to add that I may have said more about the unsatisfactory staff than the good ones. At the time of writing Summerhill has a very good staff, mostly young people with enthusiasm and an understanding of what Summerhill stands for.

MY SCHOOL
INSPECTORS

Britain is the freest country in the world. In no other country could I have had Summerhill.

But all schools are under the control of the Ministry of Education, now the Department of Education and Science (DES), and all schools, public and private, are inspected. Our first big inspection was in 1939. I printed the report in my book *Summerhill*. Then after a gap of ten years came another inspection and report.

I have never been badgered by the Ministry and the Inspectors; HMIs were always civil and friendly and helpful in their own way, though it was not my way. Their chief job is to inspect domestic arrangements and lessons. I told the first HMI we had, John Blackie, a broad-minded man, that he could inspect progress in maths and French but he could not inspect happiness, sincerity, balance, tolerance. 'I'll have a try,' said John and he made a good try. I said to another HMI: 'Your criterion is learning but ours is living. You take a short view . . . concern because Willie cannot read at twelve . . . but we take a long view. I can think of only one old pupil who can't hold down a job.' The answer: 'Maybe, but I don't see them, do I?'

The Ministry is, must be, the Establishment. It represents education as it is generally accepted by the majority of parents and teachers. If a Minister of Education were to make a decree that corporal punishment be banned the outcry from parents and teachers would make the ban impossible. If he or she ruled that there be no religious instruction in schools there would be public meetings of protest all over the country, attended, I fancy, by a majority who make no attempt to live as Christians. The Ministry is tolerant of schools like Summerhill but could not officially approve of them.

In England every private school is registered but to be 'recognised as efficient' it has to apply for recognition which is or is not granted after an inspection. I have never applied, partly because, to me, recognition means something bestowed. I also had a good notion that Summerhill would not qualify for recognition because of its failure to meet the normal standard in book learning. Indeed, the fact that every new pupil, when told that lessons are optional, immediately drops all school subjects barring the creative ones like art and woodwork, proves to me that lessons are forced on children against all their natural wishes. So that Summerhill pupils often bloom late from an academic point of view. One old boy, an engineer, seldom attended any lessons. Today he has half a dozen letters after his name. To a visiting Inspector that boy would probably have been classed as a failure.

To most folks a child's playing is a waste of time. It would be impossible to have a Ministry that did not think work of more importance than play.

I have already told about my father and the misery he experienced when inspectors came to his village school, and how I shared that misery, that fear; and to this day I have an inspector complex. The very name inspector is an insult; the one who checks tickets on a bus signifies that humanity is naturally dishonest, that every conductor is tempted to pocket customers' money. In education the word advisor would be better, and today that is what an Inspector is, even if his advice is limited to irrelevancies like methods of teaching. I have said it many times and say it again, that you cannot teach anything of importance. Maths, English, French, yes, but not charity, love, sincerity.

Inspection makes Summerhill insincere. The kids tidy up, rub out the shits and fucks on the walls; they feel self-conscious and unhappy. Some time ago when an HMI inspected the school he got a hostile reception and was troubled, and so was I. I knew what was behind it. A sensational daily paper had had an article alleging that the Ministry was gunning for Summerhill, and the kids looked on the harmless inspector as a dangerous spy who might close the school. The Ministry, of course, can close an independent school but I fancy that this seldom happens unless in cases where a headmaster is a practising homosexual or for that matter a practising heterosexual (with schoolgirls).

140

In today's paper there is an excellent example of the hypocritical Puritanism of the British Establishment. A girl in a training college was found with a man in her room. The college fired her. She appealed to the High Court; her appeal was dismissed and the seventy-two-year-old presiding judge gave her a stern lecture telling her that she was not a proper person to teach children. Her sin was to break the eleventh commandment . . . Thou shalt not be found out. How unjust is such a verdict, seeing that thousands of girl students have a sex life when they lodge extramurally in cities.

What puzzles me is why the teaching profession should tolerate inspection. The doctors and the lawyers, with their powerful trade unions, would not. True, they are not State servants as the teachers are, but since National Health began most doctors are paid by the State and I am sure would fight any attempt to make medicine an inspected profession. I belong to a profession that has no guts. I am gutless myself; I should take a stand against inspection; I should reject it on the grounds that my old pupils are nearly all successful in life; I should say to the Ministry: 'For fifty years educated and intelligent parents have sent their children to Summerhill, believing in its system, pleased with its results. Why should I have to have my school judged by an official standard that is not mine? Summerhill is primarily for living and it refuses to be judged by a body of people who think of learning and teaching methods and discipline. Let them rule about the number of water closets and baths and fire extinguishers. Summerhill accepts that ruling.'

Alas, I am not brave enough to defy the powers above, so I compromise; I employ eight teachers for sixty children, some the wrong teachers from my viewpoint – those who teach the exam subjects which I find most pupils look upon as necessary dull grinds. Not that children dislike all exam subjects. Many like English but reject maths and history.

England is the land of independent schools. There are few on the Continent, and, until the 'new school' rage in the USA, I think that the private school there was usually a military academy. Scotland never had the tradition; there are four public schools there but they are English schools with the English tradition of Eton and Harrow, and at a venture I should say English speech. John M. Aitkenhead's Kilquhanity is the only free boarding school I know of in Scotland. It also has had its troubles with the inspectorate.

Ah, well, I should not complain. The Minister has left me very

141

much alone and will do so until I die. What will happen then I cannot guess. Some Ministers may say: 'We tolerated that school until the old man died but we cannot go on allowing a school in which children can play all day without learning lessons.'

FINANCE

When I returned to England in 1924 I was almost broke, and our stay in Lyme Regis was one long financial struggle. But we had one stroke of luck there. An Australian called Cooper sent me a cheque payable to the New Education Fellowship to which I belonged. I wrote saying that I was the wrong guy and should I forward it to the Fellowship? No, he said, keep it. It was a godsend then and may have saved us from bankruptcy.

For many years we had no gifts. In 1950 William K. Elmhirst of Dartington Hall made a deed of covenant giving me £1,000 p.a. for seven years. Bill was a retiring, modest lad and I felt that he did not want his generosity to be a public matter and so I did not broadcast his gift. Some years ago a law firm sent me £1,000 from one who wanted to remain anonymous. Later again, nearer this time, Joan Baez gave a special concert for Summerhill in London and gave me the proceeds, £1,400. And recently after singing at a pop concert in the Isle of Wight she sent £2,000.

When Her Majesty's Inspectors advised our scrapping a few buildings we did not have the money to rebuild, so much against the grain I sent out an appeal. The money poured in to the tune of $30,000 and we used every penny of it erecting new teaching huts and dormitories. For many years I had poured all my book royalties and article fees into keeping the school afloat. A private school cannot make a profit; too often Summerhill has been in the red, mainly because of bad debts. Had all the debts been paid up during the last fifty years I could have lorded it in a Rolls Royce, chauffeur driven. (No, that would have meant wearing a tie.)

It is a platitude that money does not buy happiness. It buys comfort which is enjoyable; to roll up to the opera in a private car and have a stalls seat is comfort, whereas to stand in the gallery queue for two hours is, to say the least, uncomfortable. Sure, money brings more than comfort. It can bring the means for creation, for a good job, for a university career.

Summerhill has been unable to do all it wanted to do because of poor finance. We have art and handwork teachers but cannot afford a dance or a music teacher, to me of much more importance than a maths or history teacher. We long to have a fine library, a well-equipped physics and chemistry lab, a cookery department. State schools can afford all these things, which are seen as luxuries by some parents and teachers but as necessities by us, who cannot afford them. And I wish I could pay my staff more than I do. Our fees vary with the cost of living. Today (1972) they are £600 p.a. for pupils under twelve, and £750 p.a. for the over twelves, plus £10.50 for laundry each term; three terms in a year. Our inability to take poor children has been a sadness for fifty years.

Twice I have had men who wanted to finance the school. Twice I asked: 'You would want a say in the running, wouldn't you?' and to the answer: 'Of course', I said 'Nothing doing'. The situation was different when money came from Henry Miller, Joan Baez and many other kind Americans, for there were no strings attached.

Summerhill old pupils do not seem to be interested in making money, possibly because to make money one must be competitive while competitiveness in Summerhill is unknown, outside games of course.

One old boy has given a lot of money to the school to repair, mend, paint, change it. Like all true generous people he wants to remain anonymous, bless him . . . pagan blessings of course.

OLD PUPILS

I have sometimes been asked if I am prouder of Summerhill academic successes than of pupils who went into art or crafts. The answer is no, although I have often mentioned our two professors, two university lecturers, a good few doctors, one a lung specialist, another a surgeon, two lawyers – but no teachers. I only once had a pupil who wanted to be a teacher, and she was mentally defective. I mention the scholars because the usual criticism of Summerhill is that children will not be able to pass exams when free to attend lessons or stay away from them, but I am as proud of our furniture maker, our potter, our artists who show in Bond Street, our old boy who is making a name for himself with his illustrated children's books. Another of our old boys could not read at sixteen and has now invented a painless hypodermic needle for diabetics; he is also a clever engineer.

I am not primarily interested in whether they are professors or bricklayers; I am interested in their character, their sincerity, their tolerance; I like to think that they have a better chance of being pro-life than disciplined, moulded, children have.

Summerhill has often also been criticised because its graduates do not seem to be crusading to make this sick world better. I cannot think how they can. They know that spouting freedom from a soap-box in Hyde Park is a waste of time and breath; they know that marching down Piccadilly waving flags cuts no ice. One old pupil put it thus: 'All I can do is to bring up my own kids in freedom, hoping that my example may influence my friends and neighbours.' Myself, I cannot see any other way. I am sure that most of my old pupils have my distrust of politics and politicians who must find it impossible to be honest.

Yes, I am, in the main, happy about my old pupils. Many are fine men and women, hard-working, tolerant, pro-life, and only a minority have disappointed me. Summerhill did not sink in far enough with them. I think most of my pupils treat their own children in a free way. One parent who married a Summerhill boy said that Summerhill good does not appear until the second generation, an arresting and wise remark.

I have written half jokingly that when a Summerhill kid is a success it is due to the school, but if a failure the failure is due to the parents. It is nearly true. Our successes mostly came from homes with some freedom and family affection, while many of our, let me call them semi-successes, came from divided unhappy homes. More than once have I said that freedom will not cure a child who had no love as a baby; it can ameliorate the condition but the chip on the shoulder in too many cases remains. My dream of a Summerhill full of children from self-regulated homes remains a daydream.

I have often criticised universities and schools because they develop the intellect and neglect the emotions. It has been argued that Summerhill does the opposite, and it possibly does in some cases, where a child grasps freedom emotionally without having the intellectual capacity to amalgamate head and heart. I am sure that the majority of old pupils have made a synthesis of both easily and naturally. I still cannot make up my mind whether Summerhill freedom is better for the bright ones than for the ones with lesser intelligence. Bill, now a doctor, reads the weekend literary journals. Paul, now a farmer, reads the picture papers with all their kitsch. Well, if both are happy, what the hell anyway?

One feature I must record. The loyalty of all old pupils to the school is sincere and heart-warming. Recently, at our fiftieth anniversary party, the warmth and enthusiasm was tremendous.

TEACHING

I think that a teacher is born, and that all the training in all the colleges will not make one a good teacher. I have had French and Germans on the staff and foolishly appointed them to teach their respective languages. Few could do so; they had not the talent of putting their subject over the footlights. Without boasting, I say I was a good teacher although not an ideal one from an examination point of view. My teaching dwelt too much on imagination, so that when I set an essay it was not 'How I spent my holidays' but 'My false teeth fell out on my plate', or 'Give a snail's description of its journey from the front door to the school gate'. Nearly fifty years ago I said to a class: 'I am going to give you the first sentence of an essay or story or what not. Here it is: "Hell and buggery, said the bishop!" Carry on.'

A boy of thirteen wrote: 'The bishop leaned over his pulpit. "Brethren", he said solemnly, "as I entered the cathedral this morning I heard one of you use these dreadful words. I shall take take them as my text".' I certainly could not have risen to that standard; I'd have made the bishop foozle at golf. I had to give up teaching the older pupils because they protested that my method would not help them to pass the external examinations; a valid criticism, condemning not me, but the dead ones who set English papers. I could tell a child's standard in English in a half hour's talk plus a blank book in which he could write anything he liked.

There *are* skills that have to be taught – hence the good old apprenticeships, even if the first year consisted of making tea for the journeymen – but my contention is that school exams, by and large, deal with things that do not matter. Teachers become as narrow as their subjects. Maybe that is why I have so often found university professors and lecturers rather dull men. Bacon, if he lived today, might say that specialisation maketh a narrow man. This applies not only to teachers but to doctors: I have seldom met a doctor who had a wide interest or a wide area of conversation.

Several writers of books have tried to assess my work, too often assuming that I am a teacher. I am criticised because I do nothing to help teachers practically, because I have no solution to overcrowded and often violent schools, because I am not interested in organisation or exams or methods of teaching. And the critisicms would be just if I were a teacher, that is an imparter of knowledge, a moulder of character, a guide to the young. I refuse to be classified as a teacher. I might define myself as a non-believer in religion but a true believer in humanity. My message has been this one: a child's emotions are infinitely more important than his intellectual progress. I have tried, with I fear little success, to show that schools, by ignoring emotions, leave them to outside influences, the press, the kitsch of radio and TV, commercial TV ads, a plethora of magazines geared to a mentality of ten. Teachers cannot see the wood behind the trees, the wood that means life abundant, freedom from character moulding. The caning teacher is not the only one to get hold of the wrong end of the stick.

My message to teachers has been: forget the silly school subjects and look at the child, but objectively, never trying to mould it. I know that the criticism has been made of this argument that at Summerhill we mould the child by making its environment, that unconsciously the pupils are identifying themselves with me. I grant that by one's presence one moulds unconsciously, though how much one doesn't know. All I know is that I have never seen an argument in which one side was converted; imagine one between a bishop and an atheist, even if the latter thanks God that he is an unbeliever. The word mould is not the right one; influence is better. I'd concede that we influence our pupils; for even in a talk in a village pub we impress our personality on the other fellow.

I have tried, again with little success, to break down the stupid barrier between teacher and pupil, the 'sir' barrier, the obedience (on one side) barrier. I came to free education via psychology, not via the great educators who mostly had one foot in the learning and teaching camp – Rousseau, Froebel, Pestalozzi, Montessori, Dewey. I was influenced not only by Homer Lane but by Freud, Reich, Stekel; but not by Jung and Adler or Melanie Klein. Much of what I thought I had learned from the psychoanalysts has disappeared with time, but I have never departed from my belief that the psychology of the child must be the root of all education.

I have said that I have had little success in spite of the fact that things are changing. We have our new primary schools with their happy faces and chatter, their individual interests. Fine but not quite satisfying to me, for the play instinct is not fully recognised. The child must be doing something, learning by doing, but still learning, while play has and should not have any conscious element of learning. We have the outcrop of new free schools in the USA; we have the de-schooling movement. Americans like John Holt, Paul Goodman, Illich, Dennison and others are influencing American schools bravely. Kindly souls say that much reform is due to my influence, but my answer is that no one can tell. I had the good luck to run a school and write books, and if other pioneers are less known it is because they did not broadcast their results – E. F. O'Neill, Bill Curry, Kenneth Barnes (but he wrote a few books too). It isn't false modesty that makes me say that the *Zeitgeist* was more important than I am, or for that matter any individual.

Some have said that my work has been negative, and to me that is a compliment, for the other side is too damn positive with its disciplines and mouldings. If you do not know what a child should be you have to be negative, a looker-on, and that is what the Establishment will not, cannot do. It knows what a child should be. Montessori and Rudolf Steiner knew but Homer Lane didn't. And I don't know; on the other hand I have never despaired when a child seems to stand still for years. One such, a boy who in Summerhill never went to a lesson, left school barely able to read. Today he is a bright young man who has hiked all over the world. He worked for the starving in Bangladesh and is now on his way to South East Africa to see what he can do to help the natives. But he can't spell well and never heard of the Long Parliament, bringing up again the vexed question: What is education? I say it is, inter alia, forming character from the inside, not the dictated character of Eton and Harrow and the grammar schools.

I may be a teacher in the broad sense that anyone who tries to spread ideas is a teacher, but this cannot be compared with teaching in a school. My readers can take it or leave it but a child sitting under a strict teacher dare not leave it for fear of the teacher. What boy of thirteen can say to a caning teacher: 'Why don't you hit someone your own size?' Children have to accept because they are weak, frightened, docile, but adults can judge an idea without extraneous fears . . . or can they? My books cannot convert bishops or puritanical, unconsciously pornographic nosers-out of books with four-letter words. My public is a minority one. I appeal to the few who have rejected father and his authority, a fact that makes me wonder why I am a bestseller in the USA and Germany. Possibly because so many of the new generation are challenging the universal paternalism.

I am often accused of being anti-parents. I don't think that any of my present parents would agree with that. I am only against parents who cannot or will not learn how not to ruin their kids emotionally. Freedom changes them into good citizens but if the home does not change at the same time the cure takes a long time and there are many regressions.

I simply do not know how much my own experience with my parents affects my attitude to other people's parents, for the longer I live the more I realise that it is impossible to get clear of early conditioning. It can be that my alleged anti-intellectualism has its roots in my inability to live up to my father's high ideal of scholarship.

Then where do I stand? Not as a teacher; not as a great educator, far from being a clever philosopher. I'd like to think of myself as just a simple guy, with little book learning, and an infinite ignorance of life and things, but one who has some power in identifying essentials, the roots of life, believing in life so much that, to me, any attempt to change it by morals and rules and disciplines are crimes against child nature.

On Books and Writing

MY OLD BOOKS

The kind of books I have written since 1915 are milestones on a journey, things passed, left behind. That is why I cannot read my own books, and have little idea what is in them – with the exception of the kids' tale *The Last Man Alive*, the story I told some pupils in 1937, which still makes me chuckle. It was the only book in which I could bring in humour and fun, also it was fiction while most of the other books were full of opinions, many proved wrong by time and experience.

I know that it is fear that prevents my reading of the past . . . 'Good Heavens, did I really write that stuff?' Fear or shame? Some of my books have been re-published in Denmark and Germany but I would feel embarrassed if they were reissued in Britain. They were all groping books, even the most recent ones.

Long ago I wrote a novel, *Carroty Broon*, really my own boyhood fictionalised. I still think it wasn't a bad book. Another effort was *The Booming of Bunkie*, a farcical tale of a young man who set out to boom a small town in the East of Scotland. A curate's egg sort of book, good in parts. The village band could play only one tune and the locals knew it was the National Anthem because they stood to play it. And there was a mad golf course, so short that one could not use a driver. To the last green you pitched over the clubhouse. A musician, one of our parents, was to make it into a musical but after writing the first act he was killed in a street accident.

I think that a man can do only one job in life well. I have

written plays. I like to think the dialogue was witty, but I am no dramatist, nor could I write a novel of any merit. I haven't got the literary style, the word-painting, the shining metaphor.

My dramatic attempts failed, chiefly because I would explain their actions, showing the psychology behind them. Ibsen and Shakespeare explain nothing; they let the characters show themselves by their actions. There is a limitation here. The story is that when J. M. Barrie was watching the rehearsal of one of his plays, he told an actor to interpret the character by action, saying that only by action could a character be made alive.

'All right', said the actor, 'how can I explain by action the fact that I have an aunt in York who is suffering from a bad cold?'

Authorship is frustrating in one way . . . one cannot know what influence one has had on readers. I modestly think that well-known people do not read my books, and it was a mild shock when I read in Asquith's *Letters* one to a young woman in hospital saying he was sending her a book to cheer her up – *A Dominie's Log*. He was Prime Minister then and, had I known of his book choice, damme I might have got an earldom. Yet I think I would be safe to bet that my books are not in the White House Library.

In fifty years of writing I have seldom had any opposition, seldom any rude letters. My books have not been banned by any country, even narrow Catholic Eire or race-hating South Africa. I did read once that Sydney Public Library in Australia had banned one book but cannot recall which. I was not a big enough man to be doomed to martyrdom. 'The world crucifies its Christs.' I never was in that category.

I do not know what public I reach by my books. Recently I was on TV. A young lady wrote: 'I did enjoy your programme. Tell me, do you believe in corporal punishment?' The answer would be as difficult as the one I was asked to give to the question: 'Do you think that Freud was a good psychologist?' It is easier to know what reactions there are when one broadcasts. A few years ago on radio I talked to mothers and said that when you spank a child you are hating it. I asked the BBC not to send on any correspondence about the programme but heard that it got a stream of angry letters from mothers.

I have no idea how artists react to their old books, meaning by artists writers of novels and plays. It would be good to know if Hardy liked *Tess* or *Jude the Obscure*, if Lawrence liked *Lady Chatterley's Lover*. I feel sure that Tennyson did not approve much of his 'Queen of the May'.

It would be intriguing to know how many authors can read

their own books, especially their early ones, or how many sculptors can look at their own heads and torsos. When I used to make trays and bowls out of brass or copper they had no value when finished. They meant nothing and were nothing. I guess my German friend Karl Waas, the silversmith, an expert, has a different view of the fine work he produces.

My books are creations in a way but they are not works of art, only diaries, chronicles, easily dated. Freud is already dated; possibly Einstein will soon be dated. Only creators escape being dated. I am no creator; my books will die and be forgotten. I am content to think that I have reached a few million readers for good or bad, for good I hope. I am content to think that my books have helped parents to think twice before they moulded their children's characters.

MY FAILURE
AS A DRAMATIST

I once wrote a play called *One of the Family*.
Synopsis. Middle-class family of Dr Hanick: wife, son, daughter,
conservative lawyer brother. Jenny the maid steals wife's brooch.
Lawyer wants to call the police. Hanick has encouraged Jenny to
steal for his own reasons. Brother: 'All very well with a pretty
girl, but what would you do if a burgular entered the house?' Of
course the said burglar does enter the house. Law brother lifts
the phone.

> 'No, George,' said the doctor, 'I have a better plan. Mr Smith
> (to the intruder), will you be my guest for a month?'
> Wife: 'Are you mad, John?'
> Brother: 'You are off your onion.'
> Daughter: 'Wonderful!'

It turns out that the burglar, who has a revolver, is the neglected
son of the lawyer brother whom he came to shoot but was not
sure which brother was his father. A poor play, too impossible,
too full of Hanick's psychological explanations. But I think
the characterisation wasn't bad, and I like to think some of
the dialogue was good. Dr Hanick interviews the intruder the
morning after.

> Dr H: Mind if we have a chat?
> Smith: What about, the weather? A deep depression is –
> Dr H: Not descending on me anyway. Why not talk about
> yourself?

Smith: Okay, I'll try to be a guinea pig.

Dr H: I don't want to probe into your character and I guess you don't want me to. Have you the same attitude towards your profession?

Smith: Profession?

Dr H: It must be rather a fascinating sort of life. You must meet, or rather I should say avoid meeting some interesting people. Tell me, Smith, does it require any special talent, or are burglars born and not made?

Smith: Go on, I don't mind your laughing at me.

Dr H: I never laugh at anyone except myself. No, I am genuinely interested. What sort of sensation is it when you enter someone else's house? Possibly like learning to drive a car; the first few times a glorious adventure, but after that just mechanical and boring. Tell me, is burglary similar?

Smith: I don't know. I never tried it before.

Dr H: Really, this is most interesting. You mean you have branched out on a new line? Tell me, do criminals have a sort of grading? Does a crook begin by stealing milk bottles and gradually work his way up through pick-pocketing and forgery to company promoting and a title?

Smith: Go on, I can take it.

Dr H: I am so ignorant about it all. Now take the social side. Does the wife of, say, a cat burglar consider herself a cut above the wife of a pick-pocket? Possibly more of a climber.

Dear me, I do wish I had the gift of writing drama. In my work I have left the light side, the humour side of myself largely in abeyance – the comedian often longs to play Hamlet and I, the educationist, want to be the comedian.

In my play the stern lawyer brother refuses to speak to Smith. Three weeks later Evelyn, the daughter, says to Smith: 'Has my uncle spoken to you yet?'

Smith: Yes.
Evelyn: Was he friendly?
Smith: I'm not sure; all he said was pass the salt.

Dr Hanick, of course, with his psychological tricks, was myself. No, it wasn't a good play but several who read it said that it was okay to read if one treated it as a novel. It proved that a cobbler should stick to his last.

My interest in plays began when I first read Ibsen, and he is the only dramatist who has tempted me to travel a hundred miles to London to see his plays – *Hedda Gabler* with Peggy Ashcroft and *The Wild Duck* with Dorothy Tutin, both fine performances. Ibsen himself I could never get interested in. Friends in Norway often motored me over to his birthplace, Skein (pronounced Shane).

His room, where he is said to have performed his plays as a child, gave me no emotion whatever. All I read about him made me feel that I wouldn't have liked the grumpy remote man, so critical of society but so pleased to receive society's titles and honours. But how great a dramatist that man was: his technique is almost beyond criticism. (Though F. L. Lucas, in his excellent book on Ibsen and Strindberg, points out the improbability of the ending of *Hedda Gabler* when, after she has shot herself, her husband sits down with Mrs Elvstead to rescue the manuscript of the genius Lovborg whom Hedda has driven to his death.)

Strindberg interested me less than did Ibsen. Before I knew German I was taken to see his *Totentanz* (*Dance of Death*) in a Berlin theatre. I understood not a word but the play held me by the very intensity of its emotion.

In my student days I played with the idea of becoming an actor. I knew that I had little chance of success; for one thing I could not have got rid of my Scottish accent, and few Scots are required in the play world. I know I had some talent but not enough to make me reach the stars; also, I am sure that I would have jibbed at being told how to act by a director. My face was not of the brand that gets laughs and to be a comedian was out of the question. Looking back many years it occurs to me that I might have felt that acting was not creative enough; it was like working out a geometrical rider that someone else had set, like playing a piano and not composing the music. Chopin will live when the players are long forgotten – Pachmann, Solomon, Rubinstein; their gram records will wear out. Oddly enough a character in fiction might outlive the real virtuosos. In *Young Man with a Horn* by Dorothy Baker, a vivid characterisation of a trumpeter whose life was said to be founded on the life of Bix Beiderbecke, the authoress makes her hero so real that we almost hear him playing his horn. I have read the book four times.

Whatever the cause, I renounced any ambition to go on the stage and I have never regretted it. In a way, I did become an actor, speaking to thousands of students and parents and teachers. At first I had stage fright and had a phobia that I would stick and not be able to go on speaking; hence I used notes, but for many years have never needed them.

My pet aversion is the man who reads his lecture. Lecturing is an art, a trick if you like. I had an uncanny knack of feeling an audience; when I got on to the platform I knew if the audience would approve or not. The trick in lecturing is to hold your audience. One of mine was to tell a funny story if people looked bored or rustled. Once in Scotland I faced a grim crowd with set faces.

'What's wrong with you lot,' I said, 'you all look dead, so I take it you are all teachers.' Laughter and they were with me. On another occasion I began: 'I feel guilty. When I knew I was to speak to teachers with all their respectability I did a cowardly thing – I put on a tie.' I took my tie off, and again the ice was broken. So I did become an actor after all.

I have had odd chairmen in my time. Once in Scotland my chairman was the headmaster of the local academy. When I sat down he got up.

'Now the lecturer will be glad to answer questions but I warn any of the staff who are here that I won't have them trying to bring this man's ideas into my school.' There were no questions. In Johannesburg in 1936 the professor who took the chair was notorious for falling asleep on every public occasion. It was partly because he kept awake all through my lecture that South Africa treated me as a VIP. (It wouldn't today.) I once had a chairman who was vague about my name. 'I am sure that you will join me in welcoming the celebrated educationist Mr . . . O'Neill.'

The best chairman, no, host, I ever had was a rich man in a York town. 'I am not interested in education and won't come to hear you and I'll be in bed when you return. You'll find all you need at your bedside', and I did, whisky, brandy, beer.

What I liked most when lecturing in South Africa was that, in every town, my chairman was the mayor and behind every town hall platform was his room with a bar filled with rows of bottles. What I disliked most was the racialism; black teachers were not allowed to attend my lectures except once in Brakpan, a suburb of Johannesburg with a broad-minded mayor.

Once in Stockholm the hall could not hold half those who wanted to hear me so the church opposite was asked if I could speak there. Yes, but on condition that I did not mention religion or sex. It sure cramped my style. It was an odd feeling standing in a pulpit with a large Bible on the desk in front of me. The worst lecture I ever gave was in Oslo where each sentence had to be translated right away. Of course I kept losing the thread of my discourse.

I never had the gift of extemporary speaking. Even today if, at a dinner party, I were asked to propose the health of the ladies I would be terrified. My father could stand up and make a speech

157

about anything but I never had his talent in that line; I can only lecture on what I know, my work.

I cannot recall ever giving a witty answer to some interruptor. I hadn't the quickness of the suffragette who answered the shouted taunt: 'How would you like to be a man?' with a soft: 'How would you?' I once answered a question in a way that I regretted later. It was in Kimberley I think, a woman asked: 'Should I tell my child who his father is?' 'Yes, if you know', I said, and immediately kicked myself for being cruel at a poor woman's expense. With that exception I have always answered questions civilly.

WRITING AND
CRITICISM

One of my greatest pleasures is writing, or rather typing. By and large I write as I speak, without purple patches, without an involved prose style. How much I was influenced by George Saintsbury, with his aversion to the ornate style and euphuism, I cannot guess. His own style was bad, full of parentheses and digressions – a fault I have myself but I did not learn it from him.

Style cannot be taught, it is you. True, one can learn about punctuation and grammar but not about what might be called creative writing. Spelling I never had any difficulty about. I am sure that it is primarily visual. If I am not sure of the spelling of *niece* I write down *neice* and at once see which is correct. But again the theory does not always work. I have a boy of fifteen who reads all day and late into the night. He cannot write a line without a mis-spelling. My American pupils have difficulty with exams in England. Possibly some examiners do not know that in the USA 'traveller' has one l, 'humour' is 'humor' and so on. By the way it takes about two years in Summerhill for an American pupil to say: 'I am going to take a bawth' instead of a 'beth', but no American changes his or her: 'I have bin' into our 'been'.

And that brings me to a friendly argument I have had with my American publisher who changes my infinitives into split ones. Does the USA split its infinitives? To me 'He tried to correctly speak' sounds barbarous, just as the new pronunciation – con-TROversy, forMIDable, desPICable – offends me. At the same time I grant that it is pedantic conservatism on my part, for there is no ground for retaining the time-honoured tradition of the pure infinitive. In Latin amare is to love, and one cannot split amare. Another piece of pedantry is in the matter of punctuation. I always put a colon before a quotation. Every publisher I have had changes the colon into a comma. Shaw was the only writer strong enough to insist on his own forms: he refused to have any apostrophes; he wrote dont and not don't.

Why do I write? Why does anyone write? When a mountaineer was asked why he wanted to climb Mount Everest he replied: 'Because it is there'. Maybe I write because my typewriter is here, but that answer is not enough. I write because I feel I have something to say, something that others might find interesting, because I think I have a message, but a novelist or dramatist writes for other reasons, artistic ones.

Some authors have a hostile attitude to their publishers. I never had. In 1915 I wrote a series of articles for the *Scottish Educational News*. I sent them to a well-known London publisher and got a reply from Herbert Jenkins. He said that the book was too radical for his respected firm but that he was setting up his own firm and would gladly publish my *Dominie's Log*. For many years Jenkins published my books. His most famous client was P. G. Wodehouse, whose books must have been the main support of his business.

I had one big fight with Jenkins. He would change my style. If I wrote: 'I am tired,' said Mary, he changed it into: 'I am tired,' said Mary, *wearily* or *bitterly* or what not. He died comparatively young of cancer. He took no exercise; sat in his office for seven days a week.

The name of Harold Hart, my American publisher, should live if only because he saved Summerhill. In 1960, when he published *Summerhill*, we were down to twenty-five pupils and wondered if we could carry on. The publication of the book brought the invasion of American pupils and eleven years later the German translation brought the Teutonic invasion. In the preface of *Summerhill*, *For and Against* he tells of his struggle to get the book on the market; he spent quite a few grand on publicising it because he believed in it and was ready to take the risk.

I wonder what other authors do with their original manuscripts. I never once asked publishers to return mine to me, possibly because I knew they would never have any value to posterity. Had I kept my press cuttings these last fifty-seven years they would have filled a big room. I read them and then destroyed

160

them, whether they called me a genius or a corrupter of youth.

One of my chores has always been correcting proofs. An author should not correct his own proofs; he has a blind eye for minor points – mis-spelling, wrong punctuation, etc. I once heard an argument in an editorial room in Scotland. One man said that a typesetter was so mechanical that he did not know what he was setting up, and said he had proved it by giving a typesetter his own obituary; the man did not notice it. I think my informant was a liar; no man could miss his own name.

Proof-reading must be the dullest job on earth. Few ever get gems to spot, gems like: 'Queen Victoria pissed over Waterloo Bridge on her way to Westminster'. In 1913, when I was helping the editor of a washerwoman's weekly to read the proofs of a short story we had to cut a sentence. The heroine had been deserted by her unfaithful lover and, feeling suicidal, 'knew that she would never find happiness until the sod had covered her'.

A supererogatory piece of advice to young writers. Always keep a copy. Wasn't it a maid of Ruskin's who threw the MS of Carlyle's *French Revolution* into the wastepaper basket? Think of the agony of rewriting a book. When I insert the carbon copy wrongly and have to retype the page I feel furious.

It suddenly strikes me that maybe I use writing in order to think. There is something in the old phrase 'Put it down in black and white'. Certainly I think more clearly when I sit typing; why, I cannot say. It may be that print itself has a certain power, and this would account for a million Babbitts accepting the opinions of their daily newspapers. Babbitt* never knew what to think until he read his daily paper editorial, and I guess that applies to most of the voters in our fake democracy. Hence, when I look at what I have typed I may unconsciously think it is of importance because it is in print. Handwriting is the youngest brother, the inferior, only to be used in minor essays at writing, like letters to relations, letters ordering coal. In fifty years children at school will all type and the art of handwriting will die out. Pity, for, as one who can write beautiful copperplate, I would hate to see the art die. I know that today handwriting does not seem of importance. My pupils smile in a superior way when I show off my copperplate. Damn

*I am re-reading Sinclair Lewis' *Babbitt* for the fourth time; Babbitt, the picture of all the stupid and money-made middle-class men in the USA. His period is nearly fifty years ago but he still lives. In two lecture tours I met him again and again, in buses, on trains and planes, the genial, soulless Babbitt who thought that a glade of forest and lake was wasting good space for garages and restaurants and villas.

the new generation, it won't give us old uns any opportunity to swank in pride.

Writing maketh an exact man, said Bacon. It may do so but I see little proof that it does. Too many say too little in too many words. It was when I worked on the one-volume encyclopaedia, that I discovered the propensity writers have to spread themselves. I would ask some authority on history to give us two hundred lines on Cromwell. His MS would come to one thousand words and my job was to cut it down to size, excellent training I admit, which, I hope, showed in my own writing later. I like the story of the Scottish boxer who promised to wire his wife the result of his fight . . . OKKO saved sixpence on the telegram. I prefer 'He went away in anger' to 'He made his departure in a mood of considerable annoyance'. Brevity may or may not be the soul of wit but it does keep a reader awake.

In 1913 I wrote the sections on mathematics and English for T. C. & E. C. Jacks' *Self-Educator*. I had never dared to read it since it was published until I took it up recently to see what a presumptuous, ignorant fool I was then. Some of it is not at all bad. Writing on bumptious style I give the following:

'Lucy in vain sought the dreamy realms of Morpheus, but the dismal wail of feline wanderers kept recalling her to the stern realities of a grim world.'

My comment then: 'This is merely a flowery way of writing: "Lucy couldn't sleep because of a cats' concert on the tiles".' I also wrote that when I want the gardener to cut the grass on the back green, I do not write: 'Dear Mr Jones, please bring your keen blade and see to it that the sward is shorn of its luxuriance.'

In those days one was taught that repeating a word was bad style, so that news reporters, describing a visit of the King to Balmoral used the words King, His Majesty, our Royal Sovereign, in a four-line papragraph.

Even today I think that I wrote a lot of good sense about the mechanics of writing. The part I blush for is that on authors. I am sure that little of it was original but, after so many years, I cannot even guess the sources from which I cribbed it all. Shakespeare: 'He is no innovator . . . He is a conventional citizen with a conventional citizen's innate snobbery; his great ambition is to be a country squire at Stratford-on-Avon. Democracy he has no sympathy with; he ridicules popular leaders like Jack Cade; he almost invariably makes his working-class characters rogues or fools. He bows the knee to pomp and rank . . . Shakespeare appears to have no definite criterion for life . . . "Out brief candle . . .". . . his outlook is frankly that of a hedonist.'

Robert Burns: 'There is hardly one of his poems which is at once simple without being commonplace . . . His idea of freedom is platitudinous, a man who prided himself on being a Jacobite was not a democrat. He was not a deep thinker; he was ruled by heart, not by intellect . . . let us grant that he was a genius, though artistically hardly more than inarticulate.'

Mein Gott! Years later at a Burns supper in Edinburgh I said that Robbie was toasted and celebrated in Scotland, not because of his poems which few read, but because he was the symbol of the unconscious of Scotland. He was celebrated because he did all the things that repressed, Calvinist Scotland longed to do and did not dare to do, fornication chief among them. The audience did not applaud me.

Reading the pages I keep marvelling at my then erudition, or rather at the ability to take ideas from other men and pretend that they were my own. I dimly recall sitting for days in the British Museum Library with piles of books at my elbow. Nothing can have been at first-hand. I wrote of Donne, Herbert, Vaughan and Cranshaw and I am sure I never read a line of any of them. I was on better ground when I dealt with Spencer and Milton, for I had read much of them. If I were a millionaire I'd reprint my time-dishonoured section on English Literature as a warning to the young who by nature rush in where angels fear to tread.

It may be that that contribution to literature killed in me any desire to be a scholar, and I am sure that I would have been a poor one. I lacked judgement, and could never have been a dramatic critic. I recall being invited to apply for the job of drama critic by an evening paper in 1913. It gave me dress-circle tickets for a revue and for a play by Sardou – *Diplomacy*. It is mentioned in the *Self-Educator*. 'In *Diplomacy* there is a trifling pseudo-detective story of a bad woman's treachery. The characters say nothing of importance; they talk cheap platitudes . . . to an intelligent playgoer the play is boring.' I then go on to compare it with *A Doll's House* in which every character lives. I fancy the review I sent in was similar to what I wrote later. I praised the revue and Ethel Levy, the star. I didn't get the job. I asked why. 'Our readers aren't the kind to want analysis of plays and characters. They want to know if the play is a good yarn with lots of excitement.'

No. I could never have done it. In my days I have seen several Hamlets . . . Forbes-Robertson, Martin Harvey, John Gielgud, and recently Richard Chamberlain. I could not possibly decide which of them were good, mainly because I never knew what kind of man Hamlet was meant to be. It strikes me that no one else knows either. His own opinion of himself as 'a rogue and peasant slave' I discount.

But soft. I could have torn many plays to pieces even then. The artificial plays of Pinero, T. W. Robertson, H. J. Byron, Henry Arthur Jones, for then I was completely Ibsenised. It is said that a dramatic critic is a failed dramatist, and there may be some truth in it.

'He who can, does; he who cannot, teaches', Shaw again. How many teachers of English ever write a good book? How many school art teachers ever have their pictures in good galleries?

I could not have been a scholar because a scholar by necessity deals with history, with other, usually dead writers. My wish was to deal with the living, the growing, the children of tomorrow. The scholar of the cartoonist is a bowed old man with a dead face standing in a library of dead books. The man who coined the term bookworm must have had considerable perception. If scholarship is so important why don't the voters elect teachers and professors to rule a country? Homer Lane was no scholar but I make the guess that what he did with problem children is infinitely more important than the scores of books written by scholars. Edwin Muir, a fine poet, regretted that he had not gone to a university, but Willa, his wife, explained that he had missed the community living in a university rather than the scholarship.

Sour grapes. I do have an uncomfortable feeling that I missed the scholastic bus.

164

PROSE AND POETRY

          I have never liked reading poetry, I cannot say why. Some poems have attracted me – Gray's 'Elegy', 'The Ancient Mariner', 'Kubla Khan', 'The Hound of Heaven', 'La Belle Dame', 'Sohrab and Rustum', Meredith's 'Love in the Valley', 'Omar Khayyam', Shakespeare's Sonnets, Drayton's 'Since There's No Help, Come, Let Us Kiss and Part'. I never cared for Robert Burns and modern poetry leaves me cold; much of it could be written as prose. I have joyed in word painting: Shakespeare's 'And look, the gentle day Dapples the drowsy East with spots of grey', 'And look, the morn in russet mantle clad, Walks o'er the dew on yon far eastern hill'. And I like Oscar Wilde's verse in 'The Harlot's House':

> And down the long and silent street
> The dawn with silver-sandalled feet,
> Crept like a frightened girl.

I quoted it to a visiting American professor of literature. He called it phoney but I do not know why.

My preference has always been for prose. I am humbled by George Douglas Brown's descriptions in *The House with the Green Shutters*: 'He was a great fellow, my friend Will; the thumb mark of his Maker was wet in the clay of him'. Gourlay had a chest 'like the heave of a hill'. His anger 'struck life like a black frost'. I like the style of Mary Johnson in her novel *By Order of the Company*, a tale of the days of James I and the colonisation of

165

America. She caught the pictorial language of the period. No one today would write: 'Death is not more still than in this Virginian land in the hour when the sun has sunk away, and it is black beneath the trees, and the stars brighten slowly and softly, one by one.'

A phrase written by a student at St Andrews over sixty years ago has always stuck in my mind:

'Sometimes I am a grey-hooded monk who has renounced the world with love and music and all its vanities, till one day the scent of roses is blown into my face, and I find myself weeping' (R. L. Mackie). It must have been my Calvinist origins that fixed that quotation in my mind for life; terrible religion saw to it that the scent of roses did not come our way.

I never could stomach the wit of Gilbert in the Gilbert and Sullivan operas. To me it was shallow and cynical. In the *Self-Educator* I wrote: 'Gilbert's wit is based on a superficial view of society . . . Shaw, on the other hand, thinks society rotten at the core.'

I quote this not because Gilbert is of any importance, but because it reminds me that at the age of twenty-nine I was already beginning to form values about what mattered in life. Gilbert ragged society while he approved of it; Shaw disapproved of it and I was on the side of Shaw. That may have been the beginning of my challenge to life. It was at that age that Shaw and Wells were my favourite writers; possibly they had more influence on my career than all the later psychologists had. And yet, in hindsight, Wells always disappointed. He laboured a theme like the planlessness of the planners, and I kept looking for the solution that never appeared. When a solution came it was no solution at all, as in *The Shape of Things to Come*, where, after a terrible war, the world was saved by a group of scientists. I wonder what Wells would have made of the scientists today with their pollution and H-bombs and the ruin of natural life, plants and animals.

Shaw had no solution either. His brilliant analysis of society led to no promise of a new society. It must have been their analysis without synthesis that made me lose interest in Shaw and Wells. They dated themselves; neither accepted the dynamic psychology of Freud. I write this acknowledging that I have dated myself. I cannot accept the psychology of Skinner and Pavlov and Watson. Scientology seems Greek to me and I suspect it is something phoney. I have no idea what the word Existentialism means. Every man must date himself in one way or another. I like to think that I have not become dated in education.

CHANGES I HAVE SEEN

'Time you old gipsy man,
Will you not stay,
Put up your caravan just for one day?'

The wish of everyone, I fancy, to return to
pleasures long dead. It has never been a strong wish with me.
Nostalgia is not one of my virtues or vices; I can return to the
haunts of my boyhood and feel no emotion whatever. So with
tomorrow; it gives me no thrill to imagine that one day in my
native town of Forfar some town council may put up a brass
plate on the house in which I was born, 16 East High Street.
(Unlikely; I guess that very few Forfarians ever heard of me.)
Posterity means nothing to me. As Sam Goldwyn said, or rather
as some wag who attached his wit to poor Sam said: 'What has
posterity done for me?'

But to get back to that caravan and the refusal of time to stay,
I have seen many changes in my long life, not only in material
things like motors, films, radio, TV, but what one might call
cultural things, changes in human outlook. In my youth, we had
to wear costumes when bathing, and sex and swearing were taboo.
When Shaw's play *Pygmalion* was produced with Eliza Dolittle's
'not bloody likely', every paper printed the word as b . . . y. Today
even the highbrow papers will print words like shit, fart, fuck.
But why good old Anglo-Saxon words were considered obscene
I never knew. 'The permissive society' is a phrase often used
today. The adjective is objectionable; it suggests that authority is
permitting when youth is demanding, not seeking the permission
of anyone.

I have lived to see a great release of sex in women. In my early days a woman was not supposed to have any pleasure in sex, a belief sponsored by many women who had no orgastic life owing to the ignorance or selfishness of their men. Today women openly acknowledge their demand for as much freedom in sex as men. Virginity has lost its air of sanctity. It was not a woman who coined the phrase: 'A fate worse than death'.

In my lifetime the world has become more sinister, more dangerous, and here I am not thinking of hate and conquest wars, I am thinking of the diminishing power of the people and the growing power of the big businesses, the combines, the dehumanisation of industry. At the beginning of the century small businesses were common. The boss was Bill Smith who knew his hands and their families. Today workmen have no Bill Smith to approach with any difficulties they may have: they have the great bureaucratic, humanless company.

In Leiston I can go to a small factory and ask for the manager but what American can seek an interview with Mr Sears or Mr Roebuck or Mr Henry Ford? The class war has become centralised, the workers pitted against the great international combines who win the battle. And get the praise when the workers get the blame. Recently in England the postal and electrical strikes angered the nation of householders. 1984 is only a few years ahead of us.

The changes in education have been too slow for me. Anyway I have said all I have to say about education and am making no new discoveries about children and their psychology.

I think that in Summerhill we do not have the usual generation gap. Visitors ask: 'Who are teachers and who are pupils?' Though gap there would have to be if drugs came into the school. To take drugs is to escape from a miserable life, and it is the easy way. I am afraid that, instead of seeking freedom by living naturally, youth will use the quick method of the trip, and we cannot be moral about it.

Freedom in schools has grown, but not so fast as belief in book learning and examinations; the old patriarchal demand for obedience and discipline is as strong as ever in all state systems.

My pupils today seem to me to be less communal, less able to grasp and practise self-government than in the past. Some get too much money from their parents, so that saving for a rainy day is something unknown to them. Today I don't see the young, even those in their twenties, saving money. It burns a hole in their pockets. This may be due partly to the insecurity of modern life with its wars and crimes and hatreds and its possible ultimate nuclear destruction – much of diplomacy is of the eighteenth-century kind, so that in a war between Israel and Egypt backed by Russia the USA could be dragged in to wage a war that would end with the destruction of humanity and all life. Statesmen, like all of us, are more irrational than rational. Fundamentally the change in youth must be due to its loss of faith in age, in authority, in power, and for that I can cry Hurrah to the new generation.

I have lived to see – I won't say the death of God since there are many millions of Moslems and Catholics around – lived to see the decline of Protestant religion. In England the churches are not full; youth is largely indifferent to organised religion. It does not believe in sin and heaven and hell. Its gods are more or less harmless – pop stars, disc jockeys, football heroes – but the 'new religion' has one characteristic in common with the old: the hate and violence between the supporters of football teams compares with the hate and violence in religious Ulster with its Roman Catholic and Protestant teams wanting to murder each other.

It is a known fact that with age comes conservatism. Reds at twenty are blues at fifty. Without patting myself on the back I think I have escaped becoming conservative. That does not mean that I have accepted the mores and tastes of the young; its pop music and its monstrous dancing tire me, its jazz is not my jazz of the Bix Beiderbecke period. And youth's taste in literature is not mine.

Gulfs are inevitable. If conservatism means retaining what is past I am a conservative about, say, silent films, but to me it does not mean that; it means refusing to look at new facts and factors, following father's footsteps, supporting reactionary habits and measures. Britain is full of conservatives whether they label themselves Tories or Liberals or Labour. To me a conservative is one who accepted the dictates of father and hence all authority, and as I say, even the young radicals often later regress to follow the old Oedipus tradition. I missed that. I have not compromised on anything I considered fundamental. When I lecture to students I often feel that I am the youngest guy in the hall, and that is not self-deception. One compromises, becomes conservative when one has not enough belief in what one is doing or thinking, when one lacks sincerity, integrity.

Symbolically I have always been unconventional about dress and behaviour, and they put me out of the dining-room on the liner to Cape Town in 1936, when, crossing the Equator, I entered without a jacket for lunch. 'Captain's orders, sir.' Later I read of a cruise where two passengers, banned by the captain, called a meeting and were upheld by the majority vote. The captain gave way. The men were both Lords. I was mister.

My dislike of all that conservatism stands for possibly takes me too far. I hate being in a company with good manners, standing up every time a woman rises from her chair. One cannot be a democrat and a gentleman at the same time, not the gentleman of high society anyway. The men I meet in our local pubs have better manners than many guests I have seen in the Ritz or the Savoy. I hate insincerity in speech or in manners, and all our hat-lifting and door-opening is insincere. Executives do not open doors for their secretaries.

I do not like to see men with long hair or even beards. Here I am conservative, but on the other hand I like youth's freedom in dress and language. I have always disliked girls' make-up. Reared in the country where the dairymaid's beauty was real and natural I have never been able to see any beauty in a made-up face. To see ageing women trying to beat Father Time with rouged lips and cheeks is one of the saddest spectacles I know. No one is deceived. At the same time I know that it isn't fair to compare the dairymaid with the women in the city office, breathing polluted air, seldom seeing the sun.

IGNORANCE, FAILINGS
AND AVERSIONS

I have no idea how glass panes are made, or razor blades, or watches. How do they make the thread on the screws of a wristlet watch? My ignorance about books is abysmal, especially foreign books. I know more about tools although never a good craftsman; too impatient possibly. The letters BA do not make me think of a university but of a BA (British Association) thread on a radio set. In spite of getting a high mark in my final exam in History at the university I know hardly anything about it. My Hons Degree in English Literature has no significance; my views on Keats or Milton are not worth a scrap. I am ignorant about politics and finance. Statistics make me flee. When I lectured in the USA there was always some earnest questioner - 'Mr Neill, what percentage of children under ten are interested in mathematics?'

I am ignorant about psychology. Where does the truth lie? In Freud, Jung, Reich, Marcuse, Fromm, Rogers? Is sex repression the main cause of world wickedness? If Adler's power motive is right why do the masses have no power and no desire to obtain it? If original sin exists why aren't we all crooks and murderers? For fifty years I have run my school on the assumption that environment is the main factor in conditioning human behaviour, but I get two brothers, one is social, the other antisocial. True the environment is not exactly the same for both; it does not counteract the jealousy in a family. I have to conclude that environment is not enough, and sadly accept the fact that no one can do a thing about heredity.

It may be because of my ignorances that I like to ask folks about their jobs. I can listen attentively to a beekeeper, a farmer, an explorer but not to a teacher. I would like to ask an explorer a question I have had more than once from kids – how does one in the Arctic Circle do his business? Does he take his pants down in the deep freeze? I would like to ask a historian another kids' question – what did people use in the lavatory before the invention of paper? History to kids means answering the most interesting queries.

One of the regrets of my life is that I never learned French. In books most French passages are not translated; German ones are but I don't need them for I can read German. In my youth I learned small Latin and less Greek which are long forgotten. I learned German simply because my stay in Germany compelled me to. I cannot speak it well, for I have never mastered the articles – der, die and das. I taught maths for many years but today have no idea what modern maths means. The truth is that I am not educated.

I cannot understand philosophy. I have not read widely, only one book by Goethe and one by Nietzsche. The classical philosophers are Greek to me – Socrates, Plato, Aristotle, Kant, Hume. So with art and music. I cannot understand why Van Gogh's 'Yellow Chair' and Cezanne's 'Apples' are great art. I have no idea what counterpoint is.

Does ignorance matter? They say that maths teaches one to reason, but I have yet to see a school staffroom in which teachers rush to the maths man for advice. Most of us know nothing of zoology, botany, astronomy, mathematics, physics, philosophy. Charlie Chaplin did not need to know about the Wars of the Roses; Jack Nicklaus I am sure could not do a simple equation. I guess that the he-men heroes of many a Hollywood film (mostly Fascists by the way) would not know who wrote *The Inferno* or *Ghosts*. It is a fallacy that knowledge means power. I have known men who seemed to know everything, and understood nothing. Of Wilde's: 'A cynic is one who knows the price of everything and the value of nothing.' I am not saying that knowledge is valueless. My old pupil Professor Gordon Leff writes thick books on medieval history and spends many hours researching in places like the Vatican Library. It is his job to know, and knowing, to understand.

Folks who overvalue knowledge should read reports of law cases in which specialists contradict each other; as the old phrase has it: Doctors differ, but if knowledge were factual differences

172

would not appear. Knowledge is always conditioned by emotion. My knowledge of South Africa is scant; it is based on my lecture tour there in 1936 when apartheid was everywhere. I saw it as a crime against black humanity but some of the professors and teachers I met took it as a good and necessary system. It is not knowledge but emotion that makes many American citizens see Vietnam as a barbaric crime hidden behind a treaty with South Vietnam. Often very knowledgeable men are anti-Semitic, using their knowledge to rationalise their hatred. No wonder is it that the masses distrust the intellectuals; the trade unions of the USA are against the students.

Nay, it is not to know, it is to feel, and all the university degrees in the world do not help one to feel. The ideal is to know and feel at the same time. In my own case it is not my knowledge of psychology that helps a kid; it is my ability to be a kid again myself and see his point of view. 'Genius is the power of being a boy again at will', said Barrie. Not genius, which can mean anything, just ability, talent if you like.

So that I do not regret my plethora of ignorances. I know enough to let me carry on my job. To understand Einstein would not help me a bit when Peter is stealing from our larder. I won't say that ignorance is bliss but it is not a calamity, else we should all be morons. Some knowing ones solve the London *Times* crossword in seven minutes. It takes me at least ten minutes to solve one clue. They are walking encyclopaedias with phenomenal memories, but I wonder how many of them are original in thought or creative in their work. And, alas, they symbolise our education system; learn and learn, mostly about all that does not matter in life.

Philosophy means the study of what is important in life, and, as we all have different interests, our philosophies are legion. That makes for universal misunderstanding. How could my philosophy of life make any contact with that of, say, Governor Reagan, or Ted Heath, or a racialist? When you get a national philosophy as in Russia the individual ceases to exist, so maybe we should rejoice in having all our individual philosphies, even if and though they lead to class murder as in Kent University. I think my own philosophy, by and large, is to let people live in their own way, and really this sums up Summerhill. I have written again and again that no man is good enough, wise enough to tell another how to live, but I am conscious of the fact that by running a school with freedom for kids and then writing about it I am assuming that I am trying to tell readers how to live, meaning that I am conscious of being a humbug.

173

I have a privy fault – an expression taken from one of the Restoration dramatists, possibly Congreve, where a lord remarks to a guest, referring to the pretty maid who brought in the wine: 'She hath a privy fault; she farts in her sleep', a lovely neat way of betraying his relationship with the maid. I have a privy fault. I hate being opposed, and this is generally called a god-almighty complex. When I used to lecture I disliked the wise guy who got up and contradicted what I had said, disliked him intensely when I felt he was right. Tin gods don't make mistakes or at least do not acknowledge them.

I think I have too much imagination. More than once I have got in a panic. I had a short correspondence with a well-known writer in which I called him an anti-life unhappy man. Then I thought: 'Oo, is that libellous?' I saw myself in a law court being cross-examined by a clever barrister. I wondered how many thousands of pounds the damages would amount to. I am sure that it was my imagination that made my boyhood days so full of fear. The country bumpkin walked in the dark and thought perhaps of cows and corn, whereas the dark had all sorts of evil men for me. My mother was fearless but she had no imagination. I have long got over my fear of policemen but if a cop comes to the school I feel my heart flutter . . . now what have my kids been up to? In nine cases out of ten he is giving a foreign child his passport back.

I fear getting involved. The title of the German edition of *Summerhill* is *Theory and Practice in Anti-authoritarian Education*, the publisher's title, not mine. Various young Germans try to use the book in their fight for communism or social democracy or what not. I tell them that the book has nothing to do with politics. Politics mean democracy. Democracy, the votes of the masses castrated in their cradles. Without the castration we might get politics that were sincere and pro-life. All my life I could never catch crowd emotion. I could never wave a flag, never shout a slogan, never become active in any party, political or otherwise. A rank individualist dealing with crowds of kids.

I have no dignity in my job, but dignity comes out at certain times, when choked off rudely by a cop when I park in the wrong place, when I go walking in the woods with my dog and a shouting gamekeeper bawls me out. In both cases my dignity is offended, mainly because I am in the wrong. On such occasions I cannot laugh at myself.

I am not one of those brave ones who thunder: 'Do you know who I am?' No copper would know me anyway. I don't like this

174

component in myself; it belongs to the little man part of me. My annoyance may have something to do with uniforms which I detest, associating them with state power even if they are uniforms of innocent postmen. Dogs, by the way, hate men in uniform . . . ask your postman about that. Hitler's goose-stepping troops scared me in Germany. If I lived in the USA I fancy my uniform complex would be stronger. In 1948 I waited for a friend in a New York car park. He was late. I wandered round looking at the cars. A hard grip on my shoulder. A cop with a baton. 'What d'ye think you're doin'?'

'Just looking at the cars.'

'Oh yea?' His voice was nasty, and I began to fear he would run me in as a suspect.

'They are bigger than our cars', I said easily, '. . . in England.'

He softened. 'Oh, you are English.'

I disapproved of the New York cops with their guns and their swinging sticks, their arrogant indifference when asked the way. Here I'll be national and say that the London bobby is a much more friendly and helpful cop than his equivalent in New York, but a few thousands of coloured people in London might give a different picture of the London police force. I read in some paper recently that to put on uniform is automatically to become a Fascist, an exaggeration to be sure, but there is an element of truth in it.

Like many others I have always had a complex about my own name. Alexander was contracted into Alec but Clunie as a small child could not say Alec and called me Allie, which made me ashamed because a girl in my class, Allison, was also called Allie. 'Oo you've got a lassie's name.' More than once I have known married women who hated to have lost their maiden names, and quite early in life I discovered that many a woman was pleased when I called her Mary or Susan. In spite of Shakespeare there is something in a name.

I have no dignity about dress. I am never well dressed and dislike having to wear a suit and tie at a graduation ceremony. At a party I would rather be the only one not in evening dress than the only one in evening dress. I am indifferent about changing my shirts and underwear and wonder if the Nazis adopted the black shirts so that they could be worn for weeks on end and never show dirt. With a cold bath each morning for the last sixty years I take it my underwear won't get too smutty. The dignity of the London business men with their bowler hats and striped trousers amuses me. Poor devils, it is their only way of looking like gentlemen, while the artists and film directors have no need of outward dignity.

Consciously I have no racial feeling about Negroes or Jews or for that matter Scotsmen. Consciously I have no respect for titles and royalty or for presidents and politicians. I like Robbie Burns'

> 'The rank may be the guinea stamp,
> A man's a man for a' that.'

But rank has its advantages. On my passport I describe myself as author and not teacher; I get a deeper bow from the immigration guys. A teacher is not a gentleman.

Not having been reared as a gentleman I have found handicaps in social life, not only ignorance of table manners and drawing-room conversation but in such things as tipping. To this day tipping annoys and puzzles me. In restaurants the ten per cent is easy, or is it? Some waiters look askance at the ten per cent. So with taxis; one can reckon a percentage, but what about a porter who carries your luggage? When I lived in Germany fifty years ago a railway porter had a fixed charge, so many marks a case . . . it came to be about half a million DM for each case. That was the time when I won second prize in a State lottery and had to go to Berlin to collect my win. As the train fare from Dresden exceeded my win I did not collect it. I think it was about two million marks.

I always disliked hotels, partly because I never knew whom to tip. The whole tipping system is degrading to tipper and tippee. I don't know if the rumour is true that the head waiter in a West End hotel pays the management a hefty sum for the job. Could be. Certainly the system must save managements much money in wages. Like all non-gentlemen I fancy that I over-tip to protect my ego, yet I often leave a tip under the plate when I know I shall never see the waitress again. It is said that the aristocracy give smaller tips than the commoners. I once saw a lord in Forfar Station give the porter who had handled his many cases a tip of tuppence and the porter seemed to be well pleased.

I have had one tip in my life. As a private in the Scots Fusiliers I was ordered to deliver a letter from the colonel to his lady. She criticised me for not going to the back door but gave me sixpence.

I am not mean with money, only careful after a boyhood minus money. Scots really have a money complex. Like myself, many over-tip, an overcompensation for the alleged Scottish meanness, but I doubt the story that when Sir Harry Lauder used to cross to America first class he tipped the dining-room steward sixpence.

Nor do I give any credit to the story about the Scottish-American millionaire Andrew Carnegie. Andrew was sitting in a small room lit by a candle, when a young man came to ask him how to get rich.

'Oh,' said Andrew, 'then we can speak in the dark?' and he blew out the candle.

I am selfish about certain things. I don't like my car to be driven by anyone else; I never lend my typewriter, and my workshop tools are part of myself. I am comfortably off but when I get an appeal for money for some home for poor children I do not subscribe, rationalising that I need all my money for my school. I pass a beggar in Oxford Street and two minutes later enter a shop and buy tobacco at over eight shillings an ounce. Last night on TV we were told that three-quarters of a million have been killed in the Sudan war in the last three years. I felt no emotion. Distance kills emotion. If a thousand were killed in Suffolk I would have a lot of emotion, for the personal component enters . . . 'God, it might have been me'. Sure, I am writing about the material mostly, things especially, but how selfish am I in other ways? I find it almost impossible to condemn, but that is mainly due to long experience with psychology and motive, seeing in crime a sick person behind it who cannot control impulses, but again, suppose one of my little pupils were raped and murdered by a sex maniac, I fancy it would be hard to be objective then.

I am, however, unselfish with my time. I have seen and listened to thousands of visitors who had as a rule nothing to give me; they came to get from me, and I saw them patiently without, I think, a deep anger at being pumped dry, yet, here again, what is behind my patience? My armour, my facade? Neill cannot destroy his image as a nice guy who offends not even the rudest visitor? Could be. See what I mean about self-analysis? Even if we can face our faults we make the most of them in a masochistic way.

My greatest aversion is for the Roman Catholic Church. I hate it as violently as H. G. Wells did. To me it is anti-life. It is paternalism writ large. It would be comic if it were not tragic, that a Pope who never had a sex life orders millions of women not to use the Pill. I cannot associate the R.C. Church with Christianity. The savage beatings that go on in Catholic schools in, say, Eire must be expressions of bottled-up sex coming out as sadism. Christ did not say: 'Suffer the little children to come unto me . . . and get beaten up'. But why organised religion degenerated into hate of

177

life I cannot guess. I do know that Nietzsche was right when he said that the first and last Christian died on the Cross.

It is a perversion of Freud to say that when one has a violent dislike for something or someone it betrays an unconscious desire for that something or someone. Utter bosh. The logical conclusion would be that Jack Nicklaus who lives for golf hates the damn game unconsciously. Wild analysis, as Freud put it. Hence I cannot believe that my hate of Catholicism indicates an unconscious desire to flee into the arms of Mother Church. Maybe the world will not find happiness until the last religion is dead, and here I include the ugly C sisters – Capitalism and Communism. But then I can never accept anything by faith.

Like Reich I dislike small talk and gossip, and that is one reason why the new kitchen sink drama leaves me cold. Characters talk and say nothing. *Waiting for Godot* bored me; two tramps talking, just talking. Drama should be in movement. I grant that much of Ibsen is conversation, but conversation that is depicting character all the time. In a way the Godot tramps are simply saying that the world is very sick, but I cannot recall hearing any suggestion of doing anything about it. The doctor in *An Enemy of the People* tells the little Norwegian world that it is sick but he acts; he does something about it. It is because so many TV plays simply diagnose via dialect that I find them very boring, but my boredom extends to the many famous comics who have their wisecracks written for them. The wrong man always gets the kudos. The man who drives a car at three hundred miles an hour is a hero, but no one knows the name of the car designer.

I simply do not appreciate most comics. Chaplin, Buster Keaton – not Harold Lloyd, he was only an acrobat – remain for me the criterion of great clowning and fun. I can see no one today on screen or stage who can equal them.

I cannot stand the warbling voices of the women singers that are dragged into every TV show, though I love listening to opera singers – men or women – whose voices are so much better than the average soloist.

Another aversion is the TV commercial. The play stops and soap powder spoils the whole illusion. The only advantage of a TV ad is that it gives you the opportunity of going to the lavatory.

I have always hated cards. In my youth one was expected to play whist and later bridge. Many a partner must have hated my guts for I could never concentrate, being more interested in the players than in the game. Betting has never appealed to me, and horse racing wearies me, although I watch show jumping with

178

interest. I abominate performances with animals and keep wondering what cruelty goes on in their training. Years ago Jack London's *Michael, Brother of Jerry* gave me a hate of training animals for life. I cannot believe that a lion will walk along a wire because its trainer is kind. It sickens me to know that leading aristocrat members of the Royal Society for the Prevention of Cruelty to Animals in England hunt foxes and shoot deer. I was glad to see that Reich had notices all round his Maine estate banning hunting of any kind. America with its million shot-guns must spread infinite pain over the countryside. Guns and Christianity seem to go together.

I know the usual reply of the animal killers: 'You eat meat, don't you? You let others kill for you.' True indeed. Even Bernard Shaw did not get his shoe leather from animals that had died naturally. It is a good point and a fair one. The answer that our animals are killed suddenly and painlessly is certainly some kind of rationalisation, so that in protesting against hunting I am being a bit of a humbug. It is possibly the idea that killing is associated with sadistic pleasure that troubles me. As Macaulay said: 'The Puritans hated bear baiting, not because it gave pain to the bear, but because it gave pleasure to the spectator.' Humbug I may be but I know I would find a Spanish bullfight revolting.

An odd feature is that, in spite of hunting and killing, the people of England are in the main animal-lovers, and more money is raised for animal than for child protection. Recently an Alsatian guard-dog nearly killed a child, and a policeman shot it. The child's parents had scores of letters accusing them of not looking after their child and causing the death of a dog. In England a dog's life seems to be better than a child's life.

I never was a games man, neither player nor watcher. I hardly ever saw a football match until the World Cup appeared on TV and then I began to admire the skill of men like Pele and Bobby Charlton. Cricket has always been a mystery to me; it is an English not a Scottish game. I took up golf when I was a student and the irons were rusty and the shafts of hickory and the balls were floaters. I never was good and I never cared if I beat my partner or not.

One of my pet aversions is the man or woman who writes asking to visit Summerhill without enclosing return postage. Each reply costs me three new pence, the old sevenpence. Not long before he died I wrote to Bertrand Russell for some information, and although I had known him for over forty years, I enclosed a stamped addressed envelope. American correspondents are kind;

179

many send return envelopes with USA stamps on them, yes, even professors and doctors. Perhaps they really have the idea that American stamps are valid all over the globe – or should be now that the USA is the super power.

I do not like politicians and wonder how a politician can be honest. If I were an MP and my constituency consisted mainly of Catholics or Baptists I could not dare to support a bill legalising homosexuality or abortion. If I were Prime Minister of Britain and thought the Vietnam war was a crime against humanity I would have to give public support to the USA for reasons of arms and dollars and what not. The reply: 'I keep myself in abeyance; I speak for the people who elected me', suggests to me a man of no principles and no guts. If one of my old pupils became a Prime Minister I should feel that Summerhill had failed. Politics mean compromise and free people are very bad compromisers.

POLITICS AND
PIONEERING

Originally my politics were mixed up with emotion. When I threw that tomato at Winston Churchill and missed I was prompted by the bonny daughter of the local Tory chairman. Winston was then a Liberal candidate. In 1913 when I first went to live in London I joined the Labour Party and spoke ignorant rubbish in Hyde Park.

After the Russian Revolution when reports told of new freedom in schools and sex I fondly imagined that Utopia had suddenly arrived for good, but, as a canny Scot, I did not join the Party. For years I had a blind spot; I simply would not accept the stories of Stalin's mass murder by starvation of a million or more peasants who would not fit into his State farming scheme. But I did wonder why Bolsheviks of the old brigade were confessing to crimes they had never committed before they were shot in the back of the neck. The truth is that I *wanted* to believe in the new order; I wanted to think that the new education in Russia was wonderful, hence my blind eye. My disillusionment took many years.

In 1937 I applied for a visa to visit Russia. It was refused, no reason being given. By that time I had given up my hope that Communism was a cure for world sickness. I ceased to be interested in politics of any kind, but voted Labour in the belief that it was more pro-life than was Conservative, and I still hold that belief in spite of my disappointment with Labour rule.

Part of our world sickness stems from the attachment we have to the unessential, the trivial. People dare not take themselves or life seriously because it would be so appalling that they could not face it.

The millions who watch football or watch TV can think of nothing of moment – again see our daily press. Our highbrows read good journals, see good plays, and, since my readers belong to that class, I have to consider what such folks want to know about me or anyone else in the public eye. One snag is that they are for the most part liberal. Latin: liber = free. Here I stick out my neck and say that too many liberals are free only in their heads, not in their guts. A Tory will say about Summerhill: 'All wrong' but a liberal will say: 'I'm all for it, but . . .' In Britain, politically, the Tories and Liberals are of one mind in supporting the capitalist system, but I am using the word liberal in a wider sense. One must concede that most of our reforms have come from liberal legislators – abolition of slavery, of capital punishment in Britain; our new British laws about abortion and homosexuality were sponsored by liberals, or maybe I should say left-wingers. I fear that often liberal means middle of the road, because it is associated with the middle classes. I am told that some of the blacks in the USA distrust their white liberal supporters intensely.

Here it may be that the term liberal is attached to the intellectuals, those who think a lot and do little practically. Educationists like Carl Rogers, John Holt, George Dennison, might be classed as liberal men but they do something about what they believe in.

I have no politics but I vote Labour partly because of emotion, partly because Labour is against class distinctions. I should really vote Tory because the Tories will never give up their public schools. And as long as Eton and Harrow exist my own school is safe. Good old private enterprise!

I feel that the Labour members of parliament are more human in the main. But in Britain Labourites are not Socialists, or at least they cannot introduce Socialism to a country that does not want it, hence the limitations of a Labour government.

I have often been called an anarchist running an anarchist school. This puzzles me because a school with self-government, making its own laws, does not fit into the definition of anarchism. Chambers' Dictionary defines it as 'the want of government in a state'. So what am I? Just a rebel, a protester? Nay, I don't protest: I try to find practical solutions. More than once I have confessed that I am no intellectual, no great thinker. When I think out a reason for an action, I most likely give the wrong one. When the kids complained that Naomi stank and I told her her face was too clean, she took a bath, but even today, forty years later, I have no idea why I did it or why she reacted to my criticism. Intuition? But what is that anyway?

I was not really conscious of politics until in 1950 I applied to the American Embassy for a visa. I had already lectured in the USA in 1947 and 1948 and the 1950 tour had been arranged by Reich. I was kept waiting for an hour and suspected that something was wrong. Then I was called before an official.

'Are you a Communist?'

'No, I am not.'

'Have you ever written anything in favour of Communism?'

Then I knew he had phoned the Home Office and asked for my dossier.

'I have written about eighteen books but I never read them and have no idea what is in them, but I have a vague idea that I praised Russian education as it was after the Revolution. Then it was for freedom but today it is like your and our education, against freedom.'

My application was refused and my lecture tour cancelled. These were the McCarthy days of course.

I recall saying to the consul: 'I am a communist in the way Jesus Christ was one, communist with a small 'c'.' He gave me a look of shock and I guessed he was a Catholic. I found out later that he was. The sequel came when in December 1969 Orson Bean invited me to go over to take part in the Johnny Carson TV show. Again I went to the Embassy.

'It won't take more than twenty minutes, Mr Neill, please fill in this form.'

Question: Have you ever been refused a visa by the American Government? I sighed and wrote yes, in 1950, which meant that the twenty minutes was more like two hours. I was asked to fill in the complete form, and then more waits, more interviews. Finally I was given a visa for four years, and the annoying thing was that the consul said: 'We have no record of your being refused a visa.' Then I felt like kicking myself for my useless honesty.

But this is gossip, not politics. I know that some have to deal with government, finance, foreign policy. I know that democracy is phoney; our last election in Britain gave the Tories a majority but Labour and Liberal combined got more votes than those cast for the Tories. But since the alternative to democracy is dictatorship we cannot give it up. It is all so sinister. When I see on TV the primary elections in the USA with their infantile parades and bands and flags I feel dejected and hopeless. I see behind them the self-seeking lobbyists, the rat-race of Capitalism. When a President makes some gesture – Nixon going to China, for example – who knows what the motive is? Some Americans say he is thinking of the next presidential election. Some say in England that the government soft pedals its support for Israel because it has its eye on the repercussions among the suppliers of Arab oil. International politics are a dirty game and home politics can be likewise.

The Tory government is hiving off industries that the previous Labour government nationalised, a paying one like Cook's Tours. The old saying was that trade follows the flag. It is the other way round; often trade seems to control politics. The three political parties in Britain are against apartheid but if any party tried to stop relations with South Africa the trade lobbies would kill any parliamentary bill. A few years ago an American writer, Wright I think, wrote that if the Vietnam war were suddenly stopped forty per cent of American industry would collapse. Britain and the USA sell arms to both the Israelis and the Arabs.

No, I cannot see the honesty in most politics or politicians. I wonder how many great politicians have been great men. Lincoln perhaps, Churchill in the war years. Great men do not seek power. The little men are the Hitlers and Mussolinis and Stalins; the great ones are creators, the Bachs, Rembrandts, the Shakespeares, the Einsteins, the Freuds. None sought power. The Lord Mayor of London is never a workman; he is a rich business man. I doubt if any plumber could put aside his tools and take on his duties in Mansion House. There can be no real democracy when we have rich and poor.

My politics are confined to our school democracy, which is as near real democracy as it can be. We meet in a big room and make our laws by general show of hands. I know that this system could not be applied to the mass of voters across the country, yet to me a democracy in which one man is supposed to represent the opinions of thirty thousand is a fake democracy. I am aware that many politicians do much good work. I grant that many have made humane rules. What puts me off politics is the indifference of the ruling people, whatever their party.

In Britain our prison system is a disgrace. Men are treated with little humaneness. They are deprived of sex, of culture, of everything that makes life life. The barbarous system is accepted not only by politicians but by the clergy, the doctors, the lawyers, indeed by people in general. A well-fed judge will sentence men to thirty years for robbing a train and no politician protests in parliament. Another judge will sentence a murderer to life imprisonment which in practice means nine or ten years.

It is because politics do not deal with crying evils that I cannot arouse any enthusiasm about them. Schools beat kids and the politicians turn a blind eye even if they don't approve. Politics deal with what is material – trade, building houses and schools and hospitals; they do not touch humans as humans. The government will build a new school with all modern appliances and then leave it to some headmaster to run with the cane if he is that sort of criminal. When parents complain about their kids being beaten the magistrate in most cases sides with the caning teacher.

I renounce politics because they do not go down to depths. Because, even in a Socialist government, they are powered by the Establishment, the defenders of the status quo. The politicians tell us that the laws they make apply to all whatever their class. Yes, it is true; a tramp can sleep on a seat on the Thames Embankment and so can a duke.

I suddenly realise that I am quite proud of having been refused a visa by the USSR and by the USA. Maybe my claim to immortality.

I have been called a pioneer, and if a pioneer is one who does not accept crowd values, I suppose I am one. The pioneer always stands alone and is usually hated by his professional tribe, as for example Galileo, Darwin, Simpson, Freud, Reich, all of course in a category far above mine. 'The strongest man is he who stands most alone', but I fancy I have quoted Ibsen too often in my books. New ideas come from individuals; Marx was greater than the Fabian Society; Simpson was greater than the diehard doctors who rejected his chloroform. The prophet's voice always cries in the wilderness. And that makes me pessimistic about humanity. For man is a herd animal and herds seek leaders – God, Hitler, Franco, Billy Graham, even a super-swindler like Horatio Bottomley. Men are like wolves, pack animals. They are also like sheep and cattle, but only the dog-wolf herd makes man a pack leader. To my dog, Biscuit, I am his pack leader. If I go away he lies on my bed and will not eat, while my cats never miss me. Not being a zoologist I do not know why other herd animals do not make men their substitute leaders. Sheep, horses, cattle do not. It may be a question of grey matter.

It could be argued that the world is sick because man is gregarious. It is significant that the editorial in a paper is called a leader. It is the herd instinct that makes us desirous of being acknowledged by our flock. 'I have got colour TV but the Joneses haven't.' It is herd display that makes women spend billions on showing off their jewels and dresses, and men are no better with their Jaguars and Rolls Royces. The word competition means doing better than the others in the human pack, and the same argument applies to the evil Eleven Plus.

The powers above cleverly exploit our herd instinct. It is a platitude today to say that they castrate children by making them fearful of authority, make them guilty about religion and sex, so that when adult they are neutral sheep with no guts to challenge anything. Hitler castrated a nation but our overlords are much more subtle; their equivalent of 'Heil Hitler' is Law and Order, which means the defence of property and the stifling of life.

Our schools' chief function is to kill the life of children. Otherwise the Establishment would be powerless. Would millions of free men allow themselves to be sacrificed in causes they had no interest in and did not understand? How many GIs in Vietnam today could tell what the war is all about? If men were not castrated in childhood would millions work for poor wages when their masters were spending a worker's weekly wage on a lunch or sporting a £10,000 car? Down with Capitalism! Let the Workers take Control! They did in Russia. Utopia had arrived at last. A world without profit and class. That was 1917. Today, 1972, the workers are sheep led by not so gentle shepherds at the top. It alarms. Does it mean that the herd instinct is so deep that no political system can counter it? Does it mean that for ever man will be led to the slaughter whether it is symbolic – low wages – or to napalm war against another nation? Is the future of humanity one of slaves ruled by an elite of powerful masters?

But now let me be more optimistic. In fifty years of free children, I have detected not only an absence of the competitive spirit, but also a total indifference to leaders. One can reason with free children but one cannot lead them. True, my pupils lived in their own herd but not with leadership.

A headmaster can be, indeed is, a father figure but no child can make its school self-government a father figure. I say that the future success of the world will come from the rejection of the father, the crowd leader. Most people accept father and mother, meaning that the great majority joins the Establishment, the anti-progress and usually anti-life majority. Our school systems, whether capitalist or communist, foster this early moulding of the masses because wolf leaders are tough and powerful and ruthless and their main aim is to kill and eat. In the human herd we have it in replica. The wars for gold or oil or what not, the take-over bids which often make thousands unemployed, the bludgeoning of the young by sadistic cops. If the people were free such barbarities could not live.

What I do know is that as long as his long helpless childhood is conditioned by adults who accept the crowd attitude to life, man will not be free. It is good to see so many young people challenge in the West, but so depressing to see a TV film on China when a million children wave their little red books, their individuality crushed out in their cradles. Communism is the super manipulator of mass psychology; the crowd does not think: it feels. In history it has beaten the thinking ones to death, viz. the intellectuals in USSR asylums.

I know that the herd instinct can never be abolished. My concern is to see it so modified that it will cease to be a danger. Man seeks freedom and at the same time is afraid of it. Many Southern slaves were scared when they were given freedom. Old lags, after a long stretch inside, find life outside terrifying. Yet I like to think that in a thousand years the masses will have modified their crowd instinct so that competition will have been overcome by co-operation, hate by love, pornography by natural love. There will be no more lone wolves, only leaderless pack wolves seeking a common good.

PSYCHOLOGY

A word of warning to would-be therapists, amateurs. Do not try to use therapy on your friends or, most dangerous of all, on your wife and family. Art teachers are often guilty. 'That picture of yours shows that you hate your mother and want to kill her', the picture being one of a child with an axe trying to chop down a tree.

History, said Henry Ford, is bunk. Symbolism surely is bunk. I doubt if any interpretation of a dream ever helped anyone to health. It is eclectic. A bull a father image? In my boyhood it was a real horned fear object. I fancy that most therapists have dropped symbolism by now. Possibly also dream analysis, the royal road to the unconscious according to Freud.

Coming back from the psychoanalytic atmosphere of Vienna in the early twenties I thought that analysing was the answer to the problem child. I spent years analysing dreams of such children and was proud when a boy who had been chucked out of, say, Eton for stealing went out of Summerhill cured. It took me a long time to realise that Bill and Mary who had also been expelled for stealing but refused to come to me for analysis, went out cured also. I had to accept that it wasn't my therapy that cured; it was freedom to be themselves. A most satisfactory belief, for, even if therapy were the answer, the millions of kids in the world cannot all have it.

I think I had more success with the psychology that is not found in text-books. When I rewarded a bad thief by paying him a shilling for every theft I was not acting on theory – the theory came later and may have been, if not wrong, inadequate. The thief was unloved and was stealing love symbolically. I gave him a token of love in the form of a coin. The point is that the method worked again and again, but I know the situation was complicated. How much did his new freedom in Summerhill help to cure him? How eager was he to be accepted by his peers as a good guy?

When a new boy broke windows and I joined in the fun I was not reasoning. Later came the explanation: Bill wasn't breaking windows; he was protesting against adult authority, and when I joined in it put him on the spot . . . authority breaking windows? Looking back I think it was a bit unfair to spoil his fun. The simple explanation of the methods I used may be that I thought of the wrong way to treat a kid and did the opposite. Stealing – the cane or at least a moral talk in conventional schools. I made it non-moral. A boy had run away from three schools. On his arrival I said to him: 'Here is your fare home. I'll put it on the mantelpiece and when you want to run away come and ask for it.' He never ran away from Summerhill, but was it because of my attitude or the pleasure he had in being free for the first time in his life?

I have had successes but also failures. When in Dresden I told a Yugoslav girl that she was using too many nails making a box she spat at me, 'You are just like all the bossy teachers I have had'. I couldn't make real contact with her again. When giving out pocket money I said to Raymond, aged nine: 'You are fined sixpence for stealing the front door', and he burst into tears. I should have seen that he was a mental case before the incident. Telling the nine-year-olds a story about their own adventures I made Martin steal the gold we had found. Later he came to me weeping. 'I never stole the gold.' From then on I made none of them baddies.

True, I laboured under a severe handicap, for I was therapist plus headmaster. At a general meeting I'd say: 'Who the hell took my twist drill and left it to rust in the rain?' It was Willie, and in his next PL Willie shut up like a clam; I was the nasty policeman. A therapist should have no social connection with a patient, but when a Freudian or a Kleinian walks out of a cocktail party because a patient is present I think him a narrow-minded psychological snob.

I was not always the winner in the early days when Summerhill had so many crooks. One asked me for my autograph. I did not notice that the paper was folded until a local shopkeeper showed

189

it to me. 'Please give bearer fifty Players cigarettes – A. S. Neill.' For weeks Dick kept selling me stamps and only the accident of my having stained one with green ink made me aware that he had been robbing my stamp drawer. I gave him five shillings reward for his cleverness, childishly showing him that he couldn't take the old man in. Old man? I was in my forties then.

I doubt if I could use the reward trick today with a thieving pupil. There is a sophistication in the new generation; it is intangible. The new orientation in youth may stem from the spread of knowledge about psychology. Some of my older pupils, the Americans especially, juggle with terms like inferiority complex, mother fixation etc. If today, at one of our self-government meetings, a boy were charged for destroying books in the library and I made the proposal that he be appointed chief librarian, I am sure there would be a cry of: 'One of Neill's psychological tricks again'. No child would have said that forty-five years ago.

I am rather proud of the fact that in fifty years of Summerhill I know of only two old pupils who sought analysis, proud also that in that time no pupil has been brought before a juvenile court, and in the first twenty years we had many problem cases.

The new therapies of the behaviourists – Watson, Pavlov, Skinner – alarm me: 'We are the wise guys; we know how to condition kids for their own benefit.' Squeers did not say that; he practised it, as did the savage heads of our public schools for years. Of course the new conditioning is not harsh, not cruel. It is logical; rats and pigeons can be conditioned, so why not children? What troubles me is that Skinnerism could conceivably be used in a Fascist state whereas Summerhill could not. Years ago the editor of *The Daily Worker*, then the English Communist daily, was reported as saying: 'If we got Communism in England the first thing we would do would be to shut Summerhill'. Naturally I am not accusing Skinner and his tribe of being Fascists. I am just afraid that Fascism would accept the technique and adapt it to its anti-life ends. It could never use Summerhill in that way.

So where do I stand, in my old age, on therapy? I am against it because it is beginning at the wrong end. I do not deny that it can have its merits. A therapist said to me: 'My patients learn to treat their children more sensibly'. That can well be, if the therapist is for freedom. I cannot guess what effect an analysis by an Establishment doctor would have on parents. I am certain that Freud himself did not believe in freedom for children. He remained a paternalist. Remember that most patients seek therapy because of their own complexes, not because they want to rear their families unneurotically.

I have often wondered how much my psychoanalysis helped me, even the best of it: Reichian vegetotherapy as he called it then. The results cannot be fully assessed. I think it made me capable of seeing the attitude of other people, meaning that it increased my charity. For instance, when I have to sack anyone, my misery is largely due to my asking myself how *I* would feel if told I wasn't good enough, but an un-analysed person could have similar feelings.

Today the word therapy makes me think of Hermann Goering's: 'When I hear the word *Kultur* I reach for my gun.' In my time I have met dozens of people treated by all schools of psychology, and their therapy had not apparently changed them into active, creative, happy people.

It is a sad fact that the vast majority of psychologists deal with private patients, and that by and large therapy to them means treating neurotic adults lying on couches. How many Freudians have said: 'The roots of neurosis lie in childhood. I shall deal with children and tell their parents how not to ruin them emotionally'? A meagre few that I know of – Anna Freud, Susan Isaacs.

What fools we were about therapy in those days in Vienna. We were so naive. Make the unconscious conscious and the world will be a Utopia without greed and hate and crime and war. So we kept being dug into and digging into others. We never paused to think that many important people had never had analysis; Freud himself was never analysed. Great doers, great thinkers, great artists and writers had had no therapy – Beethoven, Goethe, Milton, Einstein, thousands of them. I feel that in a way they analysed themselves in their art, e.g. Blake and van Gogh. If Wagner had had analysis and had discovered what a cad he was with his anti-Semitism and his hate for others, I wonder what effect it would have had on his music. If art springs from the unconscious I wonder where *Tristan und Isolde* came from. Meaning that we are at the stone age in psychology.

One disconcerting feature in therapy is the constant undeclared war between the various schools. The Freudians for the most part dismissed Reich as a fake. A Kleinian won't see any truth in what an Adlerian says. They label themselves and when one labels oneself one ceases to grow. One is inclined to look back – What did the Master say? Today there is much wrangling among Reich's followers: 'We alone realise what the Master meant'. I am bragging when I say that, although I have been a disciple more than once in my life, I have managed to steer free of idolatry. My motto is: Take from each what you want and reject the rest, and never label yourself as one of a school. I'd hate to think that long after I am dead teachers will call themselves Summerhillians. They will thus advertise the fact that they are dead.

SEX, REPRESSION
AND PORNOGRAPHY

I call myself normal sexually, even though I
fancy I have subordinated sex to ambition. In my student days
the nice girls were taboo. 'Who touches me marries me.' So we
students picked up shop-girls, girls from the working classes. I
never once went to a prostitute – maybe because so many
enthusiastic amateurs were around. It was all wrong, all degrading.
Once after intercourse with a shop-girl on Blackford Hill she
began to cry. I asked her why.

'It isn't fair', she sobbed. 'You students take us out and we like
your manners and educated speech, but you never marry us. I'll
have to marry some workman who can only talk about football
and beer.'

That was the end of my picking up shop-girls.

Twice I nearly got married. Both girls, like myself, were of the
lower middle class. I hesitated. I was in love but reason crept in.
You want to do something important in life. Will she be able to
keep up with you? Stupidly I tried in both cases to educate them,
gave them books, talked of Shaw and Wells and Chesterton, of
Hardy and Meredith. I think it was the old snob complex my
mother had given me, transferred from social climbing to cultural
climbing. Also there was the economic factor. I was not earning
enough to support a wife and family. It would have meant settling
down for a lifetime as a country headmaster, far from city life and
culture and a career in literature. Emotionally I was wrong but I
could not act in any other way, not with my grandiose – though
unformulated – plans for success.

I got little pleasure in hole-and-corner little affairs: they were sex without love, without tenderness. My Calvinistic conscience must have made them dirtier and it must have been that conscience that more than once made me impotent. Indeed I sometimes wonder how anyone reared as a Catholic or a Calvinist can ever get away from the sex guilt inculcated in early life.

In Hellerau I danced with many a pretty girl but remained fancy-free. Violent passion was not for me and that is why I came to marry a woman older than myself. One of my pupils in King Alfred School in London was Walter Lindesay Neustätter, now a well-known psychiatrist. His father was Dr Otto and his mother was an Australian, who had been a music student in Leipzig. I got friendly with her: she had the same views on education as I had, and was well-travelled and cultured. Walter and she went to stay with Otto in Hellerau, and I have told how she became matron of my department there and in Sonntagberg, and later in Lyme Regis. After her divorce from Otto I married her because of the school: I had to be respectable. But there was another motive; she was an alien and had to register with the police, and, as a Britisher, she was full of misery and resentment. I made her a British subject. My life was full with my work and we got along splendidly. She loved travel and we went on trips to Germany, Italy, France and took cruises. I was always slightly annoyed at the expenditure; I would much rather have spent the money on a precision lathe or a shaping machine, yet the travel must have enlarged my outlook.

She worked hard and was as important in the school as I was, just as my wife Ena is today. I have been lucky with two wives who were wonderfully competent and understanding.

But to get back to sex, during the period of my first marriage the obvious happened. I fell in love with a pretty young Austrian. Then the miserable hole-and-corner business began. I had to lie, inventing trips to London to see my publisher or my agent. We stayed at out-of-the-way hotels, scared that someone we knew would enter the dining-room. On country walks we hid our faces when motor headlights shone on us. We registered at hotels under false names. It was hell, hell and damnation. Then my wife discovered the affair. Weeks of wretched argument and cruel words. I thought of walking out and living with my new love. I didn't. Again the conflict between love and my job. To have gone with Helga would have wrecked the school. And I think now that at my age then, nearly fifty, my love passion was that of what is often called the middle-age climacteric, the final attempt to

194

renew youth and romance and passion. I loved Helga, but not enough to sacrifice my work. She married a man of her own age and I am afraid she would not have been satisfied with a father substitute.

I have said that I will not write about people now living – Helga's name wasn't Helga – and I will say nothing about my second wife, Ena, barring that it was a love match, and Zoë, our daughter, a love child born in wedlock. Sex at my age is academic. As my doctor brother said just before he died at the age of eighty: 'We end where we began. As babies our penises were only for peeing with, and at eighty they are just the same.'

In a way my married lives have been easy compared with the married lives of those who live in a house and not a community. Many marriages are wrecked because of propinquity; couples are too much together, and in the best families characters clash. In a school there is no time for clashing; the common task binds together. Many men in Britain complain about women entering pubs, for the pub is about the only place where a man can get away from his family. Homes are full of ambivalence, love and hate, but the community is comparatively free from character conflict.

At Summerhill, the sex question has always been a pain in the neck. For many years I have advocated a sex life for adolescents, for any couples who are ready for it, but I had to make a *Verbot* in the school because even Summerhill cannot be free of the Establishment with its Victorian morality. The only thing I could do was to tell the kids frankly what my position was, and they realised that I was not taking a moral standpoint. Reich wrote about the sexual misery of the adolescents but I think that was an exaggeration, at least with the middle classes I have dealt with. The farthest we could go in Summerhill was to make masturbation a natural process and thus was allayed many a guilt in anxious children. We managed to destroy the shattering belief that many children have that they alone are guilty of this awful deed. Some American psychologist wrote many years ago: 'Ninety-nine out of a hundred masturbate . . . the hundredth won't tell.'

Yet, of course adolescents in Summerhill must have slept together in a school in which there is no teacher going round with a flashlight of evenings. How we have escaped pregnancies in fifty years I do not know. One explanation may be the strong feeling the kids have about the fate of the school. There may have been pregnancies that I never heard of, but I cannot believe that any parents would have hidden the news from me.

In one of my books I tell of a time when a few adolescent girls asked me if they could be fitted with Dutch Caps. I told them that I couldn't do anything without the consent of their mothers. I wrote to the mothers. Only two in six agreed and the whole six had been in the school from the age of seven or eight. That was forty years ago and I wonder how many mothers today would say yes. What I was preaching fifty years ago, he said proudly, is now accepted as normal by many parents.

The Little Red School Book, made illegal by a magistrate in London, advocated the setting up of contraceptive slot machines in school corridors. What optimism!

Looking back now I wonder if the handicap in my love life came from Calvinism or from the fact that one could never have a sex life with middle-class girls. In my youth contraceptives were just coming in and were not considered safe. In a Scottish small town virginity was priceless; an illegitimate child was an eternal disgrace and precluded any chance of getting married. Only the ploughmen and the farm lasses fornicated and often had two of their bairns at their wedding later on. I was a son of the village schoolhouse and could not make love to the dairymaids. The lower classes had very little guilt about sex but in the middle and upper classes sex outside marriage for women was sin against the Holy Ghost. In my native town quite a few married men fornicated around, but there was one law for men and another for women. Women had to be pure.

Mind you, I was an outsider, and, for all I know, there may have been a lot of sex among the toffs I saw playing tennis or riding horses. I was rather innocent in those days.

Earlier on I told of the time when my sister Clunie and I were beaten for sex play. As Reich's betrayal of his mother coloured his entire life, so, I fancy, did this beating have a most sinister effect on my own sex life. It bound me psychologically to Clunie till she died in 1919. It made the genitals the centre of the greatest wickedness. I never had any symptoms of homosexuality but I wonder if some homos could date their condition to some early incident that made a girl, and subsequently all girls, taboo.

One odd fact about sex was that in all my many sessions in analysis I never could remember when I began to masturbate, and to this day have no idea about when I gave it up. Repression with a vengeance.

To be in the swim I should write about the topic of the day, pornography. It was always there. In 1900 shabby men asked us to buy dirty postcards. Few do today; the sexy weeklies do the job for them. All I have to say about pornography is that the only cure for it is freedom from an anti-sex education. The ultimate cure for all pornography is, climate allowing, a civilisation in which we all walk about naked, in which sex has no connection with guilt. I am reasoning from the fact that the Catholic Church, the super sex repressor, is shocked by nakedness. You should have heard the Dublin priests who had seen a Summerhill film on TV with boys and girls bathing naked; you should have heard what they said to me about it in the TV bar where, by the way, they showed no inhibitions about very large whiskies and brandies. I saw more drunks on Dublin streets that weekend than I had seen since the days in Scotland when whisky was two shillings and sixpence a bottle, and on a Saturday night the town was full of drunks. God seems to approve of drink but not of sex.

In my younger days I was as pornographic as anyone else, possibly more so with my Calvinist background. At the university my stock of blue stories was a matter for envy, and although I says it as shouldn't I was a good story-teller. If I could remember even one of the stories today I am sure I would reject it as being witless and unfunny. Fifty or more years ago a Councillor Clark was in all the newspapers. He went round bathing resorts measuring women's bathing costumes. Even in those pre-Freud days we all felt that there was something unhealthy about his eagerness, and in these post-Freudian times we are apt to suspect that the anti-porn puritans must have a dirty unconscious attitude to sex. The man who ruined Oscar Wilde, Lord Alfred Douglas, in his old age nosed around for books to send to the Public Prosecutor. I had written a review of the diary of a homosexual and the publishers asked me to be a witness for the defence. It was 'Bosie' Douglas who cross-examined me.

'Look at page 58, paragraph three. Is that in your opinion pornographic?'

'If written in a public lavatory, yes, but as an illustration of the author's attitude to life, no.' Of course he won his case. I recall reading that Barrie, D. H. Lawrence and James Joyce hated sex stories. Barrie wrote a play *What Every Woman Knows*, but none of his female characters in his novels and plays had any sex, or knew anything about it. The same goes for Shaw but to a lesser extent.

The time-honoured defence of the blue story is: it isn't the dirtiness I like but the wit; even the so-called commercial traveller's jokes about waterclosets were rationalised. And, to be

just, there are blue stories that do have wit and climax. This one
for instance, one that no publisher would have printed twenty,
even ten years ago. A curate was talking to his parishioners. At
the end he said he would be glad to answer any questions. A
pause, then a woman in a mild voice asked: 'Do they have babies
in heaven?' Her husband, sitting beside her, said *sotto voce*: 'Do
they fuckin' hell!'

'One question at a time, please.'

Now to me there is nothing pornographic in that tale, although
it possibly would not be funny for anyone who had been reared
without heaven and hell. So that, fundamentally, there is an
element of sex repression in it. I tried it on some friends in New
York and it fell flat, for the Americans do not know the fuckin' hell
phrase, just as they know not the word bloody. Granted that a
curate would not be likely to say he wanted one question at a time.
Here I think of the chestnut about the deaf judge. 'Before I
sentence you', he said to the man in the dock, 'have you anything
to say?'

'Bugger all, me Lord.'

Judge to Clerk of Court: 'What did he say?'

'He said "Bugger all", me Lord.'

'Really, I could have sworn that I saw his lips moving.'

A judge would not of course accept the words 'bugger all' as
proper court language. But then every good story depends on a
switch from the normal. The incongruous enters. The Scots
ploughman fornicating with the farm girl. 'For Christ's sake,
Jean Broon, spit oot thae jujubes and tak an interest in what's
going on.' Redolent of the earth like *The Ball o' Kirriemuir*, which
I am sure J. M. Barrie chuckled over in private.

The modern, frank attitude to sex will in the end kill the porn
joke. I am told that the latest Chambers Dictionary has all the
four-letter words. Now the danger is that the sex puritan will
make excrement and sexual intercourse obscene words.

Does repression account for the non-sexual joke? What repression am I letting loose when I watch Chaplin dive into a
foot of water in *Modern Times*? Or see Buster Keaton lean on a
ship's life belt and watch it sink as it strikes the water? The incongruous need have no connection with repression, meaning
that humour is beyond analysis in spite of Freud's rather heavy
analysis of humour as letting the cat out of the bag. Scottish
humour is generally the expression of what the Englishman
considers the root of Scottish nationalism – meanness about
spending the bawbees, and it is likely that it was a Sassenach who

invented the tale of the Scots farmer. His second daughter was being married.

'Aweel, I doot we'll have to buy some confetti, for it was rainin' when Maggie was married.'

I have an idea that Scottish stories are in the main less pornographic than English ones. So many of them depend on portraying character. The Forfar to Dundee train is filled with farmers on market day. One sees a stranger sitting opposite.

'Ye'll be gaein' to Dundee?'

'No, I am not going to Dundee.' Pause.

'Ye'll maybe be gaein' to Kirkbuddo?'

'No, I am not going to Kirkbuddo.' The farmer leans forward: 'Do ye think I care a daum whaur you're gaein'?' Again a yarn that is not founded on repression.

I have been dealing with children for fifty years in an atmosphere of comparative freedom from sex repression. No child would moderate his or her language in my presence. I never hear them tell each other sex stories. In our local cinema a chamber-pot on the screen raises a howl of laughter but none of our pupils see anything funny in it. I have no contact with adolescents in the outside world and have no idea if they are as guilty about sex stories as past generations were. It may be that there has not been much advance here, for sex repression is still a powerful factor in society. On the other hand when BBC TV showed our adolescent girls bathing in the nude, no paper protested at pubic hair being shown on the screen. (How many pious letters the BBC had I cannot guess.) Things are moving in a sane direction.

The censorship campaign of our holy Willies and their female counterparts is futile and stupid. The answer is not censorship; it is rearing children with an open, amoral orientation to sex. I asked a few of my old pupils if they would go to see a porn show and the usual answer was: 'Too boring'.

Nudists often claim that nudity gets rid of sex repressions. I don't know. I asked a woman nudist what would happen if a young man got an erection. 'That happened last week and we chucked him out. A man who can't control himself shouldn't be in a nudist camp.' Nudity does not seem to be the answer either.

It is believed that pornography is for the young, that when a man's sex glands atrophy, his interest in sex diminishes accordingly. This sounds logical, and then I recall Homer Lane – 'Have you ever noticed that at a leg show the stalls are filled with bald men?' Last week a bookshop was fined for selling forbidden sex

199

books to what the papers called, quoting the judge: 'Dirty old men'. Some think that women are less interested in pornography than men. They aren't; it is rather that they have suffered more from sex repression. In a studio audience a risqué joke seems to appeal more to women than to men, to judge by the delighted screams.

WOMEN

I never understood women. What man can understand them? In some ways they are a different species. Clothes alone show the difference between a man and a woman. A man has pockets – and by the way one can almost tell a man's character by what is in his pockets. Here I turn out my own – scissors, pliers, multi-bladed penknife, pen, tobacco pouch and pipe, loose coins. A woman cannot carry such articles even if she is mechanically minded; she has at most one pocket.

A man knows the delight of pre-intercourse sex play but has no idea how a woman feels about her side of the play. I grant that if I had been reared in a pro-sex atmosphere I would have had a better understanding of the psychology of women, but as it was, women to me were beings apart, protected by a rigid sex armour that deceived the male youth. In my ignorance I thought that the shocked look a woman gave when I told her she would make a great bedfellow was genuine; I did not realise that underneath she felt it a wonderful compliment.

In my youth women were put on a pedestal and we did not realise that their feet were of common clay. I must have been about twelve when I read of a woman being killed in a train accident and I thought it could not be true because women were not human like men and not liable to fatalities. And that in spite of the fact that I had four sisters and saw their virtues and faults. Having sisters did not help me one bit to understand other women. The family sex taboo applied to the lassies over the

201

garden wall; they were all the untouchables, mysterious, unattainable.

A mere man can never understand the enormous importance a woman attaches to dress and appearance. If all men were like me the women would be wasting their time and money, for I never see what a woman wears, and at the moment at my desk could not tell what colours my wife and daughter are wearing. I see only faces, eyes in particular. I never see ankles and when some bitchy girl in my school made a remark about another girl's thick ankles I looked and saw them for the first time – she had been in the school for ten years. This feminine concern with outer appearance is slightly depressing.

Men like to be esteemed for their activities, their success in business or academics or acting, meaning that in the main they are less shallow than women. Their rewards are more permanent.

A woman may glory in her latest hat while a man may glory in the prize he won for the largest cucumber in the village Flower Show.

The difference in values must have some bearing on the political scene. A woman may vote for a handsome film star sort of candidate but I doubt if many men would vote for a beautiful film star if she stood for election. It is this difference of values that makes it impossible for a man to understand a woman, or for that matter a woman to understand a man. Men lack the frailties that make cosmetics and dress important to a woman; they feel more manly, the exhibitionism of women gives them a status.

Sixty years ago I had an affair with a woman in London, one of the upper class. She was always in the height of fashion. When we went dining in restaurants she insisted that I came in my frayed Norfolk jacket and my uncreased flannel bags. 'They look at the pair of us and then look again because of the incongruity of the partnership.'

'Meaning', said I, 'that they look at you?'

'Naturally', she smiled, and I learned about women from her. But not enough. To this day if I am in hospital I prefer to be given a bedpan by an oldish nurse than by a young pretty one. I know it is a complex – pretty girls are shocked by raw realities – but it stems from my early life; another proof that the rational cannot destroy what was acquired emotionally ages ago.

How ignorant, how stupid youth is. At eighteen I fell for a bonny lassie who did not react to my advances – I learned later that she was a Lesbian. Her sister was plain. I cultivated the sister insanely thinking that she would tell her beautiful sister what a fine guy I was. I was blind to the fact that she hated her sister like hell. I used to think that the way to a girl's heart was paved with compliments, and it took me a long time to discover that another man won her heart by telling her what a nasty bitch she was. It took many years too for me to realise that often when a girl said no she meant yes. Max Miller, the English comedian, told a story in a music-hall. A girl goes to a shoemaker to have her shoes repaired.

'Do you know what makes shoes wear out?' he asked her.

'No', she said.

'That's right', he replied.

Many in the theatre roared with laughter, but it took me two days to see the point – a girl goes out in a car with a man; she says no and has to walk home. To this day many years later I marvel at the audience's capacity to grasp the subtle point.

My slowness in understanding the nature of women has been with me all my life. I wonder if the feminine desire for outward show has anything to do with the inferior status of women in a patriarchal society. In a masculine world in which women are second-class citizens many pursuits are banned for them. There are only one or two women MPs; business executives, doctors, lawyers, are nearly all men, and the only departments in which they are equal is in teaching and nursing. So when the men build bridges and make motor cars and tend most of the sick the women can stress their importance only by being ornamental. One of the most cheering trends in modern life is the rebellion of many women against this inferior role they have to play.

It was when I first saw Shaw's *Man and Superman* that I began to doubt the time-honoured theory that man is the pursuer and woman the pursued. I began to look for the tricks women used – dropping a handkerchief, borrowing a book, accidentally crossing the legs. I did not see that the driving force of sex was as cogent, maybe more cogent, in women than it is in men. At nineteen when I read in some French book that a woman's whole interest was in her vagina I felt shocked, disillusioned. It is not the truth but it is a big part of the truth. All the cosmetics and fancy hats and dresses mean: I am desirable sexually; feast your eyes on me and take me. And yet many a woman has said that she dresses for other women and not for men. That cannot be true.

I am not trying to write an essay on women; I am only trying to analyse my attitude to women, and, as I say, it has been largely an ignorant one. It took me many years to discover that when a woman glares at a man, stamps her foot and cries: 'Get out! I

203

hate you', in most cases she is showing her love for him. But I must have had an elementary feeling for psychology. I recall a dance in the old days of programmes and white gloves, when the women stood around and the swains booked dances with them, each writing the dance in the programme with its silk string. The university beauty was besieged. I was introduced to her and didn't ask for a dance. Later she touched my arm. 'Our dance', she said. She had cut another dance. 'But', I said, 'we didn't . . .'

'I know. Damn you, you are the only one who didn't ask me.' And I learned about women from her.

Men are afraid of women. Every woman, especially a wife, is a mother substitute – many married men address their wives as Mum. The hen-pecked man is more than a music-hall joke. The man rationalises his fear by pretending that he gives in for peace. When I was a boy I knew two village schoolmasters who were not allowed to smoke in the house; they sat out in a shed on bitter nights. Not my father; he was a non-smoker, but had he been a smoker I fancy my mother would have said: 'George, your tobacco gives me a sore throat'. He often gave way for the sake of peace.

I sigh regretfully when I see the modern girl with her independence, her frankness about sex, her carelessness in dress with her blue jeans and blouse, I sigh and wish that women had been as sincere and honest in my early days. Real companionship between the sexes was almost impossible then, except maybe between two blue-stockings. The red light was sex – significant that the red light was the sign of the brothel – but in my youth young women did not give the amber and green go-ahead signal easily.

Many men are afraid of the intellectual woman, the highbrow, the scholarly woman. I never was. My old platonic friend Willa Muir was a very clever woman, a match for her poet husband Edwin. But she was never unfeminine and her sense of humour saved her from being an intellectual prig. She was a Scot and this reminds me that I have found that Scottish women are sharper in the tongue, more given to incisive criticism than their English sisters. They seem to want to take men down a peg, to assert their equality or maybe their superiority. The most aggressive questioners I have met in a life of lecturing were women in Scotland, mostly teachers I guess. Hence perhaps the strong mother complex in Scotland, seen at its best or worst in Barrie's worship of his mother in his life and in his books. To be fair to Scotland it has never had the equivalent of that sentimental and commercial abomination Mother's Day, with its suggestion that men never grow up beyond the age of ten.

I expect that it is my own mother complex that has always made me have a tender feeling for old women. I have seen a similar phenomenon among homosexuals. Many who show no interest in young women seem to love fussing around mother figures, thus giving some support to the theory that the male homo has had an unsatisfactory father and has given too much love to his mother. Owing to the incest taboo his mother is sacrosanct, and then every woman becomes taboo. I may have liked old women because they were past pretending – no longer on the defensive, therefore sincere and tolerant.

I am not brave enough to take up the question whether women have smaller minds than men. It is true that many seem to prattle about little things – their neighbours and their doings, their little gardens, their knitting, and in the loftier circles – no, not mixing in them I cannot know, but guess that they talk more of society gossip, racing, polo, garden parties than they do about Keats and Chesterton. Yes, it is easy to sneer or at least to smile at the emptiness of so much womanly talk, but I fail to see that men are any more elevated in their conversation. Relativity and psychology are not pub subjects. Men talk more about their work than women do. Naturally, for their horizon is not limited to a kitchen wall, the boundary of the modern harem with its single wife slave.

No, women are beyond me. A very clever actor buys his clever wife a necklace the price of which would support a hundred poor families for years. It puzzles me. To stage people the joy in life should be the creative art, the applause after a part well played. How an actress can value a stone bauble I cannot understand; surely she does not need so dull a status symbol. This is not meant to be a criticism of a worthy couple of world-wide fame, deserved fame; I use the illustration only to show how ignorant I am of the depth psychology of womankind. I can understand the Hollywood dumb blonde who is said to have had gold taps in her bathroom; poor kid, that was her cinderella idea of success, yet in a way is she any worse than the man who looks on a knighthood as a token of success? If offered a title I would refuse it without any hesitation, and that can be interpreted as inverse snobbery – I am above the silly, fatuous standards of fame and success.

Speaking of titles I fancy that my disillusionment with Barrie began when he became Sir James. If Shaw or Wells had taken titles I'd have been shocked, just as I am shocked when a trade union leader becomes a knight, thereby joining the Establishment. Titles hide personality. Lord Boothby to most TV viewers is Bob, I suppose because he looks so genial and human and sincere. Woman parades her vanity but man hides his by pretending that he has none.

What is the mystery about the modern fashion of long hair for men? A wish to be feminine in a man's world that has become brutal with its Belsen, its tortures in prisons, its militarism? Yet the cavaliers with their flowing locks were manly men. Or is it a realisation that woman is the stronger sex? She is, you know. As a boy I lived next door to a dentist in the days before local anaesthetics; we clustered round the door when a man went in, to hear his cries of pain, but when a woman went in we often wandered away, for she was less likely to cry aloud. If men had to bear children I fear the human race would come to an end.

Ah me! I am old now and cannot recapture the enthusiasms and ecstasies of youth, the dreams of youth, the ambitions of youth. A pretty lass is now an object of academic interest, but I still enjoy looking at one. In a Scottish tram a young lass cannot find a seat. A shepherd says to her: 'I'm an old man, so ye are quite safe to sit on my knee, lassie'. In a few minutes he pushes her off. 'I'm no so auld as I thocht I was, lassie, get off.' But it is a sad day when an invitation to go away with a beautiful blonde for a weekend has to be refused with a sigh. Myself, I haven't had the temptation. Some new Freud should write a book on post-climacteric psychology making the repression of nostalgia the driving complex.

Woman's tragedy is that she ages more quickly than a man, and her worry about her appearance betrays her frantic attempt to make the most of her sex attraction before the dark night of wrinkles and grey hair descends upon her. I hate to imagine the life of all the Hollywood stars who had nothing but their figures and faces to be proud of.

VANITY

I sometimes think that the sickness of the world is primarily due to human vanity. For generations women have bedecked themselves with furs, indifferent to the agony of trapped animals, and more money is spent on cosmetics and dress than on books and music.

What is common to both sexes is the longing for approval. A woman would not dress in the latest Paris fashion if wrecked on an island. A large part of our lives consists of this desire to be seen, to be heard, to be appreciated, to be admired. Fear of death is fear of the end of the ego. When all the egos are combined we get Nationalism and the Establishment. I am the centre of the universe, therefore my country, right or wrong, is also. Heil Hitler: Heil Nixon! The rat race for money is fundamentally a race for recognition and so is the rat race for power. Rich people are not content to leave their money in the bank; they must show that they are wealthy by their houses, cars, standard of living. One might argue that the world division into classes is due to the vanity of the few and the inferiority of the many. The poor have little to be vain about. 'My Bobby has passed the eleven plus exam but Willie next door failed.' 'We are the only ones in the street who have a colour television set.' Vanity gives us a blind eye for the miseries of the world. Keeping up with the Joneses is of more importance than all the wars and hates of the outside world. Vanity spells selfishness; it means the ccurent slogan: 'I'm all right, Jack'.

The evil of vanity is that it makes each of us view the world from our own point of view, our own interest. We read of tortures in dictator countries and then we turn the page to read the football news, and we are all guilty. We see Chicago cops beating with clubs and we switch on the TV and look at shows for ten-year-olds by Andy Williams. We evade because we are all self-centred in our vanity. So maybe Freud and Reich are not wholly right in seeing humanity's sickness as a result of sex repression, yet perhaps right in this way – that sex repression in a patriarchal society denotes the monopoly of everything, sex included, by the older generation.

I cannot recall my father showing any vanity. He had not an inch of snobbery in him and was content to be a country school-master. I fancy he put on his top hat every Sunday because he was more afraid of my mother's criticism than of public opinion. She was a vain little body; in our village we did not keep up with the Joneses: we were the Joneses, with our clean collars and shirts. One vanity the Neill family did not have; it had no desire to have its dead remembered by elaborate tombstones – we couldn't have afforded them anyway. My parents and a few sisters lie in Forfar Cemetery and there is not a stone or a cross to show the location of the grave. The town toffs lie on each side of the main drive and their stones proudly tell of their late social importance and give a hint of their status on the golden shore. The Bible tells us that there are no marriages in heaven but our local bigwigs were pretty sure that there were classes. For myself my vanity may lie in the thought that, after I am dead, my books will keep my memory alive – a thought that brings no comfort. I cannot lay the flattering unction to my soul that my books will endure as long as the tombstones in Forfar Cemetery.

Shakespeare anticipated Muhammad Ali with his Sonnet:

'Nor marble, nor the gilded monuments

Of princes, shall outlive this powerful rhyme'.

Yet an atomic war would kill the humanity that reads the Sonnets while the marble palaces would remain standing.

Vanity made man create God in his own image, the great father.

It is said that in the Far East loss of face is the most terrible of disgraces. Vanity, thy name is not woman, but humanity. It and obedience are the worst of the seven deadly virtues. And I read the lines I have written but not with a feeling of vanity; nay, my feeling is one of annoyance that I am not clever enough to analyse human behaviour.

I have been an exhibitionist in my time. Looking back now I

see that when acting in a play – and I was good, they said – I was really showing off, just as I used to do with my fancy steps in tangoes and foxtrots. The proof lies in the fact that with time the wish to act died away, possibly because of other avenues for exhibitionism – lecturing for example. Yet in 1936 when five hundred could not get into my lecture in Johannesburg, the packed hall gave me no emotion that I can remember. Same thing happened in Sweden, but, to be frank, if in either case the audience had been twenty instead of hundreds, I'd have been damned annoyed.

It is also a peculiar fact that we are conceited about the things we do not do so well, never about our best work. I am convinced that Winston Churchill was more pleased by one who admired his paintings than by one who praised his war efforts. I was never conceited about my work in Summerhill, but used to be about, say, my dancing. Fifty years ago a young lady invited me to go to Budapest to partner her in a competition for original dancing. Poor Nushi died in Belsen or Dachau. I was very conceited about that invitation knowing all the time that, compared with professional dancers, I was a clumsy clot. Luckily for my self-approval I did not go to Budapest. I used to be conceited about my acting, again realising that, compared with a professional, I was a ham actor. And a fan letter saying that the writer loved my kids' tale *The Last Man Alive* pleases me more than a letter from a professor of psychology praising my work in school.

As Barrie said: 'The greatest piece of literature is your own name in print.' But as I say, we are vain about the wrong things. Einstein may have been conceited about lots of things, I don't know, but I guess that he wasn't conceited over his relativity discoveries. Creation has no vanity in it. When one paints a picture or writes a book one thinks not of praise or success or money gain. It is when the creation is over that one thinks of appreciation and recognition, and perhaps not always then. I once knew an artist who never wanted anyone to see his paintings. He finished one, let it dry, and then painted another over it.

I have no feeling of pride about my books. I don't say that I am not pleased when they are praised, but on the other hand, when a Max Rafferty tears one to pieces in righteous passion, I react more with humour than with resentment. Criticism is always more interesting than praise; that is why I always answer a hostile letter at once, and why one does not need to be a masochist to appreciate a good criticism.

209

HONESTY AND
ARMOURING

I wonder how honest I am. And if I am honest is it because of innate goodness or fear of the police? When I had my school in Germany I hated German tobacco and every time I came home I returned with my pockets stuffed with John Cotton mixture, lying in the usual way. 'Haben Sie Tabac?' With an innocent look: 'Nein'. I was not bold enough to swindle the British Customs, nor when young had I the courage to travel without a ticket on the railway.

I think that that kind of honesty is caused mainly by fear of being caught. The wider aspect of honesty is more complicated: the honesty in human relations. Here again fear creeps in, fear of hurting the feelings of others. We are all hypocrites socially, hiding our feelings and opinions. No gentleman can say to a young lady: 'Thanks for that Etude. Your playing must have made Chopin turn in his grave.'

Social life must make us all compromise again and again. Royalty means nothing to me but I stand up when the National Anthem is played. I avoid four-letter words when Mrs Grundy comes to see her grandchild in the school. Life without tact would be hell for everybody.

How honest can one be about oneself? Our upbringing was largely one of being made ashamed . . . using the wrong fork, making a mistake in grammar, washing one's neck, picking one's nose . . . I often do this because of rhinitis that hardens matter. Not many would confess openly to homosexual fantasies or fantasies of murder. And yet I hold that none of these things matter fundamentally. True, everyone has a complex about the body. I am told that heroes who lost legs or arms fighting are ashamed of their deficiency. Most folks would hate to have their false teeth drop out on their plate. I wear a hernia truss but would be embarrassed to strip and bathe with it on.

Yet there are spheres in which dishonesty is impossible. I cannot pretend to school inspectors that I believe that learning lessons is education. If a millionaire left a will giving me a million dollars on condition that Summerhill taught religion my refusal would be instant.

Honesty can be taxed, however, in a case of friendship. When an old friend told me he had £2,000 in notes stashed away in his house, money he had not declared to the Income Tax Office, and he wanted my help in saying that I had been with him when he won the money by betting on horses, I refused to help him. Fear of being found out rather than goodly honesty.

I have no recollection of stealing when I was a kid. Then theft definitely meant hellfire. I have never been tempted to steal books or tools but I admit that I have more than once been tempted to sneak under the circus canvas, literally and metaphorically. The man who would never steal the silver spoons will cheat the Income Tax or the railway and rationalise the theft . . . they have swindled me often enough. Anyway I look honest – which reminds me of the baker who brought our bread in his horse van when I was a boy. 'Jim Fraser's face is the perfect picture of honesty', said my father, and we all agreed that it was – but I forgot what we said when later Jim was jailed for swindling his employer. Some of the worst thieves I have had in Summerhill looked like angels. No, I'd better not claim to look honest after all.

Sincerity is of more moment than honesty; it embraces it. I suppose that I am as sincere as tact will allow, meaning that insincerities such as smiling when one does not feel like smiling are very minor sins. In one of my books I wrote that to tell a white lie was pardonable and human but to live a lie is a disaster.

Dealing with kids one is forced to be sincere unless one is a disciplinarian. I find that children have a natural sincerity if they have not been conditioned into fearful, hateful little brats. Let me pat myself on the back and say unashamedly that I think I am sincere in life in its larger aspect. I could not in a TV programme advertise that some soap powder washes whiter, nor for a fortune would my conscience allow me to do so, yet, for no payment at all,

211

I could advertise something I believed in, John Cotton tobacco for instance. Having worked at one time in Fleet Street, having known left-wing journalists who, to make a living, had to prostitute their talents working for a Tory paper, I wonder how many of our TV ad people believe in the goods they are boosting.

I remember the early publicity outbreak over seventy years ago. Our village blacksmith, who was no scholar, was quoted in many a paper. 'Having suffered excruciating pain because of kidney disturbance I felt instant relief after taking Kinsley's Kidney Pills' . . . to be fair Peter Broon, although illiterate, was sincere about his kidneys.

How much does society depend on dishonesty between people? I have just had a visit from a man who wants to found a colony of dwellers who will be absolutely honest and forthcoming with each other. Some time ago one of my teachers, against my advice, started such a group. After the first meeting an adolescent girl came to me in tears saying that the others had said beastly things about her character and behaviour. My advice to close the meetings was taken.

I should think that in free and easy group therapy inevitably more faults than virtues would be pointed out. And myself, I could not take part in a group intent on being completely frank. If told that I was a self-centred poseur, disguising my innate meanness with a smile I would be angry and, even if I tried to, could do nothing about changing my character. Group criticism could work in things that did not much matter . . . Jones being told that he makes a noise when supping soup. Jones would resent the criticism but would react to it by being conscious that he was a noisy eater.

Reaction to criticism in the small group, the family, can show what a hell can be. Often I have heard a wife say: 'Peter is useless in the house. He can't mend a fuse. He has no hands . . . nor head for that matter. Thinks only of cricket . . . .' Women more than men make such statements about a partner. I expect that in extreme cases the Peters of life do some strangling. And I fear that in group criticism the same hate element would come out too often.

I try to visualise such a world of honesty, where no one had armour, no one pretended, no one had private secrets. Honesty is really a matter of good manners; one does not talk about swings when having tea with the widow of a man who has been hanged.

I acknowledge that society is sick and I am willing to suppose that it would be healthier if we were all honest with each other and spoke aloud our thoughts. Yet I cannot bring myself to try. I feel a hypocrite carrying on a conversation with some professor or his wife about – well – call it weather conversation. I have a similar reaction if I attend a local function, say, the party given by the town council chairman. People I know only by sight, like myself, withdrawn and foreign. Some with the dignity so many bureaucrats acquire by virtue of office. Innerly I feel like crying: 'We are boring each other; we are not talking the same language.' But no, I cannot say it.

Before setting up a group for mutual honesty I advise the promoters to read Ibsen's *Wild Duck* to see what happened when a fanatic for the ideal of truth thought he was giving a family true happiness, and brought it ruin instead. But Ibsen may have been wrong; I may be wrong; it could be that honesty all round would make a saner, a happier world. I am just not the man to be the pioneer.

Reich spoke of armouring, acquiring an outer shell to show to the world, hiding the depths of the personality. We all armour ourselves. Introspection is limited, and that is why a man cannot psychoanalyse himself; he dare not face his inner conflicts, his repressions. It would not be easy for, say, a prominent evangelist to face his naked soul, to find that he was selfish, mean, sadistic, and an unconscious womaniser. A balanced man is one who is prepared to discover the little man in himself, and from that angle none of us is balanced. The principle works both ways of course; Gestapo torturers of Jews petted their children and their dogs.

I wonder what form my own armouring takes. So I ask myself what lies behind my appearance of amiability. I do recognise that my altruism, say, in dealing with children covers as much selfishness as that of others, and I see no harm in that; my altruism is selfish in that it gives me a feeling of self-satisfaction. A duty altruism, like that of the unmarried daughter who gives up marriage to care for an old mother, has no component of self-interest, and must thus contain a plethora of hates and frustrations. I think of a friend I knew long ago. He was so tied to his mother that, when invited out, he refused if she were not invited also. He died and left a fortune to the Prevention of Cruelty to Animals Society and nothing to his mother. His unconscious hate of his apron strings came out in the end.

Armouring does not matter if one is conscious of using it;

as Reich often said: 'You have to be a conscious hypocrite on occasion'. It is the armouring that is unconscious that does the damage. The Salvation Army damsel grasped the idea when she went round asking people if they were saved. She came to a young man sitting alone.

'Are you saved?'

'Press', he said.

'Oh, I beg your pardon', and she moved hastily away.

I like to think that I am not too heavily armoured, that in general I speak and act sincerely and seldom tell a lie, at least never to a child. I confess that I have it easy; I am my own boss and have no need to pretend. Think of the millions who work under bosses. Bowing, saying 'sir', maybe fawning in order not to get the sack. Too often the armour comes to permeate the whole personality. You see it in the subservience of butlers and footmen . . . a dying race to be sure. When young I got most of my best dirty stories from clergymen, who, when they preached on Sundays, appeared to be holy men. Many have the knack of being dual personalities, like the Kirk Elder praising the Lord on the Sabbath and giving short weight with his sugar during the week. The best way to escape a dual personality is to be independent, a fortune given to few of us.

In South Africa, nearly forty years ago, I met a doctor who seemed to have no armouring. If invited to go out to dinner he said simply that he didn't want to. He said to me: 'Neill, I am not coming to your lecture tonight because I have no interest in what you are to talk about.' A really honest man, but I fear he had few friends. I was never so brave; it is only in old age that I can say: 'Thanks for the invitation, but I'd rather stay at home'.

According to the popular idea of repression I am repressing my hate, my scorn, my envy when I try to be gentle and kind to others. That stupid fallacy stems from the early misinterpretation of Freud. It is all nonsense. True that Uriah Heep's hypocritical smile covered a soul from hell just as Iago's soft poisonous hints did. But a writer paints in black and white whereas we are all grey.

To sum up, I begin to pat myself on the back, saying: 'You're all right, Jack. You aren't harbouring unconscious murder wishes or jealousies. You don't envy the other guy his success.'

Damn the writer of an article I have just read. He praises John Holt and George Dennison and he leaves me out. What a beastly man!

My graduation ceremony makes me think of crowd armouring. I have had three such ceremonies. They robe you in cap and

gown; you march in procession; in a crowded big hall you get your honorary degree. In spite of a few friendly professors and dons I have always felt strained, unhappy in such an atmosphere, and I think the reason is the blank impersonality of the Establishment, the formality. I make a remark to the man sitting next to me and the reply is usually monosyllabic. I cannot analyse the *Stimmung*. It is that of a law court with its solemnity . . . 'This is not a place of amusement. If there is any more laughter I shall clear the court.' Any official occasion bars laughter, bans the human touch. Once, giving evidence at an appeal tribunal on my income tax I made a light remark, and the subsequent frowns made me realise what officialdom means; it means the suppression of the emotional side of life; it means community armouring; it means the dignity of Bumbledom. I see it among local officials, town councillors, town clerks; they erect a hands-off-me barrier that excludes any familiarity. It is strong in the police force. A constable said to me: 'If the Inspector heard you address me as Bill I'd be transferred to another town immediately.' To be a cop means to have no friends.

My idea of hell would be a garden party at Buckingham Palace or the White House. Crowd armour protects against the danger of making emotional contacts, and this may be typical of England. There is less of it in Scotland where class barriers do not seem so strong. I was a member of a golf club in Suffolk for 25 years. After a round I would say to a couple of members in the clubhouse: 'The greens are fast today', and would get a stare in reply. Till the American golfers came from nearby aerodromes I spoke to no stranger. In Scotland there is no such starchiness. Last time I played in Edinburgh a man in a passing foursome shouted to me: 'Hi, man, ye're liftin' her heid!' I sure was and thanked him.

I feel somewhat guilty about taking or receiving honorary degrees, not because of Establishmental aloofness, but because I do not value the academic education universities give out, and because I have written so much criticising them. Consciously I have no pride in being a graduate. I never put my degrees on my school prospectus. I suppose I rationalise when I say that their only value is that they protect me. No Ministry can say that I am not qualified to run a school, indeed today no one can run a private school without a degree or teacher's training. I am quite prepared to face the fact that underneath I may be as proud as Punch of my MA degree, for in Scotland an MA is of great moment. And I don't want to give the impression that I failed to appreciate the honour of getting honorary degrees. They warmed

215

my heart. The students of my own university, Edinburgh, put forward my name for an honorary degree. The Senatus turned it down, and one professor was reported as saying that I was the man who was urging students to rebel. This was just after the election of a Lord Rector. I had under three hundred votes and Kenneth Allsop had over two thousand, so that Kenneth must have been the corrupter of youth. To be fair to the Senatus, I am sure their decision rested largely on my having published in a Scottish magazine the address I would have given had I been elected. It must have shocked their academic souls.

I suppose that conceit is a form of armouring, especially since we are never conceited about what we can do well.

Conceit is an armour against admitting to oneself that one is a dud. It fades with the years but never quite expires. Reich's desire to have an elaborate tomb in Orgonon was a kind of posthumous conceit; in life he scorned display and honours and pageantry of all kinds. Myself, I have no feelings about tombstones or monuments after my death. All I want is a quiet cremation with no fuss, no flowers, no black clothes, no epitaph. I should like my body to be taken away by the undertaker and have no funeral at all, but I fear that the criticism would go to my family . . . 'The hardboiled lot, not even giving the old man the respect of a decent burial.' But such a custom should come, even though in the USA the mortician lobby would fight to the death for its scandalous exploitation of the bereaved with their idiotic embalming and face-painting plus maybe a grand's worth of good oak wood that could be better employed in building.

Aphorism: death is feared and hated because it destroys the little conceited man in each of us. A modern interpretation of Christianity might run: a belief that the little man in us will die and be buried while the big man will pass to eternal glory and happiness. Or concretely, the little man equals the body and its conceits and frailties while the big man means the spirit, the soul. All religions are wish-fulfilments.

RELIGION AND FAITH

I have already told how my parents gave up their Calvinism for Spiritualism. When my sister, Clunie, died in 1919 they asked me if I could get in touch with a medium. I was then in London. With great difficulty I arranged to have an interview with Sir Oliver Lodge's medium, Mrs Leonard. She went into a trance and said things that astonished me, that Clunie had been a teacher, that she had died of lung trouble, both correct. I began to wonder if there was something in Spiritualism after all, and then – 'Have you any questions for your sister?'

'Yes, ask her if she ever thinks of Spot.'

'She says, yes; she loved Spot but then she loved all animals.'

Alas, my question had meant the village she had taught in – Spott. I did not tell my parents that part of the interview.

I have never been able to become interested in Spiritualism. I once saw a Spiritualist in a crowded hall point to a woman.

'That lady at the end of the row. You lost your father recently, didn't you?'

'Yes, six weeks ago.'

'And your mother is ill?'

'Yes, very ill.'

I approached him after the show.

'How did you know that woman had lost her father?'

'I didn't; my Control spoke with my voice.'

I was no wiser. Another time I was no wiser, either. After a lecture I had given in Stockholm a man said that he had not agreed with a lot of what I had said.

'Oh, how do we differ?'

'You are educating children for this life but we are educating them for the lives to come.' He was a teacher in a Rudolf Steiner school.

I doubt if we shall get far with the esoteric until we grasp what our conjurers do. I spent three nights in the front of the stalls trying to discover where the great conjurer David Devant got the dozens of eggs he was clutching from the air. I never knew. A friend, a member of the Magic Circle, tells me that such tricks are simple but owing to his oath he cannot tell me how they are done. But another member with less scruples explained how the levitation act is performed.

I simply cannot become interested in a life after death. My view is infantile, for example billions have died but where are they? The metempsychosis folks make it easy. The soul of the dead is parked and when a babe is born some power selects a soul to put in it. I have doubts about what are called psychic manifestations in, say, haunted houses, but am puzzled about poltergeists who throw the furniture about the room. My first wife's sister, Henry Handel Richardson, held that her house in Lyme Regis, Dorset was haunted. She and her husband, Professor George Robertson, went to the cinema one night. She had been knitting. George, an unbeliever, told me: 'When we got back Ett's wool had been draped all over the picture rail. I couldn't reach it and had to borrow a ladder from next door.'

I often heard knocks in her house but only when a German girl, said to be a medium, was present. Long after the death of George and Henry I knocked at the door and said to the new occupant, 'Do you ever hear knocks in the house?' She stared at me blankly and said of course she didn't. The poltergeist had apparently moved elsewhere.

When experimenting with table rapping, oh, forty years ago, Homer Lane was supposed to be there. I said: 'If you can tell me something I don't know I shall be inclined to believe in Spiritualism. I know you died in the American Hospital in Paris but tell me the name of the doctor or anyone there.' The table rapped out the answer 'I don't know'. But Eric Dingwall, then the investigator for the Psychical Research people, and present at the table, told me he had on more than one occasion had answers that no one taking part at the table could have known, and Eric was a sceptic about anything psychic.

I fancy that my lack of interest in things psychical may be associated with my indifference to what is called the spiritual in life. I am an earthy guy even if my head is sometimes in the clouds. I was not one of Wordsworth's little ones who came to the world trailing clouds of glory. I could not take the higher life, nor think the beautiful thoughts of the theosophists I worked with on the *New Era*, nor later could I accept the uplift of the German teachers in Dresden. I wonder if this absence of the so-called spiritual has anything to do with my inability to appreciate poetry. Nay, I am a prosy fellow, unable to fly and having no desire to take wings.

Faith . . . belief in revealed religion, says the dictionary. The word is used generally as meaning confidence; I have faith in my garage mechanic, meaning that I know from experience that he can mend my car. The mystical faith is beyond my comprehension. It denotes accepting something that is beyond rationality, some-thing that cannot be proved such as the idea of an omnipotent God, a heaven, a hell, immortality. Belief in these is founded on the word of prophets, sages, the Bible, but this is not far from the belief in Santa Claus or ghosts or witches. The puzzle to me is this: why do many learned, clever people accept, say, personal immortality? The biological law is that everything that lives dies, but man is made the exception. He is too important to go out for ever because he has a brain. No one suggests immortality for a mouse or a flea or even a dog. But when does this immortality come in? Would the bishops grant immortality to the Neander-thal Man, or before him the early humans who came down from the trees? The belief in an after-life is wish-fulfilment, or is it? Shaw said that if immortality could be proved scientifically a howl of despair would arise from humanity.

Faith and religion are geographical. Had I been born in Arabia my religion would have forbidden alcohol, and three wives would not have been a compensation. Born in Dublin I could have been a sadistic teacher in a Catholic school, though not necessarily, for I was born in Calvinist Scotland and grew out of that anti-life religion. But in the main most people accept their home religion. My pupils live without it and of the many old pupils I know of only one who sought religion later.

In my boyhood, over eighty years ago, faith was easy to accept. The earth was the centre of the universe and a kindly God had put the sun and moon and stars there to light our footsteps. He was a very personal God; he knew us all individually and when we died rewarded us with a harp or punished us with a fire. Remote from ideas we did not know that Darwin had killed the first chapter of Genesis, or later that Freud had destroyed the image of man as one who could choose good or evil. We had no idea that our earth was a minnow in an ocean of stars and planets. Because our earth was the centre of the universe so was man the supreme subject of creation, and like the stars, immortal.

I am quite aware of the limitations of rationalism. To the humanist, as to the believer, life is a mystery that cannot be solved. How did the universe begin? I look at my grand-daughter, three weeks old and marvel at her being. When she raises her hand she does something that no computer, no Rolls Royce engine can do. We have simply to accept the mystery of life knowing that it will remain a mystery. To postulate a God who was the architect of the grand design seems to me pure childish superstition. Even if we call God cosmic energy we are not solving anything. God is dead because man has taken over his energy function and has used energy to give us TV sets and pollution plus the almighty H-bomb. 'God's in his heaven; all's right with the world.' Ask the relatives of six million Jews.

To get back to faith, I cannot accept it. When Reich told me of his discovery of Orgone Energy I told him that I could not accept it simply because he said it existed. And so with the pronouncements of sages and prophets; I cannot accept what to me are fantasies. And, indeed, it is taking the hard way. It is so easy to take comfort in the hope of a blessed eternity. When one believes, as I do, that death is the end, it is annoying to say the least. It kills curiosity. I'd like to know what happens to freedom for children for instance and I shall never know. Two definitions of death. The horrible thing that kills curiosity, or the blessed thing that prevents a man from ever knowing what mess people have made of his work and ideas (c.f. Freud, Reich). What a shock I shall get if I find a devil with a fork waiting for me – 'Down those steps, Mr Neill'. But it could be worse. An angel might point a holy finger upwards. 'You will find your harp upstairs, Mr Neill.'

FATE

'Mighty events turn on a straw; the crossing of a brook decides the future of the world.' Thomas Carlyle.

I have often thought of that quotation. By one post I was offered two jobs, the headmastership of Gretna Green School and English master of Tain Academy. I chose Gretna Green because I would be my own boss. Had I chosen Tain my life would have been completely altered. I might never have met Homer Lane; certainly I would not have gone to Germany and Austria. 'The fault, dear Brutus, lies not in our stars but in ourselves.'

Or does it? Had I accepted the invitation to become a school inspector in Australia in 1912 would I ever have had a pioneer school? My star would have been a bureaucratic job of watching others run their schools. I think of the one or two bright lads in my father's village school, who, according to my father, could have had brilliant academic careers. They became slow-witted ploughmen.

My philosophy is rather like that of old Omar. It is all chance; there is no plan, no justice. A few minutes after I moved away from a railway left-luggage office an IRA bomb exploded and killed two passers-by. Poor Leslie Howard was shot down in a plane becuase the Nazis thought that Churchill was on it. So, how much do we control our fate? Henley erred when he said 'I am captain of my soul'.

I like to fantasise about the might-have-been. Had I chosen

221

Tain I could have ended up as a teacher of English in a State school until I retired at sixty-five. But what would have become of the drive within me that compelled me to challenge? Or would environment have killed the spark as it did with my father's bright pupils? All conjecture. If his environment had been different Hitler might have remained a mute inglorious dictator in his home town. The Great War made the man of many mistakes the saviour of Britain. A death made LBJ president – I guess that even his enemies are praying that no one assassinates Nixon. Nay, it is a world in which 'destiny with men for pieces plays'.

There is no logical reason why I should live to be well up in my eighties when so many died young – Chopin, Keats, Shelley, Lipatti, Chatterton; their name is legion. It is said that Lipatti, one of the most brilliant players of Chopin ever recorded, knew he was to die and feverishly recorded as much as he could to show the world his brilliance. Many a young potential genius must have died in two great wars. They were not captains of their souls.

This brings up the question of free will. In small matters possibly the will is free: I can decide whether to order whisky or beer in a pub. But in large matters I cannot see any free will. Can anyone imagine Governor Reagan using his free will to become a Communist? There can be no free will as long as conditioning of the young obtains. It is true that a small minority breaks free, the challengers of the status quo, but the huge majority, accepting its moulding, has no will to challenge anything. I am one of those who challenged yet my will is not free. I can choose to be a pioneer in education; I cannot choose to be a Communist or a Catholic or a football fan or an admirer of TV kitsch. I don't even have the free will to stop smoking when I know that my heart would be better without it. A million or two cigarette smokers know that they are in danger from lung cancer and yet few give up fags or take to a pipe. 'It won't happen to me'.

Environment alone can negate any free will. Summerhill and Eton pupils do not become crooks later, but I grant that Eton has produced many a Cabinet Minister. Middle-class morality inhibits the personal; dress alike, think alike, behave alike. At the other end of the scale what chance is there for free will in a boy born in a slum or a Negro ghetto? Maybe the chief result of therapy is that it convinces the patient that he has no free will, that his behaviour has been conditioned all the way from birth.

Then comes the dilemma. I was conditioned by religion, authority, middle-class morality, social mores, and I broke away from it. Other members of the family had very much the same

222

conditioning and accepted it. Determinism is not an answer either; under it I would have remained a conventional Scottish dominie in a village school, possibly an elder of the kirk.

And now I must make a new attempt to cut out the baccy and fail as usual. In German *ich wil* does not mean I will; it means I want to. A nasty word is the word will; a man with a strong will is usually a selfish bully bossing other people. Funny thought – here am I, a weak-willed man, doing a job that requires oceans of will without bullying anyone. I give it up, and still think that we have no free will in emotional affairs – when a young teacher I did not idealise my pupil Margaret by an effort of will. Maybe it is all a matter of semantics anyway.

HUMOUR

The greatest insult one can offer to a man is to say he has no sense of humour. Almost as great an insult is to say he is a bad driver. Such verdicts are unforgivable. One of the most humourless men I know often sums up other men – 'What is wrong with that guy is that he has no sense of humour'. There can be a criterion of good driving, but not one for good humour. Anyway humour varies with ages. In my boyhood we all laughed at the funny stories by W. W. Jacobs and at *Three Men in a Boat*, but today no young person would see humour in Jacobs or Jerome.

Like all others I like to think that I have a good sense of humour, and this includes a good sense of wit. I have always disliked sadistic humour, the kind indulged by King Edward VII and Douglas Fairbanks Senior, when they played infantile and cruel practical jokes on guests. Or by the wags of Dundee when they teased MacGonagall, the worst poet who ever achieved immortality. He was a simple scatter-brained man, and these Dundee wits sent him a letter signed by Queen Victoria making him a Knight of the White Elephant of Burma. The elephant was coming by sea and the poor man went to the docks daily to meet the ship until he got a wire from the Queen saying it had been washed overboard. That kind of humour is hangman humour, barbaric. Luckily it is seldom in evidence these days.

Possibly I like wit more than I like humour, wit that is not cruel. Wilde was never cruel as Whistler was; the nearest to cruelty

Oscar came was when a man claimed to be an old acquaintance:

'I see you don't recognise me, Oscar.'

'No, sorry, I've changed a lot.'

My favourite story of wit appears in the autobiography of Lord Beresford, if I get the name right. During the First War a distinguished American came over to England and Lord Charles gave a dinner party in his honour. When the guest's health was proposed he rose: 'Gentlemen, before I speak about the war situation I want to apologise for appearing tonight in morning dress. I came over on war business and did not expect to dine out, so I did not bring my evening clothes. When I got Lord Charles's invitation I went to a Savile Row tailor and asked if he could make me an evening suit.

'"Very sorry, sir, but I have no material and my men are all called up."

'I tried several tailors and got the same reply. Then someone advised me to go to Willie Clarkson, the theatrical costumier, and hire one, so I went to Clarkson. "Could I hire a suit of evening dress for tomorrow night?"

'Willie held up his hands. "Sorry, sir, but it can't be done; they are all out; Lord Charles Beresford is giving a dinner party".'

I told this story to a journalist friend in Scotland who was the chief guest at a Burns Supper. He had not had time to dress. He told the story, making it local.

'God', he said, 'it was received in dead silence and I had to conclude that every bloody man had hired his suit.'

I think I tell a story well, leaving out the unessentials. When my mother told a story we all sighed – 'There was a man in Glasgow . . . or was it Edinburgh . . . no, Glasgow . . .' My father had a sense of fun rather than a sense of humour. He had to explain the point of a story.

When I first lectured in the USA in 1947 I discovered that the Americans had a humour different from that of the English. A joke I made that would have raised laughter in London fell flat in New York, and more than once laughter arose when I could not see why. Every nation has its own kind of humour, which is therefore apt to become hackneyed, like the stories of Scottish meanness. When I lived in Germany the only Germans who seemed able to laugh at themselves were the Jews.

One thing has puzzled me for years, and that is that I have never once met anyone who claimed to originate a story. One the other night on BBC TV:

An old crone sitting at the fireside with her cat. Fairy appears. 'I'll give you three wishes.'

'Make me a beautiful princess.' The wand waves.

'Give me lots of money.' The wand fills the room with gold.

'Now your third wish.'

'I am very fond of my cat. Make him a handsome prince'.

The handsome prince takes the princess in his arms.

'Now I think you'll be sorry you took me to the vet.'

Someone must have made up that yarn, but who? Like the Border Ballads they are all written by anon – 'That man writes a lot', as the old lady said.

What has all this got to do with my life? Has a sense of humour helped me to face life, or is it sometimes used as an escape from facing the raw material? I do not know, but I do know that humour must have its own special time and environment. A man on his way to the gallows would not see the best joke ever made, yet old Oscar could remark, when faced with expensive treatment, that he was dying beyond his means. Of course we know that laughter is a release and the people who could not relax could not laugh. Who can think of Calvin or John Knox or Hitler laughing out loud? Maybe what ails the Bible is that there isn't a joke in its pages; maybe politicians are guys who cannot laugh. Many teachers can laugh but they dare not lest their children might discover that they were human. Too often I have seen sadistic teachers whose humour took the form of tormenting frightened little boys. It is likely that most schoolboy howlers are invented by teachers. I doubt if any schoolboy ever said that the Pope lives in a vacuum (some unconscious truth here) or that a polygon is a dead parrot.

I think that humour has been of great assistance to me in my work. I speak to every child lightly unless he or she seeks my help. Joking with a child means to it friendliness, equality, brotherhood. When someone asked me who would run Summerhill after my death I replied: 'No idea, but if he or she has no humour the school will go fut'. A school that is not a fun fair is a bad school. Alas, the dignity of teachers kills all the fun. One of my teachers was offended because a pupil called him a damned fool.

'Man', I said, 'half a dozen kids have been following me around all morning crying "Neill, Neill, banana peel". Do you expect me to stand on my dignity and get annoyed?'

I begin to think that the success of Summerhill has been due, at least in part, to this ability to be a fun kid among other fun kids.

Fun is of far greater importance than mathematics or history and all the other soon-to-be-forgotten school subjects. Humour never dies.

AGGRESSION

Reich used to tell me that I was bottling up my aggression, my rage. 'You want to be seen as the saintly Neill who is always placid.' That came after a session where he kept saying: 'Hit me, Neill', and I just laughed and said I had no desire to hit him.

The Freudians made much of aggression in children, but I think they studied the wrong children, for I see in self-regulated children much less aggression than in disciplined children. I notice that those who see much aggression in others are often projecting their own. But aggression is there in all of us. As a rule I am not aggressive – maybe Reich helped me there, for I did get rid of a lot of aggression on his couch – but I have found myself being aggressive when lecturing. When someone gets up and challenges me I react with aggression, or if you like, with hate. How dare this bastard challenge an authority like me? On the other hand I have anticipated aggression in myself when meeting people who have annoyed me. I fumed over Malcolm Muggeridge's weekly programme on TV, 'The Question Why'. Then he invited me to come on the programme and I went unwillingly, feeling that I could not get on with a man with a holy bee in his bonnet. But when I met him I liked him. I felt he was an overgrown schoolboy with an unusual schoolboy erudition, but with little grasp of what to me are the significant factors in life. No one could get angry with Malcolm Y, as I dubbed him at a time when Malcolm X was news. At that sitting I did feel aggressive when the High Master of St Paul's attacked me, but when I realised that we were talking a different language my aggression cooled off.

Aggression in a child does not usually arouse aggression in me, mainly because I am interested in the source of it, and try to understand. No therapist should react to a patient's aggression. But, dear me, when Stekel asked me to correct his pronunciation and I was fool enough to do so, he went in off the deep end.

'No, Stekel, not lof but love.'

'But, verdammt, that is what I said, lof.'

Another argument against teaching.

Maybe I have avoided being aggressive because I am not competitive. In my golfing days I never cared whether I won a match or not; my concern was with shots, and a hundred yards' drive to the green and the ball ten inches from the pin made my day.

I notice that free children have very much the same attitude to sport. The fun of the game is more important than winning. Aggression and competition. Which comes first? Aggression I suppose.

It may be that we all have our quantum of aggression and express it in different ways: the sergeant major, the bossing manager, the school bully do their expressing openly and primitively. Others do it more subtly. Do I express my aggression by lecturing and writing? 'Here, you guys, I am an important fellow. I know more than you do about kids, so you had better listen to me.' Shaw I am sure was in private life a mild, gentle gentleman, but in his writing he is one of the most aggressive writers of his time. Similarly Wells, though more aggressive as a personality. Hardy I think was unaggressive in life and writing, just as dear Wilde was. Kindly souls.

Is aggression a male characteristic? Ask any husband. An aggressive man may be feared but an aggressive woman is hated. Aggression is a male's prerogative, the primeval hunter. In a school the boys show their aggression by bullying, destroying, but the girls show theirs by being bitchy to each other. Tongue not brawn.

What I am consciously is a gentle, friendly, non-scholar with a stoop. If unconsciously I am an aggressive, hateful bully I cannot do anything about it. Circumstances might have changed the picture. In a Nazi concentration camp I might have fought like hell to grab the meagre food, yet, you know, many educated men in Belsen and Dachau sacrified their needs to the needs of others.

We simply do not know how we would react in certain situations. I met a lawyer in Oslo who had been betrayed when working in the underground. The Nazis tore off his nails, hands and feet.

'I fear I would have blurted out the names of my companions,' I said.

'And so did I, but I became so angry that I could not give them any information.' I fear I could never have reached the heights of his heroism.

In the early part of this book I told of the village school bullies, who were always rather stupid and hit with fists instead of tongues. I wonder how much this kind of frustration applies to our aggressive politicians, tycoons, headmasters. Headmasters are supposed to be scholars, but in my life I have found the least aggressive people among scholars and thinkers. I think of Jack Flugel. Prof. J. D. Bernal (Sage), Prof. Ben Morris of Bristol, many others who were kindly, gentle, tolerant.

The connection between aggression and cruelty is obvious. Was there ever a dictator who banned torture and massacre? But that is too vast and deep a subject to go into here.

DAYDREAMS AND DISAPPOINTMENTS

It may be that a man's character is best delineated in his daydreams. They are the might-have-beens, the unfulfilled ambitions, the fantasies of grandeur. Our night dreams are beyond control and can be nightmares, but the day-dream is largely in control of consciousness and is always happy. In a night dream we may be in terror of robbers, but in the daydream we conquer them.

Like everyone else I have daydreamed all my life. In youth I rescued imprisoned maidens, saved the heroine in a fire, but I never got to the length of imagining that I was really a prince boarded out as a baby to a village schoolmaster. I have had more than one pupil with that fantasy. Like others I have daydreamed of seeing people I did not like done to death; happy dreams they were. I fancy that more people have been killed in daydreams than in wars. One daydream of my youth was to watch my own funeral; that one came usually after I had been chastised by my parents – 'They'll be sorry when they see me dead'. The odd thing was that I felt no misery or sadness in that daydream; nay, on the contrary, I was pleased to be the centre of attraction at last. People were wiping their eyes as my coffin went by. When my pal broke his neck falling from a tree I recall my envy when his coffin was carried out. Why should he be the hero of the moment? This suggests that our daydreams are primarily means to assert our god-almightiness.

Later dreams are different. When in the early poverty days of

Summerhill I daydreamed of a millionaire financing the school, I was not seeking self-aggrandisement. The daydream had advanced a stage, to altruism, but not entirely. It was personal worth that the rich man was to reward.

Alas, daydreams seldom come true, and if they did the outcome might not always be a happy one. Oscar Wilde – 'There are two tragedies in life; one is not to get what you want; the other is to get it. The latter is the greater tragedy.' Maybe the large number of divorces proves Oscar's point.

Earlier I have told about my ambition to be a novelist, an artist, a dramatist, all daydreams that had no basis of talent to support them. Every man jack of us has such dreams. I assume that the humble boy in the kitchen of a mansion daydreams of being a butler one day. Some fool once wrote that if you want something badly enough you will get it. But suppose the poor kitchen lad aspired to the hand of Lady Mary, the daughter of the house, and daydreams of eloping with her?

Montessori, they say, thought that daydreaming was a kind of sickness. The fully occupied child would not daydream, or for that matter masturbate.

Oddly enough I have not daydreamed much about recognition or honours, not so far as I can recall, since my teens. Then of course I had conquered London with a brilliant play and duchesses were struggling to embrace me.

With age the daydream almost ceases to exist. In age one has no ambition, no wish for money, yet the desire to be recognised stays on even if considerably lessened. When I read the *Guardian* Tuesday Educational Section I feel a kind of sadness, not because my name or that of Summerhill is not mentioned, but because every article and letter deals with what to me is unessential. In many weeks the *Guardian* section has not mentioned the child or its psychology; it has not used the word freedom. I suppose that I am annoyed because, apparently, my work has had no influence on educationists, at least journalistic ones, which means that my daydream of public recognition has been shattered. I have sent out my message and the bloody folks have ignored it.

To stop dreaming is to die. If you are full of life you will dream. Maybe the lunatic is one who lives in a daydream that can never come true. Every Scots village has its mute inglorious Robbie Burns, and many an English village has its creator whose invention is to make him rich and famous. Success equals your daydreams coming true, at least where work is concerned. I suppose that religious people daydream about eternity. I am sure

232

that the whole invention of heaven and angels and harps originated in someone's daydream. Not being a believer my daydreams remain earthy.

I am inclined to be a pessimist in general. I'd like to daydream of a coming world of freedom, love, equality, but I cannot, and, indeed, there are few factors egging one on to optimism. With Bertrand Russell some years ago I thought that the end would come with an H-bomb blast soon. I do not think that now; I am more afraid of the universal greed that will not end pollution because that would be a loss of profit.

As I have noted earlier my youthful daydreams were about better-class girls who were unattainable. My old dog Biscuit, sex-starved as most domestic animals are, gives dream whines while he wags his tail, possibly meeting bitches in dreamland.

Bertrand Russell said that with age one loses interest in one's own personality and thinks more of humanity in general. I think this is true. One ceases to feel emotional about individuals. One cannot love or even hate as one did when young. Grief is much less poignant. Honour and recognition are much less valued, no doubt because with age one realises how small one is. Hence the old daydream about the state of humanity, not about personal success in love or work. A young man may daydream about being made a lord or a knight; an old man dreams of doing something to help his fellow men. Death kills personality and it may be that old age, with its diminution of ambition, is the end of a natural process that leads to finality. My final daydream may be the wish to die to the music of Walther's song in *Die Meistersinger*, not the *Preislied* but to me the better *Am stillen Herd in Winterzeit*; or to Lipatti playing my favourite Chopin waltz.

Have I any personal disappointments? Not now. Maybe in my earlier days when I discovered that I was not an artist nor a dramatist nor a novelist. One is only disappointed when one looks forward to some success which does not come off. At my age I look forward to nothing. Though I never give advice to the young, if I did I should say: 'Don't look backwards; don't look forwards. Face today and its joys and sorrows.'

It was said that H. G. Wells was bitter because he was never offered the Order of Merit, the only British title given for merit. I have never desired a title; I'd blush to walk down Leiston High Street and be addressed as My Lord Summerhill. In my life I have aimed at tree-tops not at stars, and so have avoided major disappointments.

233

I am disappointed because things move so slowly. In today's *Guardian* there is an article about a slum school in Liverpool which is trying out self-government, honestly confessing that it was inspired by Summerhill, but Summerhill has been going for fifty years, and apart from the new primary schools with their new freedom I know of no state school that has broken away from the old idea that schools are learning places, not living ones. Michael Duane tried with Risinghill and his attempt was killed by the anti-life brigade.

I am disappointed with teachers, most of whom, according to a journal report, want to retain the cane and the belt. I sigh when a news item tells how a headmaster sent two dozen big boys home to get their hair cut, I grieve when a headmistress sends a girl home because her hair ribbon is the wrong colour, for the attitude of such teachers is so infantile, so stupid, so arrogant.

I have had very little real grief in my life. The greatest was my grief when Clunie died. I had little when my parents died but had they died when I was young I would have had much grief. When Neil, my doctor brother, died at eighty I had no grief. As I said, with age the emotions get dull; one can neither exult nor deeply grieve, and it is unlikely that one grieves when relations and friends die of old age. When my good friends Edwin and Willa Muir died I did not shed a tear.

Distance makes a big difference to grief. If your brother dies in your arms you grieve painfully, but if he dies in Australia the grief would be less poignant. This links up with a common cure or at least amelioration of grief – flight. The rich can fly to another country but the poor have to seek flight in humbler ways. After Clunie's death I found myself doing all sorts of things that I was not accustomed to doing – washing dishes, mending chairs, anything to take my mind off my misery, but even then I recognised the selfish element in grief – 'I am left alone now'.

I cannot guess where the expression 'Good Grief' came from. It may have some hidden connection with the unconscious relief so often associated with death. I think of the Scottish funeral with its blacks and tears and the subsequent feast in the parlour with laughter and ale. I think of a military funeral with its dead march and the return of the band playing 'The Girls I Left Behind Me'. I make the guess that the family with the most hate in it gives the strongest evidence of deep grief.

234

HOBBIES

What do I do with my spare time? For years it was spent in my workshop, but a year to two back I suddenly lost interest in tools and gave all mine to the school workshop. My hobby was metal work, hammering trays and bowls out of flat circular brass or copper discs. I was never very good at it, but I know a lot about tools and machines and processes. I showed an old carpenter how to unscrew a large woodscrew that resisted all attempts with the screwdriver. I held a red-hot poker on the top of it and the old carpenter said that in fifty years he had never learned that trick. I always had a lathe but lathe work is so dull, you can only make things round.

It was because of this hobby that I tended to value tools more than I did books. Reading is, like television or watching a football game, passive, inactive. I like doing and so do children, but, having little opportunity for creation in home and school, millions of children today sit for hours with their eyes glued to the screen. In Summerhill we have TV but only at certain times, limited times at that.

I spend, or should I say, waste a lot of time watching TV although I think it is geared to a mental age of ten in every country. What do I read? Newspapers of course; I take in four dailies and three Sunday papers. I enjoy the reviews – theatre, TV, books, especially books. I am bored stiff with the old films so often presented in Britain. Even those of Garbo, yet I would walk a long way to see Chaplin's *City Lights* and *Modern Times*. There is a mystery about Charlie. I asked our local cinema to get both films and the distributors said that they were not in circulation. I wrote to Charlie in Switzerland asking why and saying it wasn't fair to the young generation to miss his greatest work and see only the old bottom-kicking, pastry-throwing shorts. I got no reply. A man who knows him tells me that Charlie does not answer letters – a talent I wish I had when my postal delivery adds up to twenty at a time.

It may be that like H. G. Wells, he cannot judge his own work, Wells thinking more of his late stodgy political novels and treatises than of his *Kipps* and *Mr Polly*.

Occasionally our TV gives us a Buster Keaton film and I laugh like hell, just as I laugh over Chaplin at his best. In general Westerns bore me, but every week I watch *The Virginian*, mainly, I think, because the characters are alive, whereas in Perry Mason no one lives; they are all sticks. The other day I discovered in my files a nice letter from Erle Stanley Gardner dated April 1927. I had sent him a fan letter praising his Ed Jenkins series in the *Black Mask* Magazine. Meaning that I discovered him before he became a household word.

Love dramas bore me now that love is for youth and not for age. Of course it is right that romance as my generation knew it should disappear, and I grant that the young will go on seeking romance but in a new way.

I seldom read a novel. Recently I have taken to reading biographies wondering if it helps one to understand writers, but have never read a biography that made a man bigger or more noble.

As a graduate in Honours English I should be reading Keats and Shelley and Milton or Dickens and Thackeray. The books are on my shelves and I shall never read them, although I do dip into Keats once in a while. Detective stories bore me. I get many books on education and psychology sent to me, chiefly from the USA. Too many are written in a stodgy style. In a way Reich killed any interest I had in reading about psychology; he went deeper than most writers. All the volumes about psychological cases seem to me now of little importance; they were about individuals and psychology should be about masses. It should be prophylaxis.

My vices these days are few. I smoke pipe tobacco, and have always ignored medical warnings that tobacco with Latakia in it is a danger for coronary. Again and again I have tried to give it up but have always failed in spite of tricks like keeping my pipe in my cottage and my baccy pouch in my office over in the main building. On the positive side the walking back and forth must have helped my health.

I like a drink but haven't been drunk for many years. Malt whisky is my favourite. When I used to drink rye with Reich I liked it but over here in England it does not appeal to me. Beer I like and some wines. Drugs I have never tried. I know nothing about them and only wonder why to smoke cannabis is a crime while smoking cigarettes is legal, seeing that few die from smoking cannabis while many thousands die of lung cancer. I never used drink as an escape. I drank for the pleasure of drinking. I can recall only one incident in my drinking life that was unpleasant. In 1936, on my South African lecture tour, I was a guest in the famous Diamond Club in Kimberley. In the bar a merchant stood me a whisky. Six other diamond merchants joined us and a did not notice that each was ordering a double for me. I was in I hole. I had often heard of colonial hospitality and how pained people were if it were rejected. I drank the lot and then rushed to the lavatory and put my finger down my throat. I must have given a lousy lecture that night. Had I been older I would have thanked them and asked them to excuse me in view of my evening lecture. Now I come to think of it, when I had too much in my student days it was because friends joined maybe two of us and all had to stand a round. I always have drink in the house but seldom touch it unless a friend visits me.

In 1922 at a dance in Vienna the band went out for its inter-mission and a young American sat down at the piano and played a foxtrot. I aked if he could play my favourite foxtrot, *The Japanese Sandman*. He played it.

'That was magnificent', I said with enthusiasm.

'I wrote it', he said. His name was Whiting, I think.

No, my musical knowledge is like that of the King of some Asiatic country who was the guest of Queen Victoria. She took him to a concert, and when the band finished tuning up he rose and clapped his hands.

Conversation. Alas, most of my conversation is one-sided. Hundreds come to Summerhill to ask me questions, and it is a joy when a visitor gives as much to me as I do to him.

My attitude to music is romantic; I have many Chopin records and no Bach ones. I would walk five miles to see and hear *Die Meistersingers* or *Tristan und Isolde*. Maybe I identify myself with the hero of *Meistersingers*, Walther, who cast aside the old stiff rules of song and sang in a new way, making his own rules.

237

COPY-CAT

        I doubt if I have done anything original in my life. Willie was a minister; I would be one. Willie drew in black and white; I also would sketch with pen and Bristol board. I copied the style of Joseph Pennell and Herbert Railton, and my sketches were a mixture of their styles. I copied Homer Lane. He had self-government in his Little Commonwealth; I would set up a school with self-government. He did therapy; I also would do therapy. I doubt if my beginning to write was an aping of Willie; more likely that by that time I was aping Barrie or maybe Wells, yet to be fair to myself my desire to write may have come from inner sources that cannot be explored. There was one factor in my favour. When I discovered that I was no draughtsman I gave up sketching, relapsing in the fifties to make a pen drawing of Summerhill for the school prospectus, again an unoriginal drawing. I gave up the wish to be a minister, but did I? Was not my freedom school a form of soul-saving without the Billy Graham tub-thumping?

I wasn't really original in setting up my school. Studies of child psychology showed me that the driving force in man is emotion, so, said I, I'll have a school in which the emotional development comes first. I have often been labelled a follower of Rousseau, but I did not read *Emile* until fifty years after opening Summerhill. Then I felt very humble to discover that what a man wrote in theory two hundred years ago I had been practising in ignorance of his ideas. Also I was somewhat disappointed. Emile

238

was free but only in the set environment prescribed by his tutor. Summerhill is a set environment but it is the community that decides, not the individual tutor.

I sometimes think that critics are too glib about attributing influence; only a man himself can know who influenced him. The great educators had no influence on me whatever. I got little out of Dewey, and was ignorant of Pestalozzi, and Froebel. I read Montessori who had only a negative influence on me, because I gibbed at her separation of work and play, her condemnation of fantasy in a child's life. I saw children in a Montessori school fitting triangles into triangles when they should have been plastering the wall with their paintings.

I don't think I copied Stekel and Reich; they came later, when I was past the aping stage. But to some extent I must have been influenced by Stekel, for I followed him in having patients, though juvenile ones.

When did I cease aping? Or do any of us ever cease aping? Oddly enough I have a complex about anyone aping me. It hurts me when some new school in the USA calls itself a Summerhill. Often I heard Reich say: 'I want no disciples', and I feel as he did. More than once I have sent letters to new educational journals in America, imploring teachers to stand on their own feet and not copy Summerhill. Of late, I am glad to say, I seldom see the word Summerhill on their pages. John M. Aitkenhead copied Summerhill when he set up his Kilquhanity School in Scotland, but then wisely went his own way, although the two schools retained and retain their fundamental belief in self-government. I heard of a school in the USA that claimed to be run on Summerhill lines. It had half an hour's compulsory religious lesson every morning, and when a boy swore they washed out his mouth with soap and water.

I used to copy clothes. My headmaster in King Alfred's School wore grey corduroy suits. I also began to wear corduroy in 1919 and have worn hardly anything else since. One thing I never copied was the English accent – I shuddered when a Scot on TV said 'Ovah theah'. In Germany I was always called *ein Englander* and did not like it. This reminds me of a Freudian slip. Stekel wrote a book and in it, he not only disagreed with my belief in freedom for children, much worse, he called me an Englishman. The book was unbound, and, as I was taking lessons in book-binding in Dresden at the time, I started to bind it. When finished I opened it. A leaf fell out – the Stekel remarks on me. That is the most astounding Freudian slip I have known; how I could bind over five hundred pages leaving one loose still makes me marvel.

Copying is not always a bad thing. We copy a writer's style, often unconsciously. But copying, alas, is not enough. I could copy Rod Laver's style for a plethora of blue moons and never win a tennis match. I long to be able to write with the word picturing of Douglas Brown, or the music of Ruskin, and I am sane enough to laugh and accept the truth that it isn't my line. Most poets have gone through an aping period, and only the great ones got out of it. Which poet Tennyson was aping when he wrote 'The Queen of the May' I cannot guess, but if McGonagall had lived in his time I might have suspected him as the inspiration.

Children have an acute sense of spotting anything that is not original. To call a child a copy-cat is equivalent to an adult's calling a man a cad. It looks as if there is an inborn repulsion against any imitation, but how children acquire their standard it would be difficult to discover. On the other hand fashion is one gigantic copy-cat. The Beatles have long hair; let's all have long hair, and no one objects to the imitation there. I am sure that if Prince Charles went to dinner in a tartan Smoking, with a pink tie, the London tailors would be inundated with orders for the new fashion. Truly, imitation is the most sincere form of flattery, but do let us confine it to hats and coats, and try to form our own fashions in art and literature and music. Our housemaid in Dresden used to spend her afternoon off in the opera and talked learnedly about Wagner. *Lohengrin* was in his Beethoven period, or was it his Mozart one? Knowing nothing of music I sat with open mouth and harkened to the authority. Emma, like her beloved Wagner, became a Nazi.

Sometimes what looks like aping is a discovery that has been discovered before. Reich, as I have said, discovered that the powers-that-be castrate children in home and school by making them obedient and frightened, guilty about sex, so that when adult they have not the guts to challenge. But William Godwin said very much the same thing around 1790, and I am sure that Reich had not read Godwin. I knew an amateur astronomer who ran down three streets in his pyjamas at three in the morning to give a fellow astronomer great news. 'I have made the discovery of the century. The square on the hypotenuse of a right-angled triangle is equal to the sum of the squares on the other two sides.' I told the late Will Hay, another star-gazer, about it and his blank look of incomprehension convinced me that he also had never heard of Pythagoras. 'There is nothing new under the sun.'

240

HEROES

I have hardly ever met great men. H. G. Wells, the hero of my youth, I met when he was an old man, and my dream was shattered; a little man with a squeaky voice and an arrogant manner. Later I sent him one of Reich's books. His reply:

You have sent me an awful gabble of competitive quacks. Reich misuses every other word and Wolfe [his translator] is a solemn ass. There is not a gleam of fresh understanding in the whole bale. Please don't send me any more of this stuff.

My reply:

Dear Wells, I cannot understand why you are so damned unpleasant about it. I considered you the man with the broadest mind in England, and sincerely wanted light on a biological matter I wasn't capable of judging myself. Your black-out letter might have been written by Colonel Blimp himself. I hoped you would give an opinion on bions and orgones, whether they were a new discovery or not, and all I got was a tirade against Wolfe's translation of Reich's German. You apply the word quack to a man whom Freud considered brilliant.

I grant that I asked for it. I intruded, I apologise, and being a Scot refund your postage. Your reputation is that of a man who can't suffer fools gladly. Apparently you can't suffer sincere research gladly either. When a New York Medical School is trying out bions and orgones on cancer patients, your 'no fresh understanding in the whole bale' sounds odd. But this is no quarrel, and I won't bother you about Reich or anyone else.

Dear Neill, No, I decline your stamps, but this business is quackery. You call me a Blimp. I call you a sucker. Bless you.

Reich was furious with me for approaching Wells. 'I don't need the approval of Wells or anyone else.'

'Then why did you send me a dozen copies of *The Function of the Orgasm* if you didn't want me to distribute them?' I asked. Reich just grunted.

A hero who did not disappoint was Henry Miller. Someone had sent him one or two of my books and Henry wrote to me and we kept up a desultory correspondence for some years. Then he came to London and we had lunch together. I loved Henry, so warm, so humorous, so obviously genuine. I have often sighed to think that thousands of miles separate us. My judgement of him might be partly conditioned by the fact that, in a booklet announcing the publication of *Summerhill*, he wrote: 'I know of no educator in the Western world who can compare with A. S. Neill. It seems to me he stands alone . . . Summerhill is a tiny ray of light in a world of darkness. . . .' But, I loved him long before he had written those words.

In my time I have met entertainers, stage and TV. One acquires an almost unconscious feeling that folks who are popular are in themselves interesting. Millions would have been delighted to meet, say, Gary Cooper, but I make the guess that Gary off the screen was just an ordinary amiable guy. My first disillusion with stage people was when I was a student. A touring Ibsen company came to Edinburgh and I wangled an invitation to supper with it. I was placed beside the leading lady who had played Nora, Hedda Gabler, Rebecca. It was to be the treat of my play-going life. The woman had no interest in Ibsen; I wondered if she knew he was a Norwegian.

I never met J. M. Barrie. He was my hero until I came under the spell of Wells. Our birthplaces were only eight miles apart. He went to Edinburgh University and so did I. He was a famous writer; I also would be a famous writer. It was a clear case of identification. I read and reread his *Sentimental Tommy*, his tales of old Kirriemuir, his Thrums.

My discipleship came to a sudden end when I read that tremendous counterblast to Scottish sentimentality, *The House with the Green Shutters*. I fancy it was then that I made a new definition of sentimentality – giving a swan emotion to a goose. The *House* became my Bible; I knew it almost by heart, I decided to write

Brown's Life and via letters to the press I got much material. Alas, it was mostly dull, peddling stuff. I could find no highlights in his life and gave up my project, sending all my material to James Veitch, the Scots novelist, who wrote it instead. But I gained a sweet experience. I visited Brown's friend in Glasgow, then an old woman, very deaf, and fell in love with her. I half think that she was too good for the rather dour Geordie. She was anxious that the life should be written by me and was disappointed that it wasn't. A few years later I called to see her again and found a boarded-up house for sale. A neighbour told me the dear old lady had died a year before. I have her letters to me, and am sending them to the National Library of Scotland with the proviso that they cannot be shown to the public for twenty years. This in case her relatives might object to their publication. I know they will be placed in the Douglas Brown file with its MS of the *House* in penny exercise-books. I used to read them every time I went to Edinburgh.

I now saw Barrie as a minor writer with flashes of insight and humour. His *Peter Pan* appealed to children because of the pirates, the adventure; it appealed to their parents because it dealt with the boy who never grew up; they had the illusion that childhood was one long rhapsody of delight. Barrie never grew up, as is shown so well and brilliantly in Janet Dunbar's biography.

He had whimsical patches. When an old lady asked him what he was going to be, he answered 'an author'. She held up her hands. 'What, and you an MA!' Talent he had, lots of it. His play *Dear Brutus* is a model of construction. But I doubt very much if I would have appreciated meeting him.

Of all the writers in the past the one I would have loved to meet would have been Oscar Wilde. To listen to his conversation in the Café Royal must have been a marvellous treat. Winston Churchill had the same wish.

Sage Bernal was a scientist with a great imagination. He used to give our pupils talks. He told them that one day the North Sea would be drained and made into arable land; he foresaw the population explosion thirty years ago and pictured the continuation of human life on the satellites. During the war Churchill thought highly of him. His first job was to examine unexploded bombs, and the tale went that he arrived at a field with a large crater bounded by barbed wire.

'Sorry, Sir', said the sergeant at the entrance, 'but no one can come in here until a big bug from London sees the bomb.' Sage, never thinking that he was the big bug, went away.

I asked Sage if the story were true.

'Not quite; I crept under the wire when the sergeant was looking the other way.'

He did not seem to know what fear was. When I asked him if he had ever been afraid in his dangerous job, he answered: 'Once, when a bomb began to make a ticking noise, I was so scared that I jumped back a yard.'

He was Sage because he always had an answer, but when I asked him why a razor on a hone sharpened better when the hone was oiled, he shook his head and said he had no idea. I wish I could have seen him dressed in naval uniform commanding a landing ship in the D-Day invasion. He did not know the difference between port and starboard and shocked his crew by crying left and right.

Sage had a stroke and the end of his life was one miserable frustration because he kept his brain until he died. I hope that someone will write a life of this fine scientist and most human friend.

So mnch for the great. My milieu has been the less exalted classes – the teachers, the students, the parents. The hoi polloi, and that has been good: so many never know what ordinary people do and think.

HEALTH

I have been very lucky as far as my health has been concerned. Apart from two painful attacks of sciatica and an operation for piles I have had no serious illness.

I lay for three months with pyelitis forty years ago and it was then I became interested in Nature Cure. It seemed to fit into my philosophy of education. Raw greens and buttermilk equalled the free child; drugs equalled the outside discipline of the schools, a false analogy of course. I used to make an annual stay in a Nature Cure Clinic and certainly felt refreshed and fit after each stay. By and large Nature Cure held that disease comes from within, that the body reacts to its poisons, mainly from bad feeding, by throwing out, so that a skin disease and a cold are methods of getting rid of the poisons, self-cleansing processes. And it sounds rational. My father and grandfather said that they owed their long lives to the many colds they had had, and some French doctor claimed that his patients with the greatest longevity were those with skin disease. The medical profession laughed what they called this quackery to scorn. The disease came from infection, outside. The germ was the centre. And the layman really does not know what to think. The Nature Cure practitioners were using oranges and lemons as cures long before Vitamin C was discovered. Some doctors, especially in Germany, used the cold compress method for sprains but did not go as far as the Naturists did with their body compresses for, say, pneumonia.

Emotionally I was all on the Nature Cure side. Yet doubts

245

arose. If diet were so important why did my father die at eighty-five after eating the wrong food all his life? Nature Cure warned against wearing flannel next to the skin. My father wore nothing else, summer and winter. But I saw a positive side. I saw women crippled with rheumatoid-arthritis scarcely able to move, but on my next visit a year later they were walking about the grounds, not cured but the disease ameliorated. Both sides in the health controversy were narrow and dogmatic. Nature Cure would have no truck with inoculations and few accepted the fact that tetanus injections had saved thousands of lives in the Great War. My doctor brother told me that after penicillin came in he had not lost one patient with pneumonia. On the other hand the medical men laughed at the idea of fasting, ignoring the fact that an animal fasts when ill. A vet told me that most of the mortality among horses and cattle in his country was due to the farmers forcing food down their throats 'to keep up their strength'.

After my South African tour, after too many drinks and no exercise, I felt like a dying man when I boarded the ship. My urine was like mud. I fasted on water for six days and arrived in Southampton the picture of health. The odd feature in fasting is that one feels so bright mentally. Then I felt I could tell Einstein where he was wrong.

Doubts increased when people who had lived on Nature Cure diet all their days died of cancer, proving that food was not enough. And I fancy that many naturopaths were unconscious moralists.

One of the best known claimed in a book that many of his cases were caused by masturbation, and they all were down on stimulants – tea, coffee, alcohol, tobacco and of course meat of any kind. I believed and at the same time did not believe, but then I have the same attitude to doctors who prescribe a salve for a skin disease without asking what is causing it. I have hardly ever seen a doctor who asked what I ate, if I took exercise, if my sex life were satisfactory. The thing was to treat the disease while the Nature Curist tried to build up the whole body. A combination of the two systems might be a solution.

There was one great difference between the two schools. The Nature Curists explained what they were doing all the way, but the average doctor does not; indeed some are annoyed when asked what is in the drug they prescribe. I have heard so many things said about the dangers of cortisone that I want to know if the pills prescribed for me contain it or not. As Shaw put it: 'Every profession is a conspiracy against the laity'.

BISCUIT

My golden labrador dog Biscuit is at the end of his tether and has lost control of his bowels. He will have to be put to sleep and I hate having to be God deciding his fate. He was an ideal dog for a school; he never bit anyone; he allowed the children to pet him and play with him. I shall miss him sadly.

The death of a cat does not as a rule give the grief that the death of a dog gives. Cats seldom show affection and persons mean little to them. Dogs flatter one; cats do not. Dogs love and do not discriminate about whom they love. I am sure that Hermann Goering's dogs loved him as much as if he had been a Gandhi. Most of us love dogs because they show love for us.

One can teach a dog obedience . . . I never could with Biscuit; if intent on some object he ignored my whistle, but one cannot make a cat obedient. Query: why can one make a horse obedient and not a cow? Or can one? Oxen in the plough, yes. But cattle in a field, no. One odd thing about Biscuit; he knew the time. Every day after lunch he knew it was time for his walk on the beach and he plagued me until I put him in the car. I recall the Skye terrier we had when I was a boy. If my father put on his hat and coat to go to the town Boulot danced around with joy, but when my father donned his tall hat and frock coat to go to church on a Sunday, he didn't even look up. Makes me wonder how much intelligence a dog has. I once asked a shepherd who had won first prize at a sheepdog trial how much his dog understood.

'He doesn't understand a bloody thing; he just obeys my

whistle. There never was a dog you could tell to put three sheep in one pen and five in the other'.

Thousands of dog owners have said that they prefer their dogs to human beings, and I understand what they mean; the boundless faithfulness and love one gets from a dog can never be got from any human relationship. A wife, a brother may criticise; a dog never criticises, never doubts. One might call it the higher animal, for it does not lie or slander, it does not make war and does not hate. If it is aggressive it is because of a bone or a bitch. Much depends on its owner's allowing self-regulation so to speak. Owners who beat dogs, send them after cats, make dogs savage. I guess that if I had put Biscuit on a chain he would have been a biter in six weeks. Cats and dogs are not natural enemies. My wife has many cats. They played with Biscuit, slept between his paws. I am not saying that in their wild state cats and dogs may not be enemies; all I say is that when domesticated there is no enmity between them.

One day dogs will be banned at least from cities. In Britain there are local laws about messing the pavements. Biscuit, by the way, never needed a law; he always left the pavement and sought the middle of the road or a grass bank. Mannerly dog was old Biscuit, and now I keep putting off that phone call to the vet, as I put off the sacking of a teacher. I am too old to get another dog but even if younger I would not have one because its life span is too short and the parting too poignant.

ZOË

Earlier in this book I said that I would not write about folks now living. But I am breaking my own resolve in the case of my daughter Zoë. I have mentioned her in more than one of my books and her name must have been read by millions. Many have written asking me about her and her life. Some have asked if she bears out the old Scots saying that the shoemaker's bairns are the worst shod. The other Scots saying is that the son of the manse is often a reprobate.

The answer in brief is that Zoë at twenty-four is as good a product of a free home and school as anyone could wish to see. She, so far, is not an academic; from earliest infancy she has had one great interest – horses. She qualified as a riding mistress and has a large stable in the school grounds, and laughs to scorn my own view of riding acquired over twenty years ago by seeing a rodeo in Madison Square Gardens. 'Cowboys can't ride; they simply sit on horses.'

Her school days were difficult. She fell between home and school. When she lived in our cottage she was an outsider to the children who boarded in the main school, and when we made her a boarder she felt that she hadn't a home. And she suffered much from the jealousy of others. My wife and I had long been convinced that teachers should never have their own children in a boarding school in which the parents work, so when she was eleven we sent her to a foreign boarding school. After her first term she said, 'Daddy, you are a swindle; you give freedom to

249

other kids but not to your own daughter. I hate school; it is fake freedom and has no real self-government.' I visited the school and brought her home. Incidentally, two other girls we knew went to that school later and both had a similar criticism, that the freedom was phoney.

I suppose at the back of my mind was the wish that Zoë would choose my own line of work and interest and run Summerhill after me. Many parents have indulged in such wishful thinking, especially fathers with big businesses. Luckily we are all wrong; luckily we have no control over our children. Luckily I came to feel that if horses were Zoë's life then her happiness was all that mattered. And after all, to be an expert on horses is as important as to be an expert in education, maybe more important, for you can ruin generations of kids by a false education of fear and authority, whereas only cruel trainers can ruin horses. Zoë's methods are gentle and kind. Her prize-winning stallion, Karthage, did not need to be broken; when she first jumped on his back he took it as another natural show of kindness. 'My stable is a horsey Summerhill.'

In September 1971 she married a young farmer and they now own a farm a few hundred yards from the school. At the wedding I had to propose the health of Tony and Zoë Readhead (pronounced Redhead) and although I can lecture for hours without any nervousness I was a little anxious about making a short speech where emotion was involved. Luckily I had a vague memory of a passage in one of my books, *The Free Child*. I read it aloud . . . .

'Yesterday was my birthday. My Zoë, who will be six next month, said "Daddy, you are old, aren't you? You'll die before me, won't you? I'll cry when you die." "Hie, wait," I said, "I will maybe wait to see you married." "In that case," she said, "I won't need to cry, will I?" ' I did not go on to read further. 'It strikes me that if a small child can take it for granted that she won't need her father when she grows up, she has automatically solved the dear old Oedipus Complex.'

250

DEATH

In these pages I have had much to say about the fears that ruled my early life, fear of the dark, of illness, of death. At eighty-nine I naturally know that death cannot be far away and I hate the idea of going out like a candle to the nothingness I think is beyond. But whether that is a fear of death I am not sure; more likely it is a fear of not living, of leaving people and things that I hold dear. And there is curiosity. I want to live to see what is to happen to children, to humanity, to the world with its hate and crime and thwarted love. It is a sobering thought that when I die the postman and the milkman will come as usual, my demise meaning nothing to them, nothing really unless to the ones around me.

I have what might be described as a grouse against death. It kills the body when the spirit wants to live. I think those people err who say that we will our own deaths, yet it may be that in sickness one can appear to do so. Keats was possibly a sick man when he wrote that he was 'half in love with easeful death'. In my old age my heart is poorly and may kill me, but my head, I hope, is alive and my interest in all things living as keen as it ever was. I should love to have another fifty years of Summerhill. Someone should found a new religion where one is allowed to revisit the earth for a week every twenty years. The chances are that after the first visit most of the departed would call off any further visits. It is an interesting speculation to think of Henry VIII

251

returning now and of his reaction to our new permissiveness about sex. Possibly he would find it his cup of tea.

There is a strong element of conceit in my attitude to death. I am the great man, not Muhammad Ali's the greatest though, and no other can do my job. Many, most, have this god-almighty complex, knowing as I do that it is purely infantile fantasy. No one is necessary, no one is indispensable. All the same the feeling is there. To go to hear a lecture about Summerhill by anyone would make me shudder, and articles about Summerhill generally give me more pain than pleasure. People ought to write about what they do in life and not about what others do . . . humbug! Haven't I written a lot about Homer Lane and Reich? yet I have tried to avoid interpreting them.

I have been lucky in having a long life with the minimum of fear stimulus from the outside. The Ministry of Education, possibly disliking my views, has been tolerant. No churchman has attacked me for keeping children from religion, or at least not giving them any. Our small town in Suffolk is peaceful and our children are safe from hoodlums and rapists. My pupils are much more fearless than I was at their age.

Someone recently asked me what incidents in my life stand out as blissful moments. In childhood there must have been many, for youth is the time for ecstasy . . . and terrible depression, say after a day at the circus. I cannot recall the early delights, the occasions when time stood still when a beloved lass smiled on me. My greatest pleasure of all was comparatively recent: my return to Summerhill after the war. The mess the army had made of the premises was forgotten in the joy of quiet happiness in being at last back in the place I loved. I had never had any emotional attachment to a place before. It may be that Summerhill is my own; I bought it, improved it; it became an extension of my own personality. It was my *House with the Green Shutters*. When I think of death now I think of it not as leaving life so much as leaving Summerhill, which after all has been my life.

Ah, I remember now. The great joy when my first book *A Dominie's Log* was published in 1915; the delight in reading the reviews and the depression I got from the hostile ones. (I hasten to add that in my long career as an author I have had very few hostile reviews.) One advantage of living in a small town is that you can get your name in the local paper, even if it is only a report of your being fined for parking, whereas in a city that cannot happen, and maybe that is why a small town seldom has youth gangs; each and everyone is known to neighbours, is a known personality, not a unit in a huge impersonal city. Today I wish I could recapture the thrill on seeing my name in print.

I cannot recall my emotion when Zoë was born, only my natural and general feeling of the unfairness that makes the mother have all the pain. I don't think I have ever had a feeling of possession about my daughter, never had the thought she was made of a clay that had a smoother texture than that of the child next door. Seeing your child grow up might be classified as a long, quiet pleasure.

Delights by a natural process tend to get repressed. The shames of adolescence . . . using the wrong fork, mispronouncing a word, being dressed in an odd way . . . in Scotland having to wear a kilt when the other boys have breeches; a thousand humiliations make youth a hell. When at sixteen I clapped my hands after the first movement of a symphony, thinking it was the end. I had an unfortunate propensity to blush. Jack Flugel pointed out the anomaly of blushing. You want to hide yourself, to sink through the floor when you have made a faux-pas – but your face being red makes everyone stare at you.

Comparative poverty was responsible for many a shame and depression. As a student having to refuse invitations to functions because I could not afford to send my dress shirt to the laundry . . . I had only one shirt. Saying that I was on the wagon as an excuse for not going to a pub with a few friends; I had not the money to stand my round. In Newport, Fife, having to travel third-class by train over the Tay Bridge to Dundee when everyone had a first-class season ticket. On the other hand I never looked on myself as a first-class person, and on the voyage to South Africa in 1936 felt so isolated from my fellow passengers that I stayed in my cabin and wrote a book – *That Dreadful School* (extracts from it appear in *Summerhill*). Tut, tut, I should have vetted it, for *Summerhill* contains a part that makes me a Freudian which I have not been for years, not Freudian or any other -ian.

I travel first-class on the railway now that I am old but I always have a vague feeling of embarrassment; the other travellers seem so stiff, so conventional compared with the riff-raff in the second-class compartments. If underneath I consider myself a first-class person, consciously I would rather travel with the vulgar – Latin vulgus, the common people. I was born in the lower-middle class and in essence I am still there, but that is partly due to my feeling that I have no fundamental contact with the toffs, the Establishment, the class-conscious, or should it be money-conscious, accepters of the status quo. An inverted snob, that's what I am.

253

If one lives to be very old nature seems to make the passing easy. I find that I have gradually lost interest in things and to a lesser degree in people. I see the gardener use the scythe I used to keep so clean and sharp and it means nothing. When I get up in the morning I feel I am a hundred and have no interest in anything or anyone, but when I go to bed I am fifty. The morning mail brings nothing to excite me; the morning papers have little interest. In old age there is nothing to look forward to. I can think of no promising event that would give me a thrill, not a cheque for a million from a rich American, not an offer of a title (which I could not accept) or a new honorary degree from a university.

Nature prepares one for the end. I have not reached the philosophy of R.L.S. with his '. . . gladly die, and I laid me down with a will'. But I begin to understand why he said it, even though he died long before his old age.

If the weakness of old age did not come I wonder how long a man could live happily, how long he could retain his interest, say, in the beauty of flowers and landscapes. I have had my school in two places of great beauty – the Austrian Tyrol and the Welsh mountains. After a few weeks I ceased to see the beauty just as the director of a musical comedy ceases to see the beauty of his chorus girls. Hence if I say to myself, 'Soon you will not see the Summerhill trees and flowers, the happy faces of the kids; soon you will leave your friends for ever, how very sad', I am not being quite sincere.

My caravanserai has rested in many a lovely spot and I am content not to wish that experiences can be repeated. In youth everything is permanent. In the old school house we children never thought that life would change, that our parents would die, our brothers and sisters would die; if anyone had told me then that I would end my life in a small English town I think I would have laughed at the absurdity of the idea. Youth is not interested in death unless some evil like Calvinism makes it a terror. My pupils, with no religious fears, think of life, of doing things, of loving, of success. The only function of life is to live, and as I have had a full life with most of my aims realised I have no wish to be nostalgic and to regret that past joys and successes are gone forever. When Charles Frohman, the theatre magnate, stood on the sinking *Lusitania*, someone is said to have asked him if he weren't afraid. 'No', he said, 'death is the greatest adventure in life', quoting Peter Pan. To me it is not, because I think with Hamlet that 'the rest is silence'. A silent adventure cannot be imagined.

I never had any feelings about leaving my own flesh and blood. One of my old pupils, a radio operator on a ship in the Second World War, told me that behind his fear of being torpedoed was the thought that he had no children to carry on his name. I am glad to have a daughter to carry on my name, though now that she is married she is no longer a Neill. I shall leave my Zoë and in time she too will die, but what I leave in work will, I hope, live for some time. I hope too that my pioneering work in education will not lead to a mass of pseudo-freedom schools, with their benign moulding of young character.

In Scotland we laughed more than somewhat about death. A farmer's wife died. As they carried the coffin down the awkward stair it hit a corner. The lid flew open and the woman woke up from her trance. Twenty years later she died a second time and the farmer stood anxiously by as they carried the coffin down the stairs. 'Canny wi' that corner, lads.'

Sad thought: death means the end of fun. If the Bible had even one joke in it I'd be inclined to believe in a heaven. Heaven for holiness, hell for company, said Bernard Shaw. Might be some fun in hell after all. If there is one I know who are in it – Shaw, Wilde, O. Henry, Damon Runyon, Mark Twain. But their light style may be cramped by the presence of St Paul, Calvin, John Knox – and of course most politicians.

I end this book with one of my favourite stories, a very old one. An Eastern merchant sent his servant to the market place to buy the day's provisions. He came running back with a face as white as a sheet.

'Master, I saw the Angel of Death in the market and he gave me a look that terrified me. Oh, Master, lend me a horse and I'll flee to Samara.'

The merchant lent him a horse, and himself took the basket and went to the market. 'Why', he said to the Angel of Death, 'why did you frighten my servant? He says you gave him a look that struck him with terror.'

'I am sorry', said the Angel of Death, 'I did give him a look but it was one of surprise to see him there, for I have an appointment with him tonight in Samara.'

My liking for this story may show that one of the major influences in my life was good old Omar Khayyam.

> The Moving Finger writes; and, having writ,
> Moves on; nor all thy piety nor Wit
> Shall lure it back to cancel half a Line,
> Nor all thy Tears wash out a word of it.

Everyman's life, including mine.

INDEX

257

260

263

Stewart, Nora, 55
Stockholm, 157
Strindberg, August, 156
Student teachers, George Neill, 5; Neill, 54–5; training and examinations, 54–5
Summerhill, 132–4, 238, 239; at Lyme Regis, 112–13; problem children, 113–14; new home for, 114; Neill's purpose, 117; influence of, 120, 125, 234; Reich and, 128–9; staff, 135–8; school inspectors at, 139, 140–1; finances, 143–4; *Summerhill, For and Against*, 160, 242, 253; philosophy of, 173; Tory and Liberal view of, 182; psychology at, 188; communism antipathetic to, 190; sex problem at, 195–6; freedom from sex repression at, 199–200; TV at, 235; imitations of, 239; pleasure of the return to, 252
Sundays, in Neill's childhood, 10–11, 34, 43; psalm-learning on, 16; family worship, 43; at Gretna Green, 90–1; in Wales, 115
Sutherland, Clunes Sinclair (Granny), and her family, 6; and Neill, 6–7, 16, 46; attitude to religion, 6–7, 42; psychic, 7–8; burial of, 45
Sutherland, Neill, 9, 45
Sutherland, Mrs, 74
Swift, Jonathan, 129

Tam, Nanzy, 24–5, 46
Tennyson, Alfred, Lord, 152, 240
Theatre, the, 67, 71, 80
Thomson, Ben, 58, 68
Thunderstorms, 26, 46
Tod family, the, 62–3

Tod, Mr, 66
Troop-train disaster, the, 91–2
Tutin, Dorothy, 155
Twain, Mark, 255

United States of America, 183–4

Van Gogh, Vincent, 191
Veitch, James, 243
Volunteers, the, Neill belongs to, 63–4

Waas, Karl, 153
Wagner, Richard, 116–17, 191, 233, 237
Wales, 114
Walker, Sir James, 74–5
Watson, Dr D. G., 87, 89, 90
Watson, John Broadus, 166, 190
Wedderburn, Dr, 41
Weddings, in Neill's childhood, 24; Neill as best man, 65
Wells, Bombardier Billy, 88
Wells, H. G., Neill and, 88, 166, 205; on death, 118; and aggression, 229; his disappointment, 233; and his work, 236; Neill's correspondence with, 241–2
Whistler, James Abbott McNeill, 224
Wilde, Oscar, 197, 255; homosexual, 116; Neill and, 126; 'The Harlot's House', 165; defines a cynic, 172; his wit, 224–5, 226; unaggressive, 229; on tragedy, 232; Neill's admiration for, 243
Wills, David, 123, 124, 125
Willsher, Harry M., 67, 70, 72
Wodehouse, P. G., 160
Wolfe, Dr Theodore, 128, 129
Wyllie, Dave, 20–1